Creation as Emanation

Publications in Medieval Studies

Edited by John Van Engen

Former Editors
Philip S. Moore, C.S.C.,
Joseph N. Garvin, C.S.C.,
Astrik L. Gabriel,
and Ralph McInerny

The Medieval Institute
University of Notre Dame

Volume XXIX

CREATION AS *Emanation*

The Origin of Diversity
in Albert the Great's
*On the Causes and the Procession
of the Universe*

THÉRÈSE BONIN

University of Notre Dame Press
Notre Dame, Indiana

University of Notre Dame Press
Notre Dame, Indiana 46556
All Rights Reserved
undpress.nd.edu

Copyright © 2001 by University of Notre Dame
Published in the United States of America

Paperback edition published in 2017

Library of Congress Cataloging-in-Publication Data
Bonin Thérèse M.
 Creation as emanation : the origin of diversity in Albert the Great's On the causes and the procession of the universe / Thérèse Bonin.
   p. cm. — (Publications in medieval studies ; 29)
 Includes bibliographical references and index.
 ISBN 978-0-268-02553-3 (hardback) — 978-0-268-02351-5 (paperback)
 1. Albertus, Magnus, Saint, 1193?–1280—Contributions in concept of creation. 2. Creation—History. 3. Albertus, Magnus, Saint, 1193?–1280. De causis et processu universitatis a prima causa. I. Albertus, Magnus, Saint, 1193?–1280. De causis et processu universitatis a prima causa. II. Title. III. Series.

B765.A44 B66 2000
213—dc21

00-032591

∞ *This book was printed on acid-free paper.*

Contents

A Note on Editions and Transliterations vii

1. Introduction 1
   1.1. Responses to Emanation 1
   1.2. Albert on the Nature of the *Liber de causis* 3
   1.3. The Nature of Albert's Paraphrase of the *Liber de causis* 5
   1.4. Summary of the *Liber de causis* 6
   1.5. A Doctrinal Problem 12

2. Emanation and Causation 15

3. God's Incommunicability to Creatures 22
   3.1. An Apparent Contradiction 22
   3.2. *Esse* and *Id Quod Est* 24
   3.3. The Interpretation of *Liber de causis* 19 27
   3.4. Resolving the Contradiction 29

4. The First Created Thing 35
   4.1. *Ab Uno Non Nisi Unum* 35
   4.2. *Prima Rerum Creatarum Est Esse; Esse Creatum Primum Est Intelligentia* 38
      4.2.1. The First Interpretation 39
         4.2.1.1. *Intelligentia* 39
         4.2.1.2. *Esse* 43
      4.2.2. The Second Interpretation 48
   4.3. Summary 51

5. Mediation in the Procession of Creatures   53

6. God's Immediacy to the Procession of Creatures   66

Afterword   79
Notes   81
Selected Bibliography   147
Index of Subjects   169
Index of Persons   173
Index of Texts   177

A Note on Editions and Transliterations

This monograph is a reworking of my dissertation, which, having been completed shortly before Fr. Winfried Fauser's critical edition of Albert's paraphrase of the *Liber de causis*, his *De causis et processu universitatis a prima causa*,[1] was based on Borgnet's edition[2] and microfilms of three early manuscripts: Lilienfeld 209 (which contains *De quattuor coaequaevis* as well), Basel F.I.21, and BN lat. 15449. While early manuscripts are not always the best, the choice of those three turned out to be a happy one, so that this book differs from the dissertation chiefly by fuller explanations and by the substitution of the critical text for citations from Borgnet with cumbersome references to manuscript readings.

Students of the *Liber de causis* have more editions to consult. Otto Bardenhewer's *editio princeps* of the Arabic text,[3] though based on a single, defective manuscript in Leiden,[4] is quite good, because made with constant reference to Proclus' Greek and to the Latin translation. ʿAbd al-Raḥmān Badawī's edition,[5] based on the same manuscript, generally takes a step backward, since he makes less use of the Greek and the Latin. The best edition is Richard C. Taylor's,[6] based on Proclus' Greek, the Latin, the manuscript of Leiden, two good, recently discovered manuscripts from Ankara and Istanbul,[7] and supplementary Arabic materials.

As for the Latin translation, Bardenhewer's edition,[8] though based on only two manuscripts and two incunabula, has been the best available, because made with knowledge of the text being translated. Adriaan Pattin provides useful notes from the commentary tradition and records many interesting variants;[9] however, he usually chooses the reading which makes more sense in Latin, whereas Bardenhewer recognizes in the *lectio difficilior* a correct if overliteral translation of the Arabic.[10] For present purposes, the most convenient edition is that which Fauser includes in his edition of Albert's paraphrase; it is Pattin's edition corrected according to suggestions Taylor has made.[11]

Arabic consonants are transliterated as follows:

ء	ʾ		د	d		ض	ḍ		ك	k
ب	b		ذ	ḏ		ط	ṭ		ل	l
ت	t		ر	r		ظ	ẓ		م	m
ث	ṯ		ز	z		ع	ʿ		ن	n
ج	ǧ		س	s		غ	ġ		ه	h
ح	ḥ		ش	š		ف	f		و	w
خ	ḫ		ص	ṣ		ق	q		ي	y

Tāʾ marbūṭa is represented simply by "a," unless the grammar requires "at."

I would like to thank the Bibliothèque nationale, the Öffentliche Bibliothek der Universität Basel, the Lilienfeld Stiftsbibliothek, and the Hill Monastic Manuscript Library at Saint John's Abbey and University (Collegeville, Minnesota) for providing microfilms: without these, many a passage in Borgnet's edition would have remained impenetrable. I owe a special debt to Professor Joel Kraemer of the University of Chicago, for teaching me to read Arabic philosophical texts during his visit to the University of Notre Dame. Above all, I wish to express my gratitude to my director, Professor Stephen Gersh, who opened my eyes to the riches of the Platonic tradition.

Duquesne University
March 1998

ONE

Introduction

1.1 Responses to Emanation

According to Wisdom of Solomon 7.25, wisdom is an emanation from God—an ἀπόρροια ("flowing from") in the Greek original, or an *emanatio* ("trickling out of") in Jerome's translation. Yet, despite the term's adoption by a biblical writer, many Christian philosophers in our day grow uneasy at the mention of emanation, feeling that it smacks of pantheism.[1]

Of course, their quarrel is not with the Bible but with Neoplatonism: those who object to "emanation" do so because it is most familiar to them from Plotinus, who, besides being a non-biblical source, may even oppose biblical teaching. Saint Basil the Great thought he did, and attacked the Neoplatonists for making God's production of the universe automatic and unwilled, like a body's production of a shadow (*Hexaemeron* 1.7 [PG29:17B-C]). And, whatever we are to make of Plotinus' remarks about necessity and the will, the image of flowing does suggest a necessary process, along with more unity between cause and effect than some may wish to admit.

But we need not read medieval philosophers for long before we notice that their reaction to emanation often differed greatly from that of Basil and our contemporaries. Pseudo-Dionysius, for one, adopted this terminology without reserve. Most striking is the case of Eriugena, who identifies emanation from God with creation from nothing, on the grounds that God is nothing—by which he means, not that God does not exist, but that he is more than being (*Periphyseon* 634A–687D). Eriugena, of course, had an undeservedly bad reputation during and after the Middle Ages, but Dionysius was accorded the authority of an apostolic Father. Boethius, too, may be added to the list of respected Greek and Latin Christian authorities who speak frequently of emanation.

In fact, many medieval philosophers not only accepted emanation but gave it new prominence. For, however freely books about Plotinus speak of emanation, such terms were far from common in the writings of the pagan Neoplatonists themselves.[2] They became common among Jewish, Christian, and Islamic philosophers.[3] And where pagan Greeks had envisioned the trickling of droplets, writers in Arabic, whatever their religion, thought in terms of flowing, flooding, gushing, bursting, and inundating. Even those who claimed the label "Peripatetic" used this language. And among Peripatetics, Albert the Great stands out.[4]

Recently, Lloyd Gerson has argued that Plotinus was no pantheist, that what he meant by the metaphor "emanation" amounted to creation, and that the necessity he attributed to emanation was not the necessity which Christians deny of creation.[5] Had Albert possessed more than indirect knowledge of Plotinian thought, he would have concurred with Gerson's assessment: as we shall see, Albert treats creation as the most perfect case of emanation and considers emanation a corrective to pantheism.

But Gerson recognizes a difference between Plotinian creation and creation as usually understood within the Judeo-Christian tradition. On his reading of the *Enneads*, the One is pure existence and causes the existence of everything, not just of Intellect, while Intellect is essence and causes the essence of everything. For believers, on the other hand, God causes both the fact that things are and what they are; God's free and wise choice determines the number and kinds of creatures. To put the problem another way, emanation — as Albert himself will point out — implies effects ranged in order over some distance; it suggests mediation. Do not that distance and the mediators which fill it remove God's causality from the diversity and multiplicity of things?

The problem is not only one of origins; it also has much to do with ends. For, procession and reversion go together; if we find well-being by returning to the source of our being, then, to the extent that our being comes from an angelic intellect or some other such creature, we ought perhaps to lower our sights and seek union with it, not with God.[6]

However Albert would have interpreted the *Enneads*, he does not admit this disagreement between his faith and philosophy. To be sure, he knows that some philosophers felt a need to introduce created creators or created causes of essence before they could explain the derivation of the many from the One; yet what he judges the best accounts of emanation at once uphold the unity of God's effect and affirm that God touches the center of each being in its distinctness and individuality.

Where can we find the best accounts of emanation? Dionysius certainly provides one. And, according to Albert, the *Liber de causis* contains another. That may come as a surprise. Many of Albert's contemporaries took the *Liber de causis* to be saying that God creates the first planetary mover, which in turn creates other things. In other words, they assimilated the doctrine of the *Liber de causis* to that of Ibn Sīnā, and pronounced it heretical. Albert, however, identifies it with the position of Dionysius, and presents it as required by sound philosophy.

Thus, Albert's theological commentaries on the Neoplatonic Dionysius hold the key to his philosophical appreciation of the *Liber de causis*. What is more, they hold the key to his philosophical appreciation of Aristotle. To prepare ourselves for understanding this last point, we need to know what the *Liber de causis* was and what Albert thought it was.

1.2 Albert on the Nature of the *Liber de causis*

Albert's project of making Aristotle intelligible to the Latins through a series of paraphrases[7] could hardly exclude the *Liber de causis*. This monotheistic reworking of parts of Proclus' *Elements of Theology*, along with Plotinian material, was translated from Arabic by Gerard of Cremona (d. 1187)[8] and attributed to Aristotle. Once William of Moerbeke finished translating the *Elements* (on 18 May 1268, according to the colophon in most manuscripts), Thomas Aquinas was able to show how the *Liber de causis* derived from it; but, before that, the *Liber* shared the good and bad fortunes of the genuinely Aristotelian writings. Of course, even prior to 1268, as Aristotle became better known, some readers saw that it could not have come directly from his pen.

While most of Albert's paraphrases go by the title of the text paraphrased, his work on the *Liber de causis* is *De causis et processu universitatis a prima causa*—not simply "The Book of Causes," but "On the Causes and the Procession of the Universe from the First Cause." Perhaps this reflects his preoccupation with the problems surrounding emanation and creation. Be that as it may, scholars have occupied themselves chiefly with Albert's report on the author and sources of the *Liber*: according to Albert, a certain Jew named David excerpted the propositions from the sayings of Aristotle (in a certain *Epistula de principio universi esse*[9]), Ibn Sīnā, al-Ġazālī, and al-Fārābī, and added the proofs himself.[10] Albert's opinion probably derived from his curiosity about the *Epistula de principio universi esse*,[11] from his recognition of the doctrinal similarities between the *Liber de causis* and al-Fārābī, Ibn Sīnā, and al-Ġazālī,[12] from the rather Platonized portrait of Aristotle which the Arabs had given him, and from notes in the manuscript(s) he had seen;[13] however, as Arabists have demonstrated, his opinion was wrong.[14] Unfortunately, the far more important question of how Albert read the *Liber de causis* lies neglected.

Such neglect is particularly unfortunate because Albert thought not just that the *Liber* was in some sense Aristotle's, but also that it was a very important Aristotelian text. There appears to have been a widespread feeling among his contemporaries that not all books of the *Metaphysics* were available in Latin;[15] and some thought the *Liber* supplied what was missing. For instance, a set of questions and answers dating from the 1230s or early 1240s and intended to help students preparing for exams, explains that metaphysics is studied in three books: the *Metaphysica vetus*, which handles being as being; the *Metaphysica nova*, which discusses divine things and the first principles in their being; and the *Liber de causis*, where divine things are considered as principles of being.[16] Albert states the relationship between the *Metaphysics* and the *Liber de causis* as follows:

> Non determinatur hic nisi de divinis substantiis, scilicet causa prima, intelligentia et nobilibus animabus, quod ad theologiam pertinet, quam in ultima parte sui et perfectissima considerat metaphysica. . . . cum de separatis substantiis, quas diversimode Aristoteles et Plato determinaverunt, sit agere metaphysici, determinatur hic de separatis substantiis secundum plenam veritatem, de quibus in XII et XIII Metaphysicae non nisi secundum opinionem determinavit Aristoteles. Propter quod et iste liber Philosophiae primae coniungendus est, ut finalem ex isto recipiat perfectionem.[17]

> Ostendimus enim causam primam et causarum secundarum ordinem et qualiter primum universi esse est principium et qualiter omnium esse fluit a primo secundum opiniones Peripateticorum. Et haec quidem quando adiuncta fuerint XI Primae philosophiae, tunc primo opus perfectum est.[18]

Accordingly, *De causis et processu universitatis*, though published by Jammy and Borgnet with the *parva naturalia*, completes and perfects Albert's Aristotelian paraphrases. Still, readers must not jump to the conclusion that Albert considered the *Liber de causis* the epitome of wisdom and the fullness of truth about separate substances. He may have; yet the many disclaimers throughout his paraphrases of theoretical philosophy forbid facile identification of Albert with the doctrines he explains.[19] "Secundum plenam veritatem" must, for now, be given a relative sense: the *Liber de causis* contains the final word of the Peripatetic school on the final part of metaphysics, whereas *Metaphysics* M and N engage Plato in probable argumentation, as an exercise presupposed to determination of the truth.[20]

1.3 The Nature of Albert's Paraphrase of the *Liber de causis*

De causis et processu universitatis (apparently composed between 1264 and 1271[21]) differs from Albert's other Aristotelian paraphrases in several ways. First, whereas others incorporate the more intelligible words and phrases from various translations (Arabo-Latin, Greco-Latin, older, and newer), here he has only the one version of the *Liber de causis* with which to work. (In fact, nothing in *De causis et processu universitatis* suggests that Albert consulted more than one manuscript of the *Liber* at the time of composition.) Second, Ibn Sīnā and Ibn Rušd left him no commentary on the *Liber* from which to borrow helpful phrases or whole interpretations.[22] In line with his opinion about the authorship of the *Liber*, however, he uses the works of Aristotle, al-Fārābī, al-Ġazālī, and Ibn Sīnā as exegetical tools. Indeed, the first book of *De causis et processu universitatis* is not paraphrase at all, but a sort of history of natural theology together with a summary of metaphysical doctrines, mostly from Ibn Sīnā by way of al-Ġazālī, which must be understood if one is to read the *Liber* well.[23] As for the second book, whereas Albert usually combines strict paraphrase and explanatory material into one continuous text, relegating longer explanations and supplementary material to "digressiones," here he labels nothing a "digressio," and he separates explanatory material from paraphrase: each paraphrasing chapter is preceded by one or more chapters clarifying unfamiliar expressions or puzzling doctrines. This most likely represents Albert's response to the difficulty of the *Liber*: the thread of the paraphrase would have been lost had he tried to intersperse explanations for everything requiring them.[24]

The following list shows where to find the paraphrasing chapter for each chapter of the *Liber de causis*:

1 = 2.1.6	12 = 2.2.34	23 (166.73–79) = 2.4.13
2 = 2.1.10	13 = 2.2.41	23 (168.64–71) = 2.4.15
3 = 2.1.16	14 = 2.2.45	24 = 2.5.4
4 = 2.1.23	15 = 2.3.6	25 = 2.5.7
5 = 2.1.25	16 = 2.3.9	26 = 2.5.11
6 = 2.2.8	17 = 2.3.14	27 = 2.5.14
7 = 2.2.13	18 = 2.3.18	28 = 2.5.16
8 = 2.2.19	19 = 2.4.4	29 = 2.5.20
9 = 2.2.24	20 = 2.4.6	30 = 2.5.22
10 = 2.2.27	21 = 2.4.8	31 = 2.5.24
11 = 2.2.30	22 = 2.4.10	

While Albert keeps the two parts of chapter 4 of the *Liber* together, as in the Arabic original, there are thirty-two paraphrasing chapters, because he divides chapter 23. This division probably reflects a peculiarity in his copy of the text, since he does not see the chapter as particularly difficult.

No commentary can be read intelligently unless the text being commented upon is also read intelligently. This is especially true of the *Liber de causis*, whose oddities have caused more than one scholar unwittingly to add his own confusions to those of the commentator under scrutiny. Moreover, Albert's doctrine may not have been what it was without the many accidents of translation and transmission. What is needed, then, is a summary of the *Liber de causis* in light of the Arabic text, indicating obscurities or errors of translation or transmission which figure in Albert's interpretation or otherwise concern us.[25] This should eliminate much repetition and clutter from the following chapters, although it will certainly not eliminate all questions as to the literal sense and the deeper meaning of the *Liber*.

1.4 Summary of the *Liber de causis*

The first chapter sets forth the truth whose implications will be drawn out in many of the remaining chapters: that a primary universal cause is more the cause of a thing than a secondary universal cause. While this may seem odd, in that the secondary cause is adjacent to the effect, still, the remote cause acts upon the effect before the secondary cause does, and it helps the secondary cause, performing every operation which the secondary cause performs, though in a higher way. (Here, the *Liber de causis* repeats the example of being, life, and humanity which Proclus uses [70] to argue for a proportion between the universality of the cause and that of the effect;[26] what significance the author of the *Liber* saw in this will become apparent in his seventeenth proposition.)

The second chapter introduces the universal causes in which this principle will be worked out. These are the real beings, and they may be distinguished according as they relate to eternity. The first cause is above eternity as its cause, since eternity is less universal than and hence participates in ("acquires," in the usual language of the *Liber de causis*) being.[27] Intellect is coextensive with eternity, because invariable. Soul, while above time as its cause, is yet below eternity, because subject to modification of its disposition; on the border between time and eternity, Soul cleaves to eternity from below.

The next two chapters apply the principle about primary and secondary causality to the hierarchy just introduced, and fill out the sketch of that hierarchy. Thus, chapter 3 presents the "noble souls," a monotheist's substitute for "divine souls," by which Proclus meant such entities as universal Soul, the world soul, and planetary and astral souls; it also touches upon bodies, both celestial and sublunary, a distinction which the Latin passes over.[28] And it explains that the first cause created the being of Soul by the mediation of Intellect,[29] which is to say that, having created the being of Soul, the first cause placed it under Intellect as a substrate[30] upon which Intellect might operate. Soul is an image of its causes, having within itself power from them; consequently, every noble soul has three operations: its own psychic operation of moving and vivifying bodies, an intellectual operation of knowing "the things" (*al-ašyā*ʾ, i.e., its sensible effects), and a divine, providential operation over nature.[31] However, the power transmitted by its causes is diminished in Soul, with the result that Soul can exercise causality only by moving its effects.

Chapter 4 opens by presenting Being, the first created thing, broadest and most unitary because closest to the One. This Being is said to be above Intellect, Soul, and Sense (with Nature, an emanation of Soul found in Plotinus *Ennead* 5.2.1); but, given the teaching of chapter 2, how can it be both created and above Intellect? In fact, it is Intellect as yet undetermined;[32] its priority to Intellect is the priority of the indeterminate to its determination (this will become clearer in chapter 24). Though closest to the One, Being is not the One, whence its unity admits of some multiplicity: it is composed of finite and infinite (chapter 8 will explain this), and whatever of it is adjacent to the first cause is perfect and most powerful intellect, containing the most universal Forms, whereas its lower part contains less universal Forms (for a reason to be found in chapter 9). In other words, Being/Intellect is a collective of beings/intellects; as a Form is to its numberless instantiations here below, so Being is to the infinite Forms (beings), with this difference, that physical individuals are separate one from another, whereas Forms, though distinct, are not separate (see Plotinus 5.9.6 and 8). Furthermore, the intellects are causally related: the first intellects pour forth the perfections they receive from the first cause upon the second intellects.

The second half of chapter 4 deals similarly with Soul. Whereas the first intellects impress permanent forms (this probably refers to their pouring perfections upon the second intellects), the second intellects impress inclining[33] forms, such as the soul, whose being is likewise composed of finite and infinite. Soul, too, is a collective, in which the more perfect souls are immediately adjacent to Intellect. As first intellects transmit perfections from the One to second intellects, so higher souls transmit perfections from Intellect to lesser souls. Of course, power is diminished in the transmission, so that, whereas higher souls cause permanent things with regular, continuous motion (the heavenly bodies), lesser souls cause things whose permanence is only through generation (sublunary plants and animals).

From chapter 5 on, the text moves systematically through the hierarchy, from top to bottom. The first cause, being first, has no cause before it through which it may be known, wherefore it is ineffable. Still, it is named by the name of its first effect, Intellect, in a higher way, since a cause is what its effect is, in a higher way.

Since the first cause is named by the name of Intellect, chapter 6 begins determining what may be said about Intellect. In the first place, Intellect is an indivisible substance, since it is neither a magnitude nor a body (in which case the collective of intellects would be a multitude) nor mobile (and thence divisible by time). For, it is coextensive with eternity; any multitude in it is in it as one thing; and, when it wants to know a magnitude, it does not extend one of its parts far from another, but rather reverts upon its essence, so that its substance and operation are one thing.

Chapter 7 adds that every intellect knows what is above it, since that is its cause, and what is below it, since that is its effect. However, it knows these things according to the mode of its own substance,[34] which is to say that it knows them intelligibly, not according to the superior or inferior mode of their substance. Hence, they are intelligible in it. For, the things in Intellect (the transcendent Forms) are not the impressions (the immanent forms), but their causes.

Chapter 8 is as much about the first cause as about Intellect, though it necessarily speaks of the ineffable in causal or negative terms. The Good establishes Intellect, gives it subsistence (*qiwām, essentia*), and transmits something of the divine power, whereby Intellect providentially rules everything below it. Indeed, nothing escapes the power of what is above it. Thus, Nature contains generation (sensible, impermanent things), and Soul Nature, and Intellect Soul, so that Intellect contains them all. As for the first cause, it is none of these and above them all, creating Intellect without a mediator and everything else by the mediation of Intellect. Again, its knowledge and power are above psychic and intellectual knowledge and power, creating them. For, whereas Intellect, Soul, and Nature have determinacy[35] and form, the first cause is only being: it is distinguished from other things, not by some form proper to it, but by its very indeterminacy and the purity of its goodness.

Chapter 9 develops themes found in chapter 4. The first intellects, being closer to the One, are more unitary and therefore more powerful than the second intellects. For, although every intellect is full of Forms, the first intellects have them in a more universal way, whereas the second look to the Forms in the first and, unable to receive them as they are, receive them by separating and dividing them.[36]

The tenth chapter argues that, since Intellect is immobile and causes through its immobile being,[37] its effects are sempiternal, wherefore things subject to generation and corruption must have a temporal, corporeal cause.

Chapter 11 expounds a principle which has already been functioning (as in chapter 9) and which will be crucial in the next two chapters: if one thing is in another, it is in it according to the mode of the recipient, not of the received. So being contains life and intellect existentially, life contains being and intellect vitally, and intellect contains being and life intellectually.[38] Thus, effects are in their causes according to the mode of their causes, and causes in their effects according to the mode of their effects: the first being/cause is in Intellect intellectually, Intellect is in Soul psychically, Soul is in Sense sensibly, Sense is in Soul psychically, Soul is in Intellect intellectually, and Intellect is in the first being existentially. Consequently, all are in the first cause in its mode.

Chapter 12 amounts to an explanation for the identification of intellects with beings/Forms, which was asserted in chapter 4. Intellect is at once the intellective subject and the intelligible[39] object, in that Intellect knows its essence. Even when it knows its effects, subject and object are together, since its effects are in it intelligibly, so that it knows them in knowing itself.

Moving down the hierarchy, chapter 13 affirms that every soul contains sensible things, in a more spiritual and unified way, as their exemplar, and intelligible things, in a multiple and moving way, as their image.[40] For, it is between[41] sensibles (its effects) and intelligibles (its causes).

Chapter 14 returns to Intellect without leaving Soul, which, as a lesser sort of self-constituted substance, may be described at the same time as Intellect. Whatever knows itself reverts upon itself in activity, wherefore its substance must also be self-reversive,[42] so that it is self-subsistent, self-sufficient, and simple. (The unstated premise may be supplied from chapter 30: a thing's activity cannot be more perfect than its substance.)

The interpretation of chapter 15, about pure and participated infinity and power, must be somewhat tentative, since "powerful" and "being" appear to have been confused rather early in the Arabic manuscript tradition.[43] The intent seems clear enough, however: to show that, though self-reversive in activity and therefore self-sufficient in being, Intellect is not thereby equal to the first cause (this theme recurs frequently until chapter 23). All infinite powers depend on the first infinite, the power of powers; created things are not powers, they have powers. For, infinity is relative: the first cause, as pure power, is infinite in all respects; Intellect's power is infinite only with repect to things below it (i.e., it causes countless effects, none of which escapes its power), not with respect to what is above it, since its cause remains above it, measuring it and all created beings with the appropriate measure. Thus, as Intellect is not power but has power, so it is not the infinite itself, just unlimited. However, the first cause is above the infinite, which is between it and Intellect.[44]

Chapter 16 continues the explanation of participated infinite powers. The more united a power, the more infinite it is, since the first infinite, Intellect, is next to the One; and the more united and infinite a power, the more wondrous its deeds. Division, on the contrary, destroys infinity. (This recalls chapters 4 and 9, where lesser intellects divided universal Forms into a multiplicity of less universal Forms.)

Chapter 17 seems to distinguish the first cause from Intellect by mode of causality. The first Being, the cause of causes who is at rest, gives all things being by way of creation; by way of form, the first Life, which is a first motion from the first being, makes all living things self-moving; and the first Intellect gives all intellectual things knowledge, also by way of form.[45] The way of creation is proper to the first cause—a crucial point missing from the Latin.

Chapter 18 provides more detail about the hierarchy of beings, and clarifies in passing how a monotheist could call some intellect divine. The perfect in each order are those which depend on the preceding order. Thus, the divine intellect receives much from the first perfections which come from the first cause, whereas the mere intellect receives by the mediation of the prior intellect. The intellective soul depends on intellect, whereas the mere soul does not. Likewise, the animate body is governed by a soul, whereas the mere natural body has no soul.[46]

Chapter 19 teaches that the first cause rules all created things without commingling with them or losing unity. For, its rule has no diversity: it pours out perfections over things by a single outpouring, but each receives according to its possibility.[47] The efflux is single because the first cause is pure goodness, and its goodness is its being,[48] and it acts by its being alone, without any relation[49] to its effect. (The unstated premise, of course, is that goodness is self-diffusive; hence, where goodness is pure and essential, self-diffusion is without a more or less, without any holding back.) For, a relation to its effect would be an addition to its uncomposed being;[50] again, were it distinct from its act of governing, its governance would be imperfect and would not penetrate things deeply.[51]

Chapter 14 concluded that every self-knower is self-subsistent, self-sufficient, and simple; now chapter 20 qualifies that. The first is self-sufficient[52] because of its unity, whereas composites need something else or their components. Nothing but the first, whether corporeal or intelligible, is self-sufficient—a denial which calls to mind the teaching of chapters 4 and 8, that even intelligible things are in some sense composites. Thus, taken together, these chapters imply that simplicity and self-sufficiency both admit of degrees.

Chapter 21 picks up the theme of chapter 5, divine ineffability, from a different perspective, while continuing the contrast between the first cause and the perfection of such beings as Intellect. The first cause is above perfection, since it is good without limit (i.e., not by participation), wherefore, unlike perfect things, which cannot pour forth perfections *from themselves* (since they have acquired them by participation), it creates all things. Consequently, the first cause is above every name, whether it signify an imperfection or a perfection.

Like chapters 17, 19, and 21, chapter 22 shows how far the causal activity of the first cause exceeds that of Intellect: God gives Intellect providential governance, governs what Intellect governs, and governs more than Intellect governs, bestowing perfections even on what has no desire to receive the outpouring of knowledge from Intellect.[53] (This is the only chapter to call the first cause "God.")

Chapter 23 brings this desire to receive together with the single efflux of chapter 19. The first cause is present to all things in one way, but things are present to it in different ways, according to their capacity to receive and delight in it, a capacity determined by their mode of being and knowing.

Chapters 24 through 28 pick up where chapter 14 left off, considering self-constituted substances. No self-subsistent substance is generated, else it would need that from which it was generated for its perfection, since generation is a way from imperfection to perfection. But the self-subsistent is always perfect, because it is the cause of its own formation. And it becomes the cause of its own formation because of its constant gazing[54] upon its cause.[55]

Since generability and corruptibility go together, chapter 25 concludes that self-subsistent substances cannot be corrupted: being their own cause, they cannot be separated from their cause.

Chapter 26 contrasts destructible substances, which are either composed (of matter and form, one assumes, not just of finite and infinite, since indestructible Intellect is so composed) or subsisting in another (as immanent forms).

Chapter 27 shows that self-constituted substances are not only incorruptible, but also indivisible. For suppose a divisible self-subsistent substance to be simple. In that case, the part is self-subsistent, just like the whole;[56] again (since the self-subsistent are self-reversive, according to *Inst.* 42), the part must be self-reversive, just like the whole.[57] Or suppose a divisible self-constituted substance to be composite. Since its components are unequal (as formal and materiate), the supposition would entail production of the nobler by the baser. Furthermore, whereas the self-subsistent are self-sufficient, composites need their components.

Chapter 28 draws a further conclusion from the ingenerability of self-subsistent substances: that they are not in time, and are above temporal substances.

Chapters 29 through 31 conclude the movement down the hierarchy of beings, introducing corporeal things and explaining their connection with the higher things, right up to the first cause. Readers of chapter 28 may have thought of a counter-example to its thesis: strictly speaking, celestial bodies are ingenerable, and yet they are somehow in time. Resolving the difficulty, chapter 29 distinguishes the sempiternal above time, which has all its operations together and is whole through its essence, from the sempiternal in time, which has a before and after in its operations and is whole through its parts, and from the transitory. Were nothing sempiternal in time, there could be no contact between the sempiternal above time and the transitory.

Chapter 30 describes another mediation, that of soul, which has its substance in eternity and its action in time. Thus, it links that whose substance and action are both in eternity with that whose substance and action are both in time. No other mediation is possible: since a thing's action cannot surpass its substance, nothing could have its substance in time and its action in eternity.

Chapter 31 reiterates the dependence of all levels of being on the first cause. Whatever is in both time and eternity in different respects is both being and becoming in different respects. Beings, the intermediate things, and things which just become are all dependent on pure Being. And all unities depend on the pure One, whose unity is unacquired.[58] There can be only one pure One, for how would two be differentiated?

1.5 A Doctrinal Problem

Many important motifs run throughout the *Liber de causis*, one of which has a special hold upon Albert's attention: that the outpouring from God is single. To draw together the threads of the argument, God is essentially good, so that his granting of goodnesses is without a more or a less. The evident gradation of beings results from their diverse receptive capacities, in turn determined by

the mode of their substance. And what determines that? God alone creates, but secondary causes can form; now, the more the mediators involved in a thing's production (or, the more "distant" it is from the first cause), the less powerful its proximate cause. Still, why this declension of power among secondary causes? Again, the answer lies in the receptive capacities of the secondary causes, and the question of what determines their mode of being and receiving returns. Perhaps Nature does form generable things, and Soul Nature, and Intellect Soul, but what forms the first created thing? God? Possibly the talk of God's measuring every being with the appropriate measure will be taken to signify that God is not absent from the process of formation; however, the source (*Inst.* 92) would suggest another interpretation. Moreover, it seems problematic to trace a being's delimitation to pure, unbounded Goodness. The only explicit statement about the formation of Intellect is that it forms itself.[59] Still, this seems to remove God's causality from the diversity of his effects, whereas the *Liber* insists that God's all-embracing power penetrates things most deeply and extends even to the last effects. The reader is left in some confusion.

The authority of the *Liber* on God's single efflux was reinforced by that of Aristotle's *De generatione et corruptione* 2.10 (336^{a}27, *translatio Vetus*): "Idem enim et similiter habens semper idem innatum est facere."[60] Many scholastics sensed heresy: if God can make only one creature, then, since more than one creature exists, creatures must create the rest. Indeed, the *Liber* seemed to say just that in chapter 3: the first cause creates the being of Soul with Intellect mediating.[61] But Albert appears not to have shared these fears: throughout *De causis et processu universitatis*, he makes strong arguments for the Peripatetic dictum; he even criticizes theologians who "misunderstand" and deny it, invoking Dionysius against them (*De causis et proc. univ.* 1.1.10 [22.1-16]).

Martin Grabmann cites Albert's repeated claims to be reporting Peripatetic teaching, not his own, and points out Albert's perfectly orthodox opinion in *Summa Theologiae* 2.1.3.3.1 (where he speaks in his own name), an opinion echoed in the writings of his disciples.[62]

Pierre Duhem finds this unsatisfactory.[63] When Albert's Aristotelian paraphrases refute Avicebron's doctrine that God's free choice determines what sorts of things are made, they refute the orthodox position; they choose the Neoplatonic theory of necessary emanation over the Augustinian tradition. True, Albert warns his readers against assuming he agrees with the opinions he expounds. But who can believe these protestations, since Albert takes sides and shows none of the historian's impartiality? If he defends orthodox views against those of Aristotle in his paraphrase of the *Physics*, that is because

sous le même froc de Frère Prêcheur, deux Albert se sont succédés.

L'Albert qui entreprenait l'exposé de la Philosophie d'Aristote et qui rédigeait la *Physique*, était tout imbu encore des enseignements de la Théologie. . . .

L'étude patiente et prolongée des doctrines gréco-arabes convertit peu à peu l'auteur de la *Physique*, et l'on vit apparaître alors un second Albert, l'Albert de la *Métaphysique* et du *Livre des Causes*. Pour celui-ci, les propositions augustiniennes que le premier Albert avait, en sa *Physique*, soigneusement sauvegardées devenaient autant d'affirmations absurdes en Philosophie. . . .[64]

But is the opinion set forth in Albert's theological works so very different from that found in his paraphrase of the *Liber*? Must one choose between his theology and the philosophy he presents? Or is his critique of the theologians more subtle than that? How does he understand this eminently Neoplatonic text *secundum Peripateticos*?

TWO

Emanation and Causation

Although readers of Aristotle's *Metaphysics* work through painstaking analyses of "principle" (Δ.1) and "cause" (Δ.2), when they turn to the completion of metaphysics in the *Liber de causis*, they encounter an obviously related and yet unfamiliar concept, "emanation," and find that the first "cause" is a source from which effects "flow." Evidently to bridge the gap between Aristotle's usage in the *Metaphysics* and the language of the supposedly Aristotelian *Liber*, Albert prefaces his paraphrase of the *Liber* with a tractate devoted to *fluere* and *influere*, beginning with the sort of lexical analysis Aristotle had performed, and proceeding to a summary of emanative systems, especially as found in Ibn Sīnā and al-Ġazālī.[1] Since Albert's analysis highlights the aspects of sameness and unity in emanation, the question about the origin of diversity takes on additional urgency.

Albert starts by distinguishing *fluere* from *causare* and *principiare*. Flowing cannot be the same as causing, he says, for, whereas causing may be either equivocal or univocal,[2] flowing is neither. It is not equivocal causation, because as a stream's waters and those of its source are of the same kind, so is what flows of one form with its origin.[3] And, despite this oneness of form, flowing is not univocal causation,[4] since univocal causes sometimes cause their effects in another, in a subject, whereas a source pours forth a simple form, without transmuting anything into a subject for that form. Here Albert apparently has in mind the way a spring seems just to pour water forth into a bed, rather than altering the bed and educing water from its potency.[5]

Of course, sometimes forms do emanate into a matter which is altered in the process. Still, Albert insists, when this occurs, an instrumental cause, not the emanative source as such, does the altering. He illustrates with one of his favorite examples, that of the artisan—a favorite because God is an artisan of sorts. A form in the mind of an artisan emanates first to his *spiritus*, then, by that vehicle, to his hands, then to his tools, and finally to the work itself. Indeed, one has to say that the artisan's idea somehow gets into his hands and his tools, otherwise his hands and his tools could not shape raw materials according to his idea. Now, "flowing" is appropriately applied to artistic production, because, throughout its travels from mind to artifact, the form of art remains *eiusdem rationis*. Yet the artisan's raw materials are altered (for instance, if he is a smith, metal is heated), that they might be fit subjects for artificial form. But they are altered by the artisan's tools (the smith's forge), and the altering is because of the matter (the metal's hardness, which would be unreceptive of the horseshoe's form); raw materials are not altered by or because of the form (the smith's idea of a horseshoe is not hot and malleable).[6] Thus, flowing implies only the procession of form from a simple formal principle.

Procession of form from a simple formal principle? Do not Peripatetics speak, rather, of educing form from matter? They do speak of educing, and that is indeed causing, not flowing. But the very form which is educed from and (materially) caused by matter may also be said to flow, inasmuch as it is an act from an act (for instance, a house from the house in the architect's mind, as Aristotle says).[7] Albert portrays change as both flowing and eduction in his *Metaphysics* as well; for instance, in answer to the question where the form of a composite goes when the composite is corrupted, at one point he gives the expected Peripatetic answer, that it goes back into the potency of the matter (7.5.10 [C16.2:388.5–9]), while at another he surprises his readers by explaining that it is resolved into the light of the intelligence which makes and informs the spheres and other causes (4.3.9 [C16.1:199.78–200.35]). For Albert, then, emanation and eduction can be two aspects of one coming-to-be; when he considers what comes to be as already present in the potency of a subject, then he speaks of eduction, and when he considers what comes to be as already present in the actuality of an agent, then he speaks of emanation.[8] And "procession" is what the ancient Peripatetics called this sort of flowing.[9]

Besides sameness and simplicity, "flowing" implies that the font remains undiminished, as the sun is not lessened by its shining (*De causis et proc. univ.* 1.4.1 [43.16–25]). Albert's shift from water to light is typical of emanationism; their similarity, revealed by our use of "pour" and "stream" for both alike, explains in part how he can weave a rich light metaphysics throughout his paraphrase of the *Liber*, which mentions light only twice (5 [91.54–56] and 15 [144.76]). The example of light indicates further that flowing must be ever in process, lest the derived lose what they have received: when the sun is eclipsed, all bodies are left without their color.[10]

Flowing and causing, then, are not identical notions. Nor is flowing the same as being a principle. For, as the very word indicates, a principle is something of the "principled," namely, its first part;[11] but this is not always the case with a font: the first font cannot be mixed with anything or enter as an element into the constitution of anything. We must return soon to this procedure of Albert's, whereby he does not simply observe water flowing and draw as many comparisons with divine activity as he can, but rather—at least in part—argues from previously established conclusions about divine activity to what flowing must be. For now, though, he adds that, because a font need not be part of its derivative, flowing may be mediate as well as immediate.

Of course, like Aristotle, Albert recognizes extended senses of "principle," senses in which the principle may be extrinsic to that whose principle it is (*Metaph.* 5.1.1 [C16.1:208.52–209.13, 25–35]). In *De causis et processu universitatis*, Albert keeps to the more proper sense of the word, as revealed by its supposed etymology; nonetheless, provided one kept the various senses straight, nothing would be wrong with speaking of an emanative principle. In fact, Albert himself is capable of writing that "principium sit id a quo fluit res primo" (ibid., 8.1.1 [C16.2:389.25–26]). Likewise, one could make a case for the expression "emanative cause"; after all, the *Liber de causis* opens with an assertion that each "causa primaria" is "influens," and Albert goes so far as to call the first cause a "fonte effectivo et formali et finali" (*De causis et proc. univ.* 2.1.2 [62.15–16]; see also 1.4.4 [46.91–47.20]). His point, then, is not that fonts are in no sense causes, but that flowing says more than just causing and does not coincide with any of the divisions of causality Aristotle makes. Not all causes are fonts, but fonts are indeed causes.

Having clarified *fluere*, Albert turns to the compound *influere*. Obviously, it means introducing the flux into a recipient; but where is the containing implied by the prefix *in-*? What, in other words, is the analog to the bed and banks receiving the spring's water? Just the possibility of the thing which receives the influx, answers Albert, since that possibility is from the thing itself.[12]

That a thing's possibility is from itself Albert has shown earlier (*De causis et proc. univ.* 1.1.8 [16.69–17.11]), and his explanations are well worth lingering over, since the doctrine is both important and easily misunderstood. The first point to note is that "from itself" is a grammatically positive way of expressing the negative "not from another": Albert means that a thing's possibility has no cause, not that it causes itself, since he considers self-causation absurd (ibid., 1.1.10 and 1.4.5 [20.6–8, 21.28–31, and 48.52–55]). Now, as Albert explains it, the proposition that a thing's possibility has no cause combines insights from Aristotle and Ibn Sīnā. Aristotle contributes the observation that we never ask why a thing is itself, for instance, why a man is a man; the question would be pointless and unanswerable because the principle of identity is self-evident (*Metaph.* 1022ª25–35 and 1041ª9–20). Ibn Sīnā contributes the equation of "what a thing is," or essence, with possibility—possibility for existence.[13]

So, when Albert writes that a thing's possibility or essence is from itself, he claims only that no cause may be sought why a thing is what it is; he explicitly cautions his readers against concluding that essence is uncaused in every respect, because when possibility is actualized, then there is at least an efficient cause to investigate.[14]

To resume, Albert was looking for the analog to the river bed which is just there receiving the waters of its source. He finds something else which is just there, unexplained, and that is a thing's possibility. When he goes on to describe the filling up of this recipient, he takes creation as his case of emanation, saying that a thing's possibility for existing, when filled by the cause of its existing, contains and serves as a foundation for the existence which has flowed into it.[15] Albert's readers may ask how, if creation is from nothing, it can presuppose a recipient. But he does not mean that God's creative emanation presupposes a patient, such as the passive potency of matter. Instead, the possibility preceding a thing's creation is merely the intrinsic possibility of anything whose notion includes no contradictions: "rational animal" was possible even before Adam and Eve, while "square circle" is not possible and cannot be created. The recipient of creative emanation is an odd sort of recipient, then, constituted as an actually existing recipient in the receiving.[16]

Besides containing existence, possibility plays a role in determining the order of fluxion, by both occasioning and limiting further flowing. For, emanation does have an order, just as the waters of a spring must fill the beginning of the stream before flowing on to its middle and end. Albert explains the order in this way. Liquids, having no bounds of their own, flow boundlessly until they come upon containers, whose shape they take. Like liquids, God has no bounds and flows boundlessly until the flux reaches a recipient's possibility. And the finitude of this possibility collects the flux until its abundance spills over, so that the emanation continues. When Albert describes *how* the emanation continues, he shifts from the image of waters spilling over to that of rivers staying within their banks. Unlike liquids and God, the recipient has limits of its own, namely, the limits of its possibility, of its essence. Consequently, whereas God flows boundlessly, the recipient flows in the measure of its possibility, until the flux reaches the possibility of the next recipient, and so on. After all, recipients cannot give more than they have received; however, if they were not determinate, they would not flow at all, since they could not even receive an inflow.[17] What Albert has done here is establish that there are secondary causes and that their causality is particular—and more particular the greater their distance[18] from the first[19]—, while God's is universal. And, as Albert carefully points out, a secondary cause flows only by virtue of its font, since of itself it has only the possibility of containing; were its font to fail, it too would run dry, though not vice versa, since a stream does not flow back into its spring.

This order of flowing may be expressed as four modes of influx. According to the first, the notion which the flowing form has in its font is preserved in the derivative. For instance, the first font is the universally acting intellect, and its outpouring constitutes and illumines intelligence.[20] By the second mode, the stream of light enters recipients according to its shadow, because of its distance from the font's pure clarity. Thus, the soul, because of its need for the body, suffers shading of the streaming light which constitutes it.[21] The third mode corresponds to the setting of the first light, in which that light is made corporeal, because it is in its recipients according to their capacity, which is for corporeality. The fourth is the streaming of light into what is mixed with darkness, as when the recipient is not only corporeal (as heavenly bodies), but also subject to contrariety and change (as sublunary bodies), which are opposed to the pure clarity of the first light.

These four states of light[22] recur throughout *De causis et processu universitatis*, and far more often than water imagery. For, Albert seems to think, light flows more truly than water. Indeed, properly speaking, water and other material things do not flow. His reason for this remarkable claim is that what flows does so on its own, without another moving it—one need not push a sunbeam to start it streaming down—, whereas material things are liable to be acted upon and moved. Thus, they flow, not by their own power, but *per accidens*, when something acts upon and dissolves them; and their flowing is but an imitation of the true, spiritual flowing. What truly flows, then, needs only its unimpeded communicability, extending itself so as to multiply itself. And only two things do this: first, the intellectual light of active intellect, and second, its copy, corporeal light.[23]

Now it becomes clear why Albert sometimes argues from what divine activity is to what flowing must be: God's creative act is the most perfect case of flowing. Talk of divine flowing may seem an obvious instance of metaphorically transferring a bodily characteristic to something spiritual, and Albert's repeated reference to rivers may seem to confirm this; however, his procedure involves looking to a bodily *exemplum* (e.g., water), observing its characteristics (e.g., flowing without apparent extrinsic impulsion), and finding those characteristics to a greater degree in spiritual beings (e.g., though water appears unmoved, its flowing in fact requires something to warm and keep it liquid, whereas God communicates himself while absolutely unmoved).

In a sense, Albert's argument should come as no surprise: he speaks of emanation throughout this and other philosophical works and yet repeats Aristotle's disapproval of metaphors in philosophy,[24] as if there were no question of emanation falling under that head. Still, Albert's assertion that "what is material does not, properly speaking, flow" seems excessively strong, especially when compared with his usual treatment of non-metaphorical divine names. In his opinion, all the words in Dionysius' *On the Divine Names* apply literally to God, and the perfections they signify are at their most perfect in God, yet they apply literally also to the creatures through which the human mind learns of these perfections. Thus, he does not deny that a wise man is properly speaking wise simply because God is wise in an infinitely better way.[25] Why, then, even if God does flow most of all, should Albert deny that water flows? Again, if his attitude is such that he takes flowing and the like to apply literally to spiritual realities, then there is something peculiar in the fact that, although Augustine presents the illumination of angelic intellects as the literal interpretation of "let there be light," Albert's theological works label that reading symbolic and metaphorical.[26]

On the other hand, one passage calls Augustine's reading "mystical,"[27] a term Albert usually contrasts with "symbolic": God's symbolic names are taken from sensible things, to which they apply first and foremost, whereas his mystical names are taken from intelligible things, and signify perfections which belong properly and primarily to him. His symbolic names are metaphorical; his mystical names, though proper, are not said of him and of creatures in the same way. For, two things are involved: the perfection signified and the mode of signifying. And while the nature of the perfection is always in God before and more properly than it is in creatures, nevertheless, the complex mode in which the human mind understands and signifies it falls short of God's utterly simple reality.[28] Hence, mystical terms apply to God and creatures analogically.[29] And if so, then either Albert speaks loosely when he calls Augustine's exegesis mystical, or he is somewhat hesitant whether light is metaphorically or literally and analogically said of spiritual beings.

Signs of hesitance again appear when Albert discusses action in his *Summa theologiae*.[30] Flowing, which Albert has said God does without a previous undergoing, seems to fall under the category action, about which Augustine made similar claims: "Quod autem ad faciendum attinet, fortassis de solo Deo verissime dicatur: solus enim Deus facit et ipse non fit, neque patitur" (*De Trinitate* 5.8 [PL42:917C]). Albert comments on this text in a tractate "on things said of God through metaphor and likeness." The solution declares that, among the categories, only substance and relation are said literally of God. However, replying to the Augustinian objection, Albert explains that action may be considered in two ways: as from the agent *qua* agent, or as performed by lower agents because of some need. Augustine's words are true of action considered in the first way, which, by passing over the agent *qua* patient suffering need, opens upon an action exceeding the bounds of the category and losing its note of accidentality. This *actio ultra genus* is predicated substantially of God, whose action is his substance.[31] Now, these two ways of considering action apparently correspond to the perfection signified (productive action) and the mode of signifying (which reflects the imperfect agents we know first), a distinction Albert uses to explain analogy, not metaphor. And, several paragraphs later, he seems to remove action from the list of categories predicated only metaphorically of God: of itself, he writes, action implies neither dependence nor imperfection, but rather most perfect being, upon which others depend; therefore, action may be said of God, though the needs driving created agents to action may not.[32]

Even if Albert does use metaphors in philosophy,[33] he minimizes their philosophical drawbacks by translating them into plain speech. Metaphor is obscure "quia nescitur qua similitudine transferatur" (*Top.* 6.1.2 [B2:433a], paraphrasing Aristotle *Top.* 139ᵇ34); however, Albert's tractate on flowing does his readers the service of pinpointing the likenesses between material and spiritual flowing. Distance and shadow he also explains: they amount to dissimilitude and difference (see nn. 18 and 21). And light imagery has to do with intelligibility: form, since it makes a thing knowable, is a sort of light.[34]

As Albert's remarks about true, spiritual flowing make clear, the best "translation" for *fluxus* is self-communication: "communicabile in eo quod communicabile, fluere habet" (*De causis et proc. univ.* 1.4.4 [47.21–22]). Still, in what sense is God communicable? In other words, to what extent may God be said to emanate?

THREE

God's Incommunicability to Creatures

3.1 An Apparent Contradiction

If font and efflux are of one form, then, given the radical distinction between Creator and creature, it is hard to see how God can flow at all, much less flow into a multiple and diversified creation. Far from evading the difficulty, Albert repeatedly declares both that God is most communicable and that he is utterly incommunicable. On the one hand, he must be communicable, because he is undoubtedly good:

> Dicit Areopagita Dionysius, quod 'bonum est sui communicativum et diffusivum.'[1] Largitates autem sive processiones primi super omnes sunt magis communicabiles et ideo sunt maxime bonitates bonitatum habentes rationes. (*De causis et proc. univ.* 2.3.15 [152.5–9])

> Quidam posteriorum, sicut Avicenna et Alfarabius et Algazel, quaedam adhuc [i.e., praeter posse, scire, et velle] debere addi contenderent. Dicunt enim addi debere bonitatem. Bonitas enim, ut dicunt, dispositio est ad emittendum. Si enim ponatur, quod aliquis possit et sciat et velit, non sequitur, quod fluat vel emittat in opere. Invidia enim potest impedire [Plato *Tim.* 29E; Aristotle *Metaph.* 983ª2–3]. Sed si bonus sit, cum bonum sit communicativum sui et suorum, statim in bonitatibus fluet et emittet. (Ibid., 1.3.5 [40.47–54])

> Si autem quaeritur, quid facit primum fontem emittere hunc fluxum, cum possit nihil agere in primum, dicendum, quod ipsa communicabilitas primi, cum semper sit in actu et ex copia bonitatis semper exuberet, hanc facit emanationem. (Ibid., 1.4.1 [43.26–30])

On the other hand,

> Omnino enim incommunicabile est [primum principium]. . . . (Ibid., 2.2.18 [111.77–78])

> Inter omnia incommunicabile est [primum] secundum 'id quod est.' (Ibid., 2.4.5 [160.31–32])

> Ipsa [causa prima] secundum seipsam incommunicabilis est. . . . (Ibid., 2.4.7 [161.8–9])

> *Deus benedictus et sublimis* . . . propter incommunicabilitatem super omnia sublimatur. (Ibid., 2.4.10 [163.80–164.1], glossing "Deus, benedictus et sublimis" from LC 22 [163.84])

If consideration of God's goodness causes Albert to affirm communicability, what would make him negate it? One begins to guess the sort of problem involved while examining the third chapter of his tractate on flowing, where he presents emanative communicability as a later Peripatetic alternative to the pantheism of the earliest Peripatetics. For, the first metaphysicians, such as Hermes Trismegistus[2] and Asclepius, held that the first principle penetrates all things, so that whatever is in them is either God or matter or an accident; and even while God's essence remains the same, his mode of being is diversified as matter casts ever deeper shadows upon it.[3]

Albert finds this opinion abhorrent, not only for errors about the divine nature, but also for an error about created nature: the opinion does away with the gradation of things by making God's essence the form of each and every thing.[4] Indeed, throughout *De causis et processu universitatis*, Albert seems preoccupied with pantheism, at least in part because it was not confined to the most ancient Peripatetics:

> Et hic quidem error antiquissimorum fuit, quem postea Alexander renovavit, et alii quidam dicentes Iovem esse omnia. . . . Quidam autem, qui materiam primam esse dixerunt primum principium, dicebant Palladem esse omnia et in templo Apollinis inscriptum esse, quod Pallas est, quidquid erat et quidquid est et quidquid erit, cuius peplum nullus umquam revelare potuit. (*De causis et proc. univ.* 1.4.5 [49.27–36])

Who were the "alii" who said that Jove was all things, or the "quidam" who spoke of Pallas Athene? Lucan wrote that "Iuppiter est quodcumque vides," and Plutarch of Chaeronea reported the inscription in the temple of Isis/ Athene, ἐγώ εἰμι πᾶν τὸ γεγονὸς καὶ ὂν καὶ ἐσόμενον· καὶ τὸν ἐμόν πέπλον οὐδείς πω θνητὸς ἀνεκάλυψεν; but, much closer to Albert's day, David of Dinant repeated Lucan's words and apparently translated Plutarch's.[5] Now, Albert did consider David both a follower of a certain Alexander[6] and a pantheist; moreover, the suspect parts of David's work, if rightly interpreted as pantheistic, are pantheism of the very sort Albert most often attacks in *De causis et processu universitatis*, namely, identifications of God, mind, and matter.[7] And Albert knew well that, although David had been condemned in 1210, his influence lingered: "Discipulus autem ejus quidam, Balduinus nomine, contra meipsum disputans..." (*Summa* 2.1.4.3 obj. 7 [B32:109b]).

3.2 *Esse* and *Id Quod Est*

To understand the reconciliation of God's communicability and incommunicability, or even to feel the force of the question, one must first observe Albert commenting on *Liber de causis* 19, since that is at once a rejection of pantheism and an exposition of the intimacy of divine governance. For there the anonymous writer argues that, were God to commingle with his effects, he would lose his unity and would govern, not by his being, but by an act of governing and according to some relation. Albert could have agreed, since he does hold that God is utterly simple and acquires no real relations from his activity *ad extra* (*De causis et proc. univ.* 1.1.10 and 1.2.5 [20.21–34 and 31.53–58]); however, mistakes and infelicities in the Latin version[8] kept him from recognizing this as the chapter's literal meaning. Nevertheless, he also simultaneously rejects pantheism and asserts divine immanence. This he does, not through the original contrast between agents composed of being and action or relation with those not so composed, but by examining a more fundamental composition, that between *esse* and *id quod est*. All agents, he says, are composed of *esse* and *id quod est*, with the single exception of God, whose unparalleled simplicity both distinguishes him from all things and makes him most communicable.

The substitution of this composition for the other, mistranslated one appears to have been suggested to him by the occurrence of both *esse* and *ens* in *Liber de causis* 19: "Et bonitas prima... non est bonitas nisi per suum esse et suum ens" (158.79–80). Here *esse* is the Arabic *anniyya*, and *ens* is *huwiyya*; while *anniyya* and *huwiyya* are carefully distinguished in some texts, in the *Liber de causis* they are often practically synonymous. Albert, of course, could not have known that; indeed, no one can work out the relations between *esse*, *ens*, and *essentia* from the Latin text, since Gerard of Cremona did not set up a one-to-one correspondence between the Arabic and Latin words pertaining to being (as neither did the Arabic translate Proclus' Greek consistently).[9] At any rate, Albert took the side-by-side occurrence of both *esse* and *ens* to be significant, and revealed what he thought the significance was by substituting his preferred terminology in his paraphrase: "*bonitas* eius, quam influit, *est per suum esse et* per *suum ens* sive 'id quod est'" (*De causis et proc. univ.* 2.4.4 [158.58–59]).[10]

All of this is complicated by the fact that Albert's terminology is not entirely consistent either. That results partly from the inevitable and desirable flexibility of natural language, partly from allusion to several authorities, who themselves use a variable language, and partly from Albert's stylistic shortcomings. Therefore, to comprehend his exegesis of *Liber de causis* 19, we must examine some fluctuations in his vocabulary. Since various studies have scrutinized his ontological vocabulary in general or in his other works,[11] the following remarks can be brief and mostly confined to relevant texts from *De causis et processu universitatis*; additional passages will demand attention later.

The pair *esse* and *id quod est* come from the axioms in Boethius' *De hebdomadibus*; at times, following Gilbert of Poitiers and later authors, Albert uses *quo est* for *esse*: "Et hoc iterum dicit Boethius, et multi dicunt, quamvis non intelligant, quod 'in omni eo quod est citra primum, aliud est esse et "quod est," sive aliud est "quo est" et "quod est"'" (*De causis et proc. univ.* 1.1.8 [17.19–22]).

One could not ask for a clearer identification of *esse* as existence than "*esse, de quo quaeritur per 'an est'*" (ibid., 1.1.10 [19.35]; see also 1.1.8 [16.76–85] and 2.1.17 [81.19–24]). As for *id quod est*, it clearly means "essence" in the following text:

> Omne enim quod ex alio est, aliud habet esse et 'hoc quod est.' Quod enim animal sit animal vel homo homo, hoc est 'hoc quod est,' pro certo non habet ex alio. Hoc enim aequaliter est homine existente et homine non existente secundum actum. . . . Patet ergo, quod omne quod est, 'id quod est' habet a seipso. Esse autem suum in effectu, si ex nihilo est, a seipso habere non potest. (Ibid., 1.1.8 [16.69–17.3]; see also 1.4.5 [49.6–13])

This argument from the existential neutrality of essences is, of course, Avicennian (see especially *Philosophia prima* 5.1–2); yet Boethius, not Ibn Sīnā, gets the credit when, several lines down, Albert explains that this is what Boethius intends by writing, in the axioms of his *De hebdomadibus*, that what is can have something besides what it is.¹² But Albert does not always read Boethius in this Avicennian sense. Thus, just a few pages later, and with what seems a reference back to 1.1.8 and 1.1.10, he writes, "Iam enim habitum est, quod primum est necesse esse, quod nec subiectum alterius est nec in subiecto est, sed idem est sibi esse et 'quod est'" (*De causis et proc. univ.* 1.2.1 [26.2–4]), and the reader is left asking what the identity of God's being and essence has to do with his being neither a subject nor in a subject. Does *quod est* correspond to the "subjectum alterius," and *esse* to what is "in subjecto," and do they still mean "essence" and "existence," respectively? In other words, is Albert implying that, in all but God, existence is in that subject which is essence? Or does he mean something else?

Whatever he means there, when he comments on chapter 8 of the *Liber de causis*, he plainly means something else. For, the *Liber* says that "intelligentia est habens *yliathim* quoniam est esse et forma" (112.76), and, though *yliathim* translated μορφή, "form," it looked suspiciously like ὕλη, "matter."¹³ Accordingly, Albert needed to find something matter-like yet compatible with immaterial intelligence. Now, matter plays a role, not only in change, but also in individuation, so that Aristotle can extend the notion and make an "intelligible matter" account for the existence of more than one geometrical circle (*Metaph.* 1036ª1–11). Albert extends the notion of matter still further: since only particulars act and undergo (Aristotle *Metaph.* 981ª16–17), and since intelligence acts and receives emanations, intelligence must be a particular, a "this something," a supposit or hypostasis (a supposit being what is "placed under" a common nature, such as intellectuality); and, while there is no matter among incorporeal things, the supposit, in determining the commonness of the nature to this or that particular, exhibits a property of matter, wherefore certain philosophers call it "*hyliatin*," a word they derive from ὕλη.¹⁴ *Id quod est* is no longer essence; here, it is this *hyliatin* which underlies essence; it is also what the first cause produces for the reception of *esse*. As for *esse*, it is something resulting from the common nature.¹⁵ And this, Albert now says, is the meaning of Boethius' axioms.¹⁶

The *Liber*, having attributed *hyliatin* to intelligence, to soul, and to nature, both affirms and denies it of God:

Et causae quidem primae non est *yliathim*, quoniam ipsa est esse tantum. Quod si dixerit aliquis: necesse est ut sit ei *yliathim*, dicemus: *yliathim* suum est infinitum et individuum suum est bonitas pura.... (112.77–78)

Albert agrees: since God, like intelligence, acts (though he does not also undergo), and since he is distinct from all things (despite what David of

Dinant claims), he must be a "this something," wherefore he does have a supposit; on the other hand, his utter simplicity requires that this supposit or *id quod est* be the same as his *esse*. Consequently, though he is distinct from all things, he is not cut off from anything; rather, he is omnipresent, as is *esse*.[17] And since *"hyliatin"* and "individual" ordinarily point to the incommunicability of an instance of a kind, which kind is of itself apt to be communicated, they are said of God only improperly: because infinite, he can be neither a kind nor an individual instance thereof nor anything limited to a category.[18] Both the *Liber* and Albert, then, allow God *hyliatin* only in a paradoxical way according to which it is not other than that from which it is in every other case distinguished.

3.3 The Interpretation of *Liber de causis* 19

The doctrine worked out in connection with chapter 8 of the *Liber de causis* reappears in Albert's exegesis of the crucial chapter 19. When the *Liber* states that governance does not weaken or destroy the unity of the first cause, that, Albert thinks, is because God's deity is the divine supposit, and both are his providential goodness ("non est bonitas nisi per suum esse et suum ens" [LC 19 (158.80)]). To clarify this, Albert contrasts the providential rule of secondary causes. Because they are created out of nothing, they are nothing and in potency according to their supposit; but no cause acts according as it is nothing and in potency; therefore, secondary causes act, not according to their *id quod est*, but according to their *esse*. *Esse* in which sense? Form or essence, apparently, since that is from itself (see pp. 17–18 above). For a secondary cause, then, *esse* or *quo est* is also *quo agit*, "that by which it acts," while *id quod est* is *quod agit*, "that which acts." God's providential activity, however, does not thus divide him or manifest any duality in him since, as the first cause, his supposit is no more out of nothing or potential in relation to some prior cause than is his essence; for him to act by his *esse* is for him to act by his *id quod est*, since these are the same in him.[19]

The reader is now in a position to follow Albert's argument why God is altogether incommunicable; it, too, forms part of his exegesis of *Liber de causis* 19. That text opens by claiming that the first cause rules all created things without commingling with them, and gives as the reason for this that governance does not weaken his unity. Albert, again contrasting secondary agents with God, takes their duality as the reason why they do mingle with their effects. Indeed, they must mix with their effects, since action requires contact.[20] And the mixing must be formal, because *id quod est*, as the root of particularization, is incommunicable, while *esse* or *quo agit* is communicable.[21] Thus, when fire acts upon an object, it mixes with the object by heat; and when an intelligence or noble soul constitutes a thing, they mix by the light of form. But God, unlike fire, intelligences, or planetary souls, acts by his *id quod est*, with the result that he remains incommunicable in his every action and unmixed with his effects.[22]

Albert considers that *esse* and *id quod est* explain yet another aspect of *Liber de causis* 19, although now he takes less care to make his explanations fit the actual words of the text, which runs as follows:

> Redeamus ergo et dicamus quod inter omne agens, quod agit per esse suum tantum, et inter factum suum non est continuator neque res alia media. Et non est continuator inter agens et factum nisi additio super esse, scilicet quando agens et factum sunt per instrumentum et non facit per esse suum <...> et sunt composita. Quapropter recipiens recipit per continuationem inter ipsum et factorem suum et est hunc agens seiunctum a facto suo <...>. Agens vero inter quod et inter factum suum non est continuator penitus ... non agit nisi per ens suum.... (159.70–76)

As detailed above (p. 10), this text describes an agent—Albert takes it to be God alone[23]—which acts immediately by its being, not through any relation to its effect, since such a relation would be an addition to its uncomposed being. "Redeamus et dicamus" suggests that this second half of the chapter is partly repetition as well as development of the first; accordingly, just as Albert thinks that the pair *esse* and *id quod est* figure in the first half, so he finds them in the second, though with more difficulty. The *Liber* describes the agent who acts without a *continuator* as he who "agit per esse [*anniyya*] suum tantum" and then as he who "non agit nisi per ens [*huwiyya*] suum"; Albert, apparently suspecting that the language of the text as he has it is loose or corrupt or the result of mistranslation, tidies it up for expository purposes by introducing his preferred terminology. Paraphrasing "inter omne agens, quod agit per esse suum tantum," he adds the other member of his pair: "*inter omne agens, quod agit per esse suum* et '*id quod est*' *tantum*" (*De causis et proc. univ.* 2.4.4 [158.69–71]). For he knows that God acts without a *continuator*, but, in his terminology, created agents are the ones who act "per esse suum tantum." The *continuator*, of course, must be something which is in both the agent and its effect (thus accounting for the mixing of agent with effect), and that would have to be the communicable essence.[24] Once more, Albert must do some violence to the text to make this clear: the original "et non est continuator inter agens et factum nisi additio super esse" ("and a relation between agent and effect must be an addition to its being") becomes "*continuator* enim *inter agens et factum* sive causatum *non est nisi* in his in quibus est *additio* naturae, qua agit, super 'id quod est' sive *super esse* 'eius quod est,' secundum quod est" (ibid., 158.73–159.3; this would be translated: "a cause of continuity between an agent and its effect is found only where there is the addition of a nature, by which the agent acts, to the agent's supposit, i.e., to the being of the individual existent as such"). In other words, in this clause from the *Liber*, Albert takes *esse* as a misleading designation for the supposit, and would translate: "a cause of continuity between agent and effect is an addition to the supposit," i.e., it is essence. When the *Liber* continues this sentence with "scilicet quando agens et factum sunt per instrumentum et non facit per esse suum," Albert must again substitute *ens* or *id quod est* for *esse:* "Et hoc non est nisi *quando agens et factum* fiunt *per* quoddam medium, quod est ut *instrumentum et non facit per* ens suum sive 'id quod est'" (ibid., 159.3–6). In line with this, the words "est hunc agens seiunctum a facto suo" must mean that a composite agent is separate from its effects according to its supposit, though conjoined to them through its essence: "in talibus omnibus *agens* secundum 'id quod est' *seiunctum est ab* eo quod fit, quod *factum suum* vocatur, sed per esse factor continuatus est facto" (ibid., 9–11).

Now, God cannot be at once separate from his effects according to his supposit and conjoined to them through his essence, because, in his unique case, supposit and essence are the same. Consequently, Albert concludes, God must be entirely separate from his effects, in both supposit and essence, not conjoined to them by a *continuator*.[25]

3.4 Resolving the Contradiction

As exegesis, Albert's conclusion gets things exactly backward: the *Liber de causis* actually argues that the agent without a *continuator* is closer to its effects than the agent with a *continuator*, since the first acts upon its effects directly by its being, not through a relation. But far more than accurate exegesis is at stake, for, Albert seems to have proved too much: if, as he has said, action requires contact, how can an entirely separate God act at all?[26] Is any room left for divine communicability, and so for self-diffusive divine goodness, for emanation? To put the problem another way, while form is communicable, Albert expresses reservations about calling God a form because, although form is uncaused according to what it is, it is not an altogether uncaused cause, since it has efficient and material causes (see chap. 2 n. 14). Still, denying that God is in any sense a form would seem to do away with his efficient and final causality as well.[27]

Yet Albert may not be so very far from the teaching of the text before him. While he does reverse the sense of "est hunc agens seiunctum a facto suo," his intention in asserting God's separateness is not to deny the intimacy of divine governance. Rather, he means to reject pantheism, as do the opening words of *Liber de causis* 19. This becomes clearer in the course of his exposition of *Liber* 23, which deals with omnipresence. There he exposes the pantheistic consequences of explaining divine governance through a *continuator*: since the *continuator* would be a communicable essence, present in both agent and effect, there would be one form of all things, and all things would be univocal in that form.[28] And however much Albert stresses the anti-pantheistic side of *Liber* 19, he does teach God's closeness to his effects as well.

Indeed, Albert often tempers his anti-pantheistic remarks with assertions of God's omnipresence. Though incommunicable and not mixed with his effects by a *continuator*, God penetrates them through his very self; he is immediate and proximate to each thing, deserting nothing which is. All things are in their divine font, who is extended through all things essentially and by the presence of his light and the power of his might—extended through all things, acknowledges Albert, but not so as to become part of the essence of anything.[29]

As in *Liber de causis* 19, so too with Albert what accounts for God's closeness to his effects is the very simplicity which ensures that he remains unmixed with them. That is, because his *esse* is his *id quod est*, he is unmixed with his effects, since in them *esse* and *id quod est* are distinct; and, again because his *esse* is his *id quod est*, he is unbounded and therefore penetrates all things.[30] Apparently, the idea is that God, as indeterminate, is not cut off from any of what being can be.[31] In fact, he is nearer to things than are their nearest principles. After all, their proximate principles are immediate and proximate because penetrated by his power, and what is proximate through itself is more proximate than what is proximate through another.[32]

This simplicity which is an indeterminacy allowing God to penetrate all things accounts for his communicability, the sole vehicle for his emanation:

> Et si quaeritur, quid sit vehiculum fluentis, nihil est quaerere. . . . emanatio a primo fonte intellectualis et simplex est. . . . Propter quod vehiculum non habet nisi suiipsius communicabilitatem. Primum enim, de quo locuti sumus, propter suam nimiam simplicitatem penetrat omnia; et nihil est, cui desit ubique et semper existens. (Ibid., 1.4.1 [43.48–56])

Yet, looking carefully at this text, one sees that the "suiipsius" which has communicability is not the first font, but his emanation. Such was also the case with the opening quotation in this chapter: God's gifts or processions are what is most communicable. On the other hand, the very next quotation and that in the third note made the good communicative of his gifts and of himself too.

This tangle of conclusions—that God is incommunicable, though penetrating all things, that his processions are communicable, and that he himself is communicable—begins to sort itself out in light of the tractate on emanation. There Albert explained that the possibility of a thing serves as the recipient of emanation, and that only the first font flows universally, whereas other things flow in the measure of their possibility; Albert gave the example of liquids, which, having no bounds of their own, flow boundlessly until they come upon containers, whose shape they take (see p. 18 above). Now, since God, as utterly boundless, flows boundlessly, he is, in this sense, most communicable.[33] Yet the boundless flux cannot remain boundless, nor does God's communicability make all things God; and this is not because of any lack in the flux or any defect in God's communicability, but only because influx is into a recipient, which must have limits.[34] In other words, God is wholly present to his creatures and gives himself wholly to them—how, indeed, could he give himself in part, when he has no parts?—but he is not wholly received.[35]

Still, how is he received at all if he is not wholly received? Albert cannot mean that only a part of God is received, again because God has no parts. What, then, is received? This problem leads Albert, following Dionysius, to speak of processions from God. It also accounts for why, in the texts about God being extended throughout his creation, he writes about the "praesentia luminis sui," for *lumen* refers to the effect in another of the *lux* in a source.[36]

"Processions" will concern us later, in connection with the first created thing. First and by way of preparation, another Dionysian term demands attention: analogy. Once more following the Areopagite,[37] Albert often speaks of a thing's rank and of its corresponding receptive capacity as its "analogy." That he then has this and not the more familiar Peripatetic meaning[38] in mind is especially plain when he speaks of "a thing's own analogy."[39] For, the Peripatetic notion deals with something had in common, not with one's "own." Nonetheless, the two meanings are not entirely unrelated. Thus, having enumerated various perfections of God's knowledge, Albert writes that intelligences and souls participate in these perfections according to the analogy of each or its proportion to God:

> In intelligentiis autem et ordine intelligentiarum per participationem sunt secundum uniuscuiusque intelligentiae propriam analogiam sive proportionem ad primum. In anima nobili animaliter sunt secundum talis animae, qualis dicta est, proportionem et possibilitatem.[40]

Aristotle uses "analogy" to mean proportion, that is, a likeness of ratios (*Poet.* 1457b16–18); and he recognizes proportion as one reason why a word might come to be "said in many ways" (*Eth. Nic.* 1096b26–29). In the above text, Albert considers the "analogy" of a thing—its grade of being with its consequent receptive capacity—its ratio or proportion to God.[41] One could easily supply the four terms of the proportion: for instance, as a noble soul and its capacity are to God, so is psychic knowledge to divine knowledge. And that emanations are received according to the analogy (capacity) of each recipient has much to do with "analogous naming," though, as will soon appear, not quite of the sort Aristotle describes.

Both kinds of analogy figure in Albert's answer to the question how finite creatures receive God's total self-communication and, thus, how emanation can occur. As he maintained in his tractate on flowing, font and flux must be of one form, not equivocal. But he also denied that they were univocal, and his denial is more than justified when the font is God, since God has no communicable essence to serve as *continuator* between himself and his creature so as to make them univocal. Therefore, in good Peripatetic fashion, Albert has recourse to what is between pure equivocity and pure univocity. In other words, we should expect to find flowing, not among altogether equivocal causes, nor among completely univocal causes, but rather among things which share a name through analogy, such that some get the name primarily and others secondarily:

> [Fluxus] non requiretur in genere causae efficientis aequivocae omnino, quia tunc non esset unum in forma, quod fluit per ipsa et ex ipsis. Et cum primum iterum non sit in eodem genere cum aliquo secundorum, patet iterum, quod non erit inter ea quae omnino univoca sunt. Erit ergo inter ea quae dicuntur per analogiam sive per prius et posterius. . . . (*De causis et proc. univ.* 1.4.6 [49.75–50.1])

"Per prius et posterius" refers, of course, to Aristotle's *Metaphysics*, where Albert reads that "healthy" is predicated of a medicine secondarily, because it benefits the body, which is healthy first and foremost (1003a33–b18). Yet "healthy" as said primarily and secondarily of the body and of medicine does not exactly parallel, for example, "wise" as predicated of Creator and creatures;

no body just *is* health, and no body has all the health there is to have, while God just *is* wisdom. Therefore Albert, commenting on Dionysius, warns against misinterpreting analogy: in the case of Creator and creatures, analogy does not imply something in which God participates first and foremost, while creatures participate in it secondarily; rather, since nothing precedes God such that he can participate in it, one must say that God is this or that *per prius* because he is substantially this or that, whereas creatures are this or that *per posterius* according as they are like their Creator.[42]

Truly, creatures are like their Creator, Albert repeatedly says, all the while denying that the Creator is like his creatures;[43] the receptive capacities of the various grades of being are analogies or proportions to God, yes, but God is not proportioned to them. Explaining the "omnes virtutes" with which *Liber de causis* 15 opens, Albert writes that "all powers" carries no implication that God's power falls under some one genus with, say, the power of an intelligence. Indeed, to say that God's power had something in common with that of creatures even by analogy would be misleading, because the analogy is grounded in creatures, not in God; after all, creatures imitate God, not the other way around. Albert finds the key in the works of Dionysius: creatures participate, not in God or in any aspect of God, but in something of what flows from God.[44] More on the "something of what flows from God" later, but, for now, that causes are not proportioned to their effects is again a Dionysian teaching.[45] However much "analogy" may mean proportion, then, the analogy which interests Albert here is an odd sort of proportion, and, argues Albert while commenting on Dionysius, the Peripatetic theory of analogy applies to talk about God only in an extended sense. For, the analogy familiar to Peripatetics would require something common to God and creature: as things of the same genus or species share some one thing in the same way (thus, "animal" means the same thing when said of a cat and a dog, or "man" when said of Peter and Paul), so things named analogously share some one thing in different ways. But, were anything common to God and creature, God would not *be* that thing; he would only have it, and would therefore be composite. In the case of God and creature, then, analogy must imply, not that some one thing is in both in different ways, but only that a likeness of what is in God is in the creature.[46]

To put this another way, creatures flow or formally proceed from God, not as from a generic or specific form, but only as from an exemplar form. Still, since God is the exemplar of creatures, then, however much they resemble him by only a weak sort of analogy, he is in some sense their univocal cause, as containing their Ideas.[47] Consequently, God bears the title "universal cause" for two reasons: on the one hand, he is universal, not as pantheistically said of all, but as cause of all; on the other hand, the definition of a universal—what is in many and said of many—does apply to God because he is omnipresent and because, being more or less a univocal cause, he communicates to things what they are and are called.[48] And, if God truly is in many and said of many, then, even though he is incommunicable and remains forever unique, we may rightly describe emanation as divine self-multiplication.[49]

FOUR

The First Created Thing

We have seen that Albert abhorred the earliest philosophers' pantheistic account of emanation, not only for its mistaken notion of God, but also because, by making God's essence the form of each thing, it destroyed the gradation of beings. Yet equally true is that an inability to explain the gradation of things can lead to pantheism, with its denial of that gradation.[1] Accordingly, Albert devotes much attention to the origin of diversity throughout *De causis et processu universitatis*.

4.1 *Ab Uno Non Nisi Unum*

Albert puts the problem especially well in his tractate on flowing. Having described the order of emanation in terms of distance from the light, shadow, the setting of light, and the admixture of darkness (see p. 19 above), he asks where the shadow comes from in the procession of the very first creature from the light of God's mind. Certainly not from God, but what else precedes the first creature? Yet if there is no shadow, so that the first creature is just as lightsome as God, then whence the shadow covering the effects of that first creature? It begins to look as though there can never be any shadow at all.[2]

Albert's reflections on divine incommunicability confirm that no supposed darkness in God causes the first shading of light; rather, the complexity essential to a creature (as recipient with received existence) rules out the creation of an equal to the utterly simple God. But perplexities remain. For, the origin of diversity poses a twofold problem: besides the special difficulties occasioned by the procession of the first non-God, further questions surround the variety and multiplicity of the successive non-Gods. To put it another way, it is one question why God makes anything other and less than himself, and quite another why he makes things other and greater or lesser than each other.

Indeed, granted that God does create something less than himself, still, it would seem that he can create only one such thing. After all, agents produce their like, and God is most one; how, then, could his effect not be one? We have seen (p. 13 above) that Aristotle seems to lend his authority to this proposition, as at *De generatione et corruptione* 2.10 (336ª27, *translatio Vetus*): "Idem enim et similiter habens semper idem innatum est facere." Who more than God is always the same and disposed in the same way, without variation of thought or volition or power?[3]

Of course, Aristotle is not talking about some unique first creature, but about the impossibility of explaining both generation and corruption by a single celestial motion; that requires the duality of approach and retreat found in motion along the ecliptic.[4] Motion is Aristotle's concern at *Physics* 8.6 as well, where he argues that the unmoved mover causes things to move always and not just sometimes: "Illud autem, quod est non motum, quia est, sicut diximus simplex, et permanens in eadem dispositione, movet uno motu simplici" (260ª18–19, *translatio Arabico-Latina*). Even at *Metaphysics* 12.8 (1073ª27–28, 1074ª31–37), where he argues against a plurality of heavens on the grounds that each heaven would need its own prime mover, whereas there can be only one pure act, it is not exactly a question of one God being unable to produce more than one heaven. However, these Aristotelian texts did evolve into a doctrine that the One can produce only one thing. The steps in this evolution have yet to be traced satisfactorily; doubtless, Eleatic, Platonic, and Neoplatonic themes played their part. Most notable is Plotinus' question how, since a thing cannot give what it does not have, the One can originate a plurality.[5] At any rate, explicit statements of the doctrine appear in Arabic texts, most importantly Ibn Sīnā's: "Ex uno, secundum quod est unum, non est nisi unum."[6] And Maimonides (2.22) attributes it to Aristotle and all philosophers, specifying (and rejecting) the conclusion Aristotle allegedly drew: not that God moves the one and only heaven, but that he produces one simple intelligence, which in turn produces the next intelligence, and so on. Consequently, Albert feels sufficient confidence about its pedigree to conjecture that Aristotle had formulated it in an untranslated theological treatise:

> Ab uno simplici non est nisi unum. Haec enim propositio ab Aristotele scribitur in epistula, quae est de principio universi esse, et ab Alfarabio et ab Avicenna et Averroe suscipitur et explanatur.[7]

Indeed, he writes that, among philosophers, only Ibn Gabirol denied it, holding that from one comes two (*De causis et proc. univ.* 1.1.6 and 1.4.8 [13.68–14.5, 55.72–80 and 57.65–58.4]).

Since, to Albert's mind, that *Epistula* and the writings of Ibn Sīnā and al-Ġazālī were among the materials from which David the Jew constructed the *Liber de causis*, he is not surprised to discover the same doctrine there. He finds it in precisely the chapter which has already occupied so much of his attention, the nineteenth, with its argument that the efflux of perfections from pure goodness must be single (see pp. 10 and 12–13 above, and *De causis et proc. univ.* 2.4.2). Most of Albert's contemporaries took this in such a way that God would create only the first created thing, an intelligence, which would then carry on the creative work; that seemed to them the meaning of passages like "et causa quidem prima . . . est creans intelligentiam absque medio et creans animam et naturam et reliquas res, mediante intelligentia" (LC 8 [112.71–73]). And that, of course, is heretical,[8] so that "ab uno unum" would eventually appear on Etienne Tempier's list of condemned theses:

Quod ab uno primo agente non potest esse multitudo effectuum. (44)

Quod effectus immediatus a Primo debet esse unus tantum et simillimus Primo. (64)[9]

Albert, however, boldly attacks theologians who attack "ab uno unum" and backs the Peripatetic dictum with Dionysius' near-apostolic authority. Listing the properties of necessary being, he writes that only one thing can issue immediately from it and that Dionysius said as much when he taught that creatures are differentiated by their distance from God but are one and the same in him:

Decima proprietas *est, quod* a primo, quod est *necesse esse,* immediate *non* potest esse *nisi unum.* Et hoc quidem iam omnes concesserunt Peripatetici, quamvis hoc quidam non intelligentes negaverint theologi. 'Idem enim eodem modo se habens non est natum facere nisi unum et idem.' . . . Nec hoc est contra theologum, quia Dionysius dicit, quod ea quae sunt a primo, per distantiam ab ipso accipiunt differentiam. Relata autem ad ipsum et in ipsum unum sunt et idem. Similiter Peripateticus concedit, quod a primo per primum et immediatum, quod aliquo modo distat ab ipso, tota producitur rerum universitas. . . . (*De causis et proc. univ.* 1.1.10 [22.1–15], alluding to *Div. nom.* 5.6 [PG3:820D–821A])

Obviously, Albert's unconventional stance[10] must remain puzzling at least until we determine his understanding of the "one" and "same" and "first" and "immediate."

4.2 *Prima Rerum Creatarum Est Esse; Esse Creatum Primum Est Intelligentia*

"The first created thing" figures in many Arabic texts as a designation for what the Plotinian One originates.

According to Plotinus, whatever is, produces something from itself, as fire produces heat and perfume diffuses its fragrance (5.1.6.30–40). Now, the One is utter fullness. It is all things and no thing, because all things come from it; it is not being, in order that it may generate being. And being is generated when the superabundance of the One overflows, making something other than itself. Were this flowing motion away from the fullness of the One and toward something other to continue indefinitely, it would end in utter emptiness. However, the motion stops, the Other halts; the result is Being, less than the One and yet full. And not only does this Other halt; it also turns to the One and is filled, looks toward it and becomes Intellect (5.2.1.1–13). In this way, Being constitutes itself as Intellect (5.1.7.13–14), and generates all the beings (Ideas/intellects) within itself (ibid., 27–35; 5.9.8). For, Intellect, wishing to think the One, ends by conceiving something else (ἄλλο, "other"; i.e., itself, Being) made multiple in itself (5.3.11), since the One exceeds its receptive capacity (6.7.15.13–22). This self-constitution of Intellect may be described as the imposition of the Forms on intelligible matter, that is, on Being (2.4.5.28–34).

The brevity of the *Liber de causis* assumes rather than explains Plotinus' vision. Nonetheless, even readers without access to the *Enneads* can reconstruct parts of his system. For, while the fourth proposition of the *Liber* has it that "prima rerum creatarum est esse" (88.63), there are equally explicit declarations about *intelligentia*:

Esse quidem creatum primum est intelligentia totum. (LC 4 [88.72])

Intelligentia quidem non recipit divisionem quoniam est primum creatum quod creatum est a causa prima. (LC 6 [101.81–82])

Ens primum creatum, scilicet intelligentia ... (LC 15 [144.65, repeated with slight variations in ll. 67–68 and 71])

Causatum primum ... est intelligentia.... (LC 15 [144.78])

Intelligentia est primum creatum et est plus similis Deo sublimi. (LC 22 [163.84–85])

Obviously, *esse* and *intelligentia* go together somehow, so that the first created thing is also an *intelligentia*.

Most of Albert's contemporaries, it seems, rightly took this to mean that the first created thing was a separate, intellective substance.[11] And, adding the premise that from the One only one can come, a number of them wrongly concluded that the *Liber* made everything else the creature, not of God, but of a created intelligence.[12] With Albert, the situation is reversed. Refusing to attribute this particular heresy to Aristotle, he rightly reads the *Liber* as teaching that everything other than God is God's creature; but he defends his reading by means of a twofold interpretion of the first created *intelligentia*. While recognizing that, in most of the chapters cited, *intelligentia* means "separate, intellective substance,"[13] he denies that this is always the case.

4.2.1 The First Interpretation

4.2.1.1 Intelligentia

Explaining *Liber de causis* 4, Albert examines both *esse* and *intelligentia*. To take *intelligentia* first, it often designates the ten planetary movers, but Albert finds another sense in James of Venice's translation of Aristotle's *De anima*: "Indivisibilium igitur intelligentia [νόησις] in his est circa quae non est falsum" (430ª26–28, quoted from memory at *De causis et proc. univ.* 2.1.19 [83.70–71]). Here, *intelligentia* refers to simple apprehension, the first act of the mind, and so to the concept.[14] Thus, *intelligentia* is an equivocal name (ibid., 2.1.21 [85.72–76]). And Albert decides that, in the clause "esse quidem creatum primum est intelligentia totum," *intelligentia* must have the second meaning, so that the first created thing is the concept of being. As for the second and third *intelligentiae*, they would be the next most universal concepts, namely, "living" and "sentient":

> Quando autem dicimus esse intelligentiam simplicem, non intelligimus, quod sit intelligentia, quae substantia intellectualis est in decem ordines multiplicata, . . . sed quod est intelligentia, hoc est, forma a lumine intellectus agentis in esse producta et in simplici illo lumine per intentionem accepta, sicut dicimus esse intelligentiam primam et vivere intelligentiam secundam et sensibile intelligentiam tertiam et sic deinceps. (Ibid., 2.1.19 [83.61–69])

But on what grounds does he decide this? As we shall see later, the choice will allow him to defend "ab uno unum," but it is not the manifestation of some desire to read orthodoxy into heresy. Rather, it seems dictated by the very description of *intelligentia* in *Liber de causis* 4.

To recall that description, being, the first created thing, is above intelligence, soul, and sense. It is broadest and most unitary because closest to the One; nevertheless, it is not the One, whence its unity admits of some multiplicity: it is composed of finite and infinite, and whatever of it is adjacent to the first cause is most powerful intelligence, containing the most universal intelligible forms, whereas its lower part contains less universal forms. Thus, being is entirely intelligence, and being/intelligence is a collective of intelligences or intelligible forms, which, though distinct, are not separate. Furthermore, the intelligences are causally related: the first intelligences pour forth the perfections they receive from the first cause upon the second intelligences. And these latter impress such forms as the soul.

When the anonymous author of the *Liber de causis* so describes *intelligentia*, he undoubtedly means what Plotinus means: that the Forms, as immaterial, are thinking intellects (*Enn.* 5.4.2.44–50, 6.6.6.19–26), and that all the Forms are one Intellect. He is not discussing separate intellects as opposed to intelligible forms, or intelligible forms as opposed to separate intellects, since these are but the subjective and objective aspects of the one intelligible world. Albert, however, has no such theory of intelligences; the planetary movers of which he learns from other "Peripatetic" texts do not make up a hierarchy of genera and species. Now, the foregoing description of *intelligentia* would cause great difficulties to any commentator trying to expound it in terms of planetary movers; but it does lend itself to exposition in terms of more and less universal concepts, since that is part of what its author had in mind.

Accordingly, Albert understands by the unity of *esse* its not being composed of genus and difference.[15] This gives it unparalleled predicative breadth, since differences are divisive (*De causis et proc. univ.* 2.1.18 [83.31–48]). In this sense, the *Liber* places it above the more particular concepts of intelligence,[16] soul, and sense. It is composed of finite and infinite because of its relations: with respect to what it comes from (the Creator), it is finite—more on that shortly—but with respect to what comes from it, it is infinite.[17] More precisely, it is potentially infinite, since it can be divided indefinitely into substance and accident, genera, species, and subspecies. And this first intelligence, the concept *esse*, pours forth perfections upon the subordinate intelligences/concepts in that it contains less universal intelligible forms (such as the concepts of living, sensing, and reasoning) in a more universal way. Subordinate intelligences/concepts also pour forth perfections, albeit they have somewhat less to give. Though distinct, the "intelligences" are not separate from each other, since their distinction arises from determination of the confused, not from spatial distance; for example, "life" determines the confused notion "being," so that the two are distinct, but "being" contains "life" nonetheless, in its own confused and potential way. The second half of *Liber de causis* 4, about the collective hypostasis Soul, receives like treatment: in Albert's view, it deals with the concept of soul (ibid., 2.1.19 and 23).

Albert shows extraordinary ingenuity as he works out how each detail of *Liber de causis* 4 can be taken of concepts; yet what does he gain by it? For, when he writes that *"esse creatum simplex* conceptus mentis *sit"* (ibid., 2.1.18 [82.53–54]), his readers must wonder how a mere concept can be created at all, never mind created first. Plainly, Albert cannot be talking about "mere" concepts, about the sort which depend for their existence on a human mind, of which they are accidents.

When Albert calls *esse primum creatum* a "form brought into being by the light of the agent intellect and considered as in that simple light" (see p. 39 above), the agent intellect in question is not a faculty of the human soul. Rather, it is God, the universally acting intellect. For, as Eustratius and Ibn Sīnā teach, forms or universals are of three sorts, since they may be before, in, or after the particular things of which they are forms. Forms in things are only potentially universal. Forms after things are logical universals, concepts arising in the human mind through abstraction; they are after things because men derive their knowledge of things from things. Forms before things are also concepts in minds, but in such minds as do not have their knowledge caused by things but rather cause things by their knowledge; Ibn Sīnā refers to these forms as intellectual genera, meaning that they belong to pure, separate intellects.[18]

Albert presents the *universalia ante rem* as Plato's way of saying what Aristotle says at *Metaphysics* 1032b11–14, namely, that the form with matter comes from art, the form without matter, so that, for instance, a house comes from the house in the architect's mind (*De causis et proc. univ.* 2.1.20 [85.8–16]). Of course, Aristotle is speaking about the art which is a form in the human soul (1032a32–b1), but Albert habitually extends the text's application to the divine artisan who makes the universe.[19] At any rate, in order to understand the first created thing, this Platonic and more or less naturalized Peripatetic *universale ante rem* must be examined at greater length. And, just as universals are of three sorts, so universals before things may be considered in three ways: as one in the source of emanation, as notionally different from each other in the light streaming from the source toward things, and as really diverse where things receive the stream.

Tales autem formae tripliciter accipi possunt, scilicet ut in principio processionis huius, et sic omnes accipiuntur ut unum; et ut in lumine extenso a primo procedentes, et sic differentes sunt ratione; et tertio ut in lumine terminato ad res, et sic accipiuntur secundum esse diversae. (*De causis et proc. univ.* 2.1.20 [85.39–44]; see also 1.3.6 [42.6–30])

Secundum esse autem, quod habet in lumine fluente, fluxus vocatur vel processus. (Ibid., 2.2.12 [105.9–10])

Considering form in the first way reveals how erroneous it would be to take intellectual for logical universals. For whereas the products of human abstraction may be said of things, exemplars may not: their universality is causal, not predicative. Moreover, abstraction yields genera and differences, which the simplicity of the divine mind cannot admit.[20] Still, however profound the first consideration, the second occasions the most perplexity and demands close scrutiny.

Albert compares forms in the second consideration to rays proceeding from a single point of the sun, and reports Plato as saying that these forms differ in genus and species according as they are taken confusedly or determinately in that procession (ibid., 2.1.20 [85.65–68]). In this case, "Plato dixit" announces, not Plato's words, but what Albert believes to have been his opinion. The words, in fact, are closer to those of Dionysius, who points out how the radii of a circle are perfectly united in its center but ever more differentiated from each other the farther they move from that center (*Div. nom.* 5.6 [PG3:821A]—the passage with which Albert fortifies "ab uno unum" against hostile theologians). Indeed, in the very next chapter, describing how the "second intelligences" (the less universal concepts) pour out more determinate perfections in their procession from God than do the "first intelligences," Albert notes that the more determinate perfections are more separate from each other and tend more toward particulars; for this reason, the procession of perfections does not stop with the concepts as in the streaming light (the second consideration), but only with the immanent forms (the third consideration).[21]

This last point is crucial. The intelligences/concepts are not genera and species subsisting in themselves somewhere between God and the universe; that would be the error which Aristotle, rightly or wrongly, attributes to Plato and, rightly, refutes. Rather, forms exist only mentally—whether as exemplars in God's mind and in planetary intelligences, or as abstractions in human minds—and as the forms of individual creatures. This and other of

Albert's teachings about the procession of form become clear as he explains the concept of *esse*.

4.2.1.2 Esse

That *esse* is the first created thing appears from the definition of *creare:* to produce from nothing or, in other words, to cause without presupposing anything by or with which one causes. This implies that what is created must presuppose nothing. But reasoning presupposes sensing, sensing presupposes living, and living presupposes being; *esse* alone presupposes nothing, since it is the term of every sort of resolution.[22]

Albert draws his readers' attention to linguistic morphology for a moment: *esse* is a verb, expressing an act; more specifically, it is an infinitive, with the simplicity of indeterminacy. The *Liber de causis* calls the first created thing *esse*, not *ens* or *entitas*, because it is a simple and completely indeterminate concept, answering the question whether a thing is.[23]

Of course, the simplicity of a term of resolution cannot compare with that of the first cause. By definition, the first created thing is from nothing and produced by the Creator; consequently, it has relations to both nothingness and the Creator. Admittedly, the Creator also has relations, and many more than the first creature (for, the Creator is related as Creator to every creature), but these do not detract from his utter simplicity, since they are merely logical. The relations in the first created thing, by contrast, are real.[24] Still, they are just barely real: they are not two component essences of the first created thing, but only the relations of one and the same thing to diverse things.[25]

Because it is from nothing, the first created thing is not utterly pure *esse*, as God is.[26] Consequently, *esse* said of the Creator is not univocal with created *esse:* the first created thing, not God, is the term of resolution when one analyzes creatures into their essential principles, since God is not an intrinsic constituent of creatures.[27] Again, were created *esse* and the *esse* said of the Creator in some common genus, that genus would precede the Creator, who, on the contrary, is absolutely first. No, *esse* is common to Creator and creature only by the analogy of imitation.[28]

Nor is created *esse* the genus of the creatures following it; rather, it is their principle. For, every genus is composed of difference or, in the case of the highest genera, of something analogous thereto with what is differentiated (else one genus would not be distinct from the others); and no composite can be ultimate in resolution.[29] The universality of created *esse*, then, is not according to any of the five relations of universality known as "predicables," but according to analogy:

Latissimae universalitatis est, quamvis universalitas sua non sit generis vel diffentiae [sic] vel speciei vel proprii vel accidentis, sed principii primi ingredientis in esse rerum omnium, quod per analogiam refertur ad entia.[30]

But, if the first created thing is not some univocal form of being hovering above the many beings, where and how is it found? When Albert calls created *esse* the principle of creatures, he wants "principle" taken in its strict sense, as the first part of the "principled," so that created *esse* is in the creatures following it; hence his "ingredientis in esse rerum omnium." That he does indeed intend this is confirmed when he contrasts the ways in which God and creatures are called "being": unlike God, universal being is contracted and determined in each of the things that are and has no actual existence apart from them.

Si [primum, i.e., Deus] dicatur ens, non illo intellectu dicitur ens quo ens vocatur, quod est universale ens. Hoc enim contrahitur in omni eo quod est, et determinatur et nullum esse habet extra ipsum secundum actum. (*De causis et proc. univ.* 1.3.6 [41.38–42])

Here, of course, it is a question of *ens*, which is only sometimes synonymous with *esse*; still, the conclusion is demanded by Albert's understanding of forms. Thus, for instance, when explaining Plato's *universalia ante rem*, of which *esse* is the first, he notes that these ideal forms are borne into each thing:

Plato in lumine intellectus universaliter agentis formas ideales rerum posuit. . . . Et has dixit esse universalia ante rem existentia. . . . Lumen enim agentis intellectus primi, quod extenditur in omne quod est, vehit eas in omnem rerum multitudinem. (Ibid., 2.1.20 [85.17–27])

We shall need to inspect more such texts later; however, the clearest by far are not in *De causis et processu universitatis*, but in *Super Dionysium De divinis nominibus*, because Albert's doctrine of *universalia ante rem* owes at least as much to Dionysius as to Eustratius and Ibn Sīnā (something the use of "procession" suggests). To recall Dionysius' teaching, God, as cause of all things, precontains them: he contains and, in his simplicity, is being itself, life itself, and so on with his other names. But, again as cause of all things, he transcends them: he is above being and causes being itself, the first of his gifts; he is above life and causes life itself, which participates in being itself, and so on. In other words, God is being itself and life itself, but, in him, these are imparticipable, as he is; in order that creatures may participate in them, God pours them forth. Whatever Proclus thought, these processions or emanations are not gods or separate, subsistent forms and causes; rather, the one God causes all being, and they are providential manifestations of his power. Thus, while God (with the archetypes as in him) is unparticipated—incommunicable, Albert would say—his gifts (or the archetypes as proceeding from him) are participated (see *Div. nom.* 1.7, 5.5, 11.6, and 12.4).

Dionysius' teaching causes puzzlement because he insists with equal fervor upon two apparently incompatible aspects of God: transcendence and immanence. Albert addresses the difficulty most directly where Dionysius does, at *De divinis nominibus* 11.6 (953B–956A). There Dionysius turns to the queries of his dedicatee, Timothy—namely, what "life itself" means and why God is sometimes called that and, at other times, the cause of its substance; so too for the other per se perfections. Albert, like Timothy, frames his questions primarily in terms of life but intends them and their answers of all the per se perfections,[31] including being itself. Two of his questions shed light on *De causis et processu universitatis*.

One is how Dionysius can call life itself a primary being (πρώτως ὄν) and then assign it a cause, God; after all, first causes do not themselves have causes. Albert replies by distinguishing the absolutely first cause, God, from the first among created causes, the per se perfections proceeding from God:

> Per-se-vita . . . non dicitur prima causa viventium absolute, sed in genere procedentium a prima causa absolute, quia est prima causa formalis, qua omnia creata viventia vivunt, sicut etiam dicitur, quod 'prima rerum creatarum est esse.' . . . (*Super Dion. De div. nom.* 11.24 [37.1:423.21–26])

For present purposes, the notable thing here is that Albert places the first created thing of the *Liber de causis* in parallel with Dionysius' "life itself"; "esse creatum primum" is the "being itself" which Dionysius terms the first of God's gifts, in which the other processions and their effects participate. In his *Metaphysica*, too, Albert remarks that the first effects and the divine effluxes, such as the first *esse*, are called "divine processions" by Dionysius.[32]

Now, Dionysius' distinction of the unparticipated God from his participated processions and the participants was a monotheistic adaptation of Proclus' triad, τὸ ἀμέθεκτον ("the unparticipated"), τὸ μετεχόμενον ("the thing participated in"), and τὸ μετέχον ("the participant"). The author of the *Liber de causis* omitted Proclus' mean term, apparently because it referred to the henads, that is, to gods (see chap. 1 n. 58). But Albert, by following Dionysius, effectively reintroduces τὸ μετεχόμενον—now no longer polytheistic—into the *Liber*. Apparently, then, Albert's threefold consideration of *universalia ante rem* is more or less equivalent to the Procline-Dionysian triad. The forms as one in the source of emanation correspond to τὸ ἀμέθεκτον; the forms as notionally different from each other in the light streaming from the source correspond to τὸ μετεχόμενον; and the forms as really diverse where things receive the stream correspond to τὸ μετέχον.

The second pertinent question is whether God has indeed made a "life itself." One would think not, because the life proceeding from God exists, not by itself, but as received in living things. True, Albert says, but not the whole truth. For, while it is the case that natures, such as life, have no real existence (*esse naturale*) apart from their supposits, they do nonetheless have a sort of being proper to them (*esse naturae* or *esse essentiae*): this is what Ibn Sīnā proves when he argues that instantiation is accidental to an essence.[33]

Why the reference to Ibn Sīnā? Because Albert finds the three considerations of forms or natures in Ibn Sīnā as well as in Dionysius. True, Ibn Sīnā does not present them as a threefold consideration of the forms *ante rem*; rather, they appear among many other items within a list of the meanings of "nature" and of expressions derived from it. Nevertheless, Albert seems to find Ibn Sīnā's remarks especially clear, since he uses them more than once to explain Dionysius. Thus, commenting on Dionysius' reflections about how God may be called being (PG3:824A), he says that *esse creatum primum* may be considered in three ways: with respect to the principle whence it flows; according to its proper notion, that is, as flowing from its principle but not yet received in things; and as received in things. Now, in the first two considerations, created *esse* is one and common and therefore discovered only by the mind; however, as received, it is particularized and really exists. For these points about its existential status, Albert refers his readers to Ibn Sīnā, who says:

> Natura non habet esse ex hoc intellectu [i.e., abstraction]: nec in essentia primi principii, inconveniens est enim ut habeat in sua essentia aliquid quod sit extraneum a sua essentia: sicut scies postea. Nec sunt unum in via veniendi ad res: ad modum alicuius fluentis antequam perveniant: nec habent esse unum aliquod in rebus sine diversitate.[34]

Here, then, is the threefold consideration of *esse*. As in the source whence it proceeds, it is identical with that divine source and one with the other Ideas. As proceeding from its source, it has the *esse naturae* and is one but notionally diverse from the other processions. And as having reached the term of its proceeding, it is particularized and has *esse naturale* in creatures.

If Albert understands the first created thing of the *Liber de causis* as the first procession of *De divinis nominibus*, a procession he explicates in accord with Eustratius' teaching on intellectual universals and Ibn Sīnā's on existentially neutral essences, he has yet another source besides. Supposing the *Liber* to be a Peripatetic work, he finds this first created thing in Aristotle too: *esse*, broadest in predication, is the *ens commune* in which Aristotle finds the subject of metaphysics.

> Esse enim, quod haec scientia considerat, non accipitur contractum ad hoc vel illud, sed potius prout est prima effluxio dei et creatum primum, ante quod non est creatum aliud. (*Metaph.* 1.1.1 [C16.1:3.1–4])
>
> Ens autem scimus esse causatum primum causae primae. (Ibid., 1.4.8 [57.69–70])

This is just as we should expect. For, Albert takes the *Liber* to complete Aristotle's *Metaphysics*; the *Liber* deals with divine things, because the science of metaphysics, in its last and most perfect part, considers theology (see p. 4 above). Why in its last part? Because divine things are, not the subject of metaphysics, but what it seeks. Its subject is being, which is said of all; its goal is the corresponding cause of all, which explains that subject.[35] And so, as a matter of course, when the *Liber*, the last part of metaphysics, reaches this first cause and describes its production of the first effect, the latter will already be familiar to us as the subject of metaphysics.

Here arises a problem whose solution we must put off for a while. As we have seen, Albert finds it significant that the *Liber* calls the first created thing *esse*, not *ens*; yet identification of *esse primum creatum* with the *ens* of Aristotle's *Metaphysics* would seem to forbid his making much of the infinitive. Albert describes *esse* as an act, as a concept not formed or determined to anything, and as the answer to the question whether a thing is (see n. 23); but, however tempted we may be to translate *esse* "existence" in contradistinction to "essence," still, the subject of metaphysics is said of all, and *per prius* of essence. In light of this, "being," and "being" in its vaguest sense, would seem the best rendering for *esse*; and, when Albert denies that the concept *esse* is formed or determined to anything, vagueness—not contradistinction from essence or from anything at all—would appear to be his meaning: "Ambitus ergo suae praedicationis a nullo restrictus est."[36] Has Albert changed his mind in the short time between his composing *Metaphysica* and *De causis et processu universitatis*? Or is he consistent, if obscure?

4.2.2 The Second Interpretation

Be that as it may, mention has been made of Albert's twofold interpretation of the first created *intelligentia*. According to the first, this *intelligentia* is the concept of *esse*, an intelligible procession from God's mind. The relevance of this interpretation to the dispute over "ab uno unum" will occupy much of chapter 6 below; but, to understand exactly what was disputed, we must look at Albert's second interpretation and its relation to the first.

When Ibn Sīnā, al-Ġazālī, Ibn Rušd, and Maimonides mention "ab uno unum," the context always has to do with the emanation of planetary intelligences and, more particularly, with the doctrine that God immediately produces only the first such intelligence. Not a few of Albert's contemporaries found this doctrine in the *Liber de causis* as well. Albert disagrees, but not through failure to see that, in the *Liber*, a separate, intellective nature is the first created thing.

When, in the very next chapter of the *Liber*, he reads that the first cause is named by the name of its first effect, intelligence, though in a higher way, he comments that God's proximate effect is intelligence according to its being, that its substance is intellect, and that God, therefore, is intellect in the highest way, as the artisan of all things:

> Effectus autem proximus eius secundum esse est intelligentia, cuius substantia intellectus est. Et propter hoc meliori modo, quo potest, causa prima dicitur esse intellectus universaliter agens, ad omnia habens se sicut intellectus artificis ad artificiata. . . . (*De causis et proc. univ.* 2.1.24 [90.78–83])

Albert could hardly make it clearer that he is no longer speaking of *intelligentia* as a concept than by writing "according to its being," "whose substance," and "the artisan's mind."

However, this first created thing is not the first of the planetary intelligences. The *Liber de causis* tends to speak generally: it says of intelligence what plainly holds for every intelligence and never identifies an intelligence as Saturn's or Jupiter's. For, its intelligence is a collective of intelligences. Albert recognizes that "intelligentia" often stands for "omnis intelligentia," and so he makes each intelligence a one produced by the One. Intelligence does not cease to be one, he says, until another form enters into its constitution, as, for example, the human mind belongs to a soul. And this whole rank of simple intelligences is what comes second after the first cause. Thus, explaining "intelli-

gentia quidem non recipit divisionem quoniam est primum creatum quod creatum est a causa prima" (LC 6 [101.81–82]), he writes:

> Ab uno non est nisi unum et a simplici non est nisi unum simplex.... Et sic constat, quod intelligentia primi ordinis et omne quod in forma intelligentiae constituitur, unum est et multiplex non erit nisi alia forma, quam intelligentiae lumen in constitutione eius apponat, sicut est forma animae vel naturae. In communi autem quidquid in forma intelligentiae tantum est, secundum est a causa prima. Primum enim causatum causae primae est intelligentia.... (*De causis et proc. univ.* 2.2.7 [100.27–37]; see also 2.2.15 [108.33–40])

Nonetheless, for Albert as for the author of the *Liber*, this order of being exhibits degrees of excellence and unity:

> In hoc tamen secundo ordine sicut in quolibet ordine multi sunt gradus..., et semper superior maioris unitatis est quam inferior. (Ibid., 2.2.7 [100.47–50])

Later, we will need to determine the relations between the members of this order. But a more obvious question is how both the series of intellective substances and the concept of *esse* can be the one from the One. The phrases "according to its being" and "whose substance" (p. 48 above) suggest an answer which Albert had worked out years earlier. Faced with an interpretation of Genesis 1.1 according to which the heavens and the earth created by God in the beginning were the angelic nature and prime matter, he asked how these can be the first creatures when the *Liber de causis* says that *esse* is first; he replied by distinguishing what is first as the simplest notion (*esse*) from the first among actual existents (the first intelligence):

> Primum dicitur duobus modis, scilicet, secundum rationem formae et simplicitatis, et secundum ordinem substantiae in essendo. Secundum rationem formae et simplicitatis nihil est ante esse: quia omnia aliquo modo se habent ex additione ad ens, etiam unum, et verum, et bonum, ut in libro I *Sententiarum* est ostensum. Sed secundum ordinem substantiae in natura et esse, opinio omnium Philosophorum est, quod intelligentia prima sit primum causatum a Creatore universitatis. Quod autem illi intelligentias, nos vocamus Angelos:[37] et tunc stat expositio illa, quia creatio potius respicit esse, quam ordinem simplicitatis. In

abstractione autem fit per intellectum. (*Sent.* 2.1.1, ad id quod objicitur de tertia, 1 [B27:8b–9a])

In other words, *esse* is first in simplicity as the term of all resolution; creation is not simplification, however, but production of something into real existence; and *esse* has real existence, not as a concept preexisting in or proceeding from God's mind, but as received in things. Consequently, the concept *esse* is created only in its third consideration. As for what is first "according to the order of substance in being," Albert elsewhere explains that it must not have the sort of simplicity the concept *esse* has. After all, very little belongs to the notion of *esse*, else it could not be predicated of everything; but what is closest to God should be most like him, and that likeness comes about through its participating in all perfections.[38]

Still, if creation does have to do with existence rather than simplicity, why does Albert ever call simple *esse* the first created thing? Precisely because creating is causing something to be, not to be an intelligence, so that even if the first creature is an intelligence, it is created *qua* being, not *qua* intelligence. As noted above (n. 22), when Albert argues that *esse* is the first created thing because creating is causing without presupposing anything and *esse* alone presupposes nothing, his premises suffice for the further conclusion that *esse* is the only created thing; *esse* is first in all creatures, and their other perfections are produced, not by creation, but by information, by the forming of *esse*:

Quod autem ultimum est in resolutione, primum necesse est esse secundum viam compositionis. Esse igitur primum est in omnibus illis quae procedunt a primo. . . . Quodlibet enim sequentium cum supponat in intellectu suo praecedens se, non ex nihilo, sed ex aliquo producitur, in quo est incohatio sui esse. Nihil ergo sequentium potest fieri per creationem. Sequens enim se habet ad praecedens ut informans ipsum et determinans. Productio igitur istorum non per creationem, sed per informationem est. Relinquitur igitur, quod *esse sit primum* et *creatum* et quod *alia* causata *non creata sint*. . . . (*De causis et proc. univ.* 2.1.17 [81.12–46])

This distinction between creation and information comes from *Liber de causis* 17 (151.74–77), which Albert anticipates in order to make sense of *Liber* 4. And, apparently, the sense he proposes is that, strictly speaking, *esse* is the first and indeed the only created thing, yet intelligence is the first created thing in that it is first among the recipients of created *esse*.[39]

4.3 Summary

Given the complexity of Albert's understanding of the first created thing, it may prove useful to review it before further analysis.

Plotinus, reasoning that a thing can give only what it has, described the emanation of a one from the One. This emanated one was Being, which, by contemplating the One, became Intellect. For Plotinus, then, Being and Intellect were two aspects of a single hypostasis. And Intellect was a collective of intellects, which were identical with the Ideas. The same teaching inspired the anonymous author of the *Liber de causis*, although, in his religious belief, he specified that this first emanation was created. Now, Albert had no access to texts detailing the Neoplatonic theory; instead, he faced a bewildering set of assertions that *esse* was the first created thing, that *intelligentia* was the first created thing, and that *esse* was *intelligentia*.

Quite naturally, he assumed that this "Peripatetic" text was speaking of planetary intelligences. But he also recognized that much of what the *Liber* said about *intelligentia* made good sense when said of concepts. That was the case because the intelligences of the *Liber* were indeed concepts—not human abstractions, to be sure, but Platonic Ideas—as well as knowers. Had Albert been aware of and accepted this, he could have conflated the Aristotelian and Neoplatonic opinions, so that intelligences would be both concepts and planetary movers. That was not to happen. Rather, he argued that *intelligentia* was an equivocal term, whose meaning must be determined with care at each occurrence. The two possibilities were "knower" and "concept," the former requiring little explanation, and the latter receiving elaborate development.

On Albert's reading, when the *Liber* identifies *esse* and *intelligentia*, then *intelligentia* means "concept." This first created thing, the concept of being, is an intellectual universal, not a logical universal, Albert says, borrowing the threefold universal of Eustratius and Ibn Sīnā. Dionysius and, to some extent, Ibn Sīnā provide him with a threefold consideration of this intellectual universal. Considered as in and identical with the divine mind, *esse* is imparticipable; that is why Albert formulates the notion of analogy through imitation, whereby what is in creatures is not the same thing as what is in God, but only a likeness thereof. Considered as proceeding from the divine mind, *esse* is a perfection in which creatures may participate, and it is common to creatures by the sort of analogy with which Aristotle establishes the subject of his *Metaphysics*, for, the *esse* of the *Liber* is none other than the subject of Aristotle's *Metaphysics*. While this identification will enable Albert to rebut a charge of heresy brought against the Peripatetics (see chap. 6 below), that is not why he makes it; rather, the role of the *Liber* as theological completion of the *Metaphysics* demands that the former account for the very effect examined in the latter. Of course, as an exponent of Peripatetic thought, he cannot admit that the common has real existence as common; created *esse* is really found according to its third consideration, as received by its participants.

FIVE

Mediation in the Procession of Creatures

Interpreting the first created thing as *esse* allows Albert to elucidate the Creator's nearness to each creature; interpreting it as the series of celestial intelligences allows him to uphold the order of secondary causality, that is, the influence one recipient of created *esse* has upon another, as well. Let us turn to the questions why and in what sense Albert insists upon secondary causality, since the answers will put us in a position to investigate how God is no less near his creatures on that account.

Albert argues, not just that *esse* is the only created thing (see p. 50 above), but also that God is the only creator. That follows from his being the first cause and from the definition of creation, for, "first" means what presupposes nothing, and creating is causing with nothing presupposed. But if God is the only creator and *esse* the only created thing, then the *esse* in all things is his proper effect.[1] What, in that case, remains for secondary causes to do?

Certainly not what al-Fārābī and Ibn Sīnā proposed, because they disagreed that only God can create. Albert reports that, whereas "certain ancients," Plato among them, maintained that power, knowledge, and a will untouched by envy make God a perfect agent, al-Fārābī, Ibn Sīnā, and al-Ġazālī[2] found something lacking. For, if the One produces only one, how do specifically and numerically distinct effects arise? On their theory, it seems that, besides power, knowledge, and will, God requires the intervention of such mediators as intelligences, spheres, and elemental qualities in order to be a perfect agent.[3]

Briefly, the theory, in its Avicennian form, runs as follows. God's contemplation is creative, producing the first intelligence and making it necessary in the sense that, if God creates it, it must exist. The contemplation of this first intelligence is likewise creative; however, its contemplation is not as simple as God's. For, while its necessity is the one produced by the One, the first intelligence includes something else as well, namely, its possibility; this it has, not as a second thing from the One, but from itself.[4] Therefore, its contemplation is threefold and produces three things: when it contemplates God, the absolutely necessary being — and this is its noblest contemplation —, it produces the second intelligence, its noblest effect; when it contemplates itself as necessary through God, it produces the soul of the outermost sphere; and when it contemplates itself as possible in itself, it produces the body of that sphere. The second intelligence also has a triple and creative contemplation: when it contemplates God, it produces the third intelligence; when it contemplates itself as necessary through the first intelligence (necessary because, given that the first causes its existence, it cannot but exist), it produces the soul of the sphere of the fixed stars; and when it contemplates its own possibility, it produces the body of that sphere. So too with the intelligences, souls, and bodies of Saturn, Jupiter, Mars, the sun, Venus, Mercury, and the moon.[5] As for the intelligence produced by the intelligence of the moon, it is the agent intellect which governs the lowest, terrestrial sphere.[6]

Albert must reject this theory insofar as it makes creative power communicable to creatures; nonetheless, he does not utterly reject it. Indeed, he sometimes ridicules al-Biṭrūǧī, whose astronomy does away with intelligences as mediators and has God himself move all the spheres. For, to Albert, both Ibn Sīnā and al-Biṭrūǧī represent extreme views, in which (as often happens with extremes) he finds a shared error.

Al-Biṭrūǧī was among several twelfth-century Spanish Arabs and Jews who rejected Ptolemy's theory of the spheres, with its epicycles and excentrics, in favor of a homocentric theory. Not that his homocentric theory was entirely a return to Aristotle's. Whereas Aristotle thought the higher spheres slower (*Cael.* 2.10), al-Biṭrūǧī hoped to explain the same phenomenon as Ptolemy — an apparent eastward motion — by positing one mover, whose impulsion would be received according to the distance of the mobile body, so that the lower a sphere, the slower its rotation. In other words, God would move the first sphere from East to West, and the remaining spheres would participate in its motion, though sometimes seeming to move from West to East because of their tardiness.

This theory has some merit, which Albert acknowledges in various texts. But Albert has objections too, at least one of which pertains to mediation.[7] He expresses astonishment at people who deny the order of mediators and make divine power the immediate cause of all things; such people — he takes al-Biṭrūǧī to be their inspiration — fail to give sufficient weight to the gradation of beings. For, since the goodness flowing from God is not sometimes greater and sometimes lesser (LC 19), al-Biṭrūǧī's followers must mean that a uniform goodness flows immediately from God into greater and lesser receptive capacities. In that case, all things would have a universal efficient cause, but would lack proper efficient causes for their greater or lesser perfections. The implication is that al-Biṭrūǧī's "science" ends by making scientific knowledge impossible: God would be the answer no matter what the question, with the result that we could have no distinct knowledge of diverse things through their proper causes.[8]

In light of this, Albert's objection to Ibn Sīnā cannot be that mediators are needless. Rather, to his mind, both Ibn Sīnā and al-Biṭrūǧī failed to see that things need their proper causes. In the case of al-Biṭrūǧī, this failure led to his doing away with proper causes. In the case of Ibn Sīnā, however, the problem was not that he found proper causes completely needless, but that he thought the need God's: he posited mediators in the belief that God could create only the first intelligence. Albert considers the opinion that God needs mediators un-Aristotelian. After all, if secondary causes receive all of their power from the first cause, how can they add to the power of the first (LC 1)? No, the role of secondary causes becomes clear when Aristotle, explaining why the outermost sphere has but a single movement while intermediate spheres have a multiplicity of motions, argues that the less perfect require more means if they are to attain to their end (*Cael.* 292^{a}22–^{b}24). The Aristotelian view, then, is that the need for mediators is on the side of the effect. Although God's power, knowledge, and will do indeed make him a perfect agent, secondary causes are still required, not by the perfect agent, but by his effects, the lesser of which cannot receive his gifts in their original purity and simplicity. Secondary causes add determinacy and composition to these gifts, thus proportioning them to the lesser receptive capacities of lesser effects.[9]

How does Albert understand this task of the secondary causes? He speaks of mediation in two not unconnected ways, corresponding to formal and efficient causality. The first comes to the fore as he paraphrases *Liber de causis* 3, with its description of how

> causa prima creavit esse animae mediante intelligentia [et alatyr],[10] et propter illud facta est anima efficiens operationem divinam. Postquam ergo creavit causa prima esse animae, posuit eam sicut stramentum intelligentiae in quod efficiat operationes suas. Propter illud ergo anima intellectibilis efficit operationem intellectibilem. (79.77–80.78)

What can this mean? Not, as some among Albert's contemporaries interpreted it, that the first intelligence creates the soul, since only God can create, as Albert has shown and as the author of the *Liber* believed (LC 17). Instead, Albert thinks of a meaning for "mediante" which would be contrasted with "inchoante" and "terminante," and offers the following interpretation. A definition may include two differences, in which case the definition has a beginning, a middle, and an end. For instance, man is a "vivum sensibile rationabile"; here, the term in the middle, "sensibile," forms the genus "vivum," whose final determination comes from the ultimate difference, "rationabile." Likewise, noble soul—Albert rightly takes this to mean "celestial soul"—requires intellectuality in order to move the heavens, and so "intelligentia" must be placed in its definition. But intellectuality does not suffice to make a mover, because mover and moved must be proportioned to each other (Aristotle *De an.* 407^{b}17–19), and so the definition or the essence is incomplete until one adds an inclination toward the moved, which, in this case, is "alatyr," a celestial circle. On this reading, "causa prima creavit esse animae mediante intelligentia et alatyr" means that, when God created celestial souls, he created intellectual beings inclined toward their spheres. (Apparently, "esse" is the beginning of this definition and functions as though it were a genus.)[11]

Readers who agree that only God can create may yet think—probably in accord with the intention of the author of the *Liber*—that what God creates is the beginning of the soul, its bare being, while its formation to intellectuality comes from a celestial intelligence; the soul, then, would be constituted partly by God and partly by an intelligence. But this opinion that God makes only the beginning of things, just as much as Ibn Sīnā's opinion that God makes only the first thing, implies that God is an imperfect agent, requiring mediators if he is to produce a universe; Albert has argued that any need for mediators is on the side of God's effects, and so he must hold that God gives all things being and gives it perfectly, even if they need mediators in order to receive it.[12] Accordingly, Albert offers four arguments that celestial intelligences have no part in constituting celestial souls in being. First of all, if God created a potential soul which intelligence then actualized, then the soul, which is a form, would be generated; whereas Aristotle proves that only composites, not forms, can be generated (*Metaph.* 1033^{a}23–^{b}9, 1069^{b}35–1070^{a}3). Again, on the same supposition, the most perfect cause would produce something imperfect, which the second and less perfect cause would bring to perfection.[13] Moreover, on this supposition, the soul would have two equally immediate efficient causes, although the first causes, as sources of order throughout the universe, should themselves manifest the greatest possible order. Finally, the second cause has nothing to give which it did not receive from the first cause (LC 1); therefore God, the universally acting intellect, can give soul intellectuality at least as well as a celestial intelligence could.[14]

The question *how* it can be that God creates the soul without the help of an intelligence, when the One produces only one, must await chapter 6 below; so far, Albert has made clear only *that* it must be so.

The presence of "intelligentia" as "medians" in the definition of celestial souls opens the way for a second sort of mediation. For, because celestial souls are intellectual, they can receive illuminations from celestial intelligences. These latter, then, although they do not constitute celestial souls in being, do perfect their intellectual powers. Such, Albert thinks, is the meaning of the *Liber* when it continues, "postquam ergo creavit causa prima esse animae, posuit eam sicut stramentum intelligentiae in quod efficiat operationes suas."[15] And by perfecting their intellectual powers, intelligences perfect the souls' causal power as well.[16]

This second sort of mediation receives more attention elsewhere in *De causis et processu universitatis*. Indeed, at times Albert sounds almost, though never exactly, like Ibn Sīnā. We have seen that the composition inherent in creatureliness rules out the creation of an equal to God. To put that another way, by the very fact of proceeding, what proceeds is at some distance from that whence it proceeds. This distance or diversity appears in that the essence of what proceeds is not its own existence; rather, the essence is, of itself, potential, requiring a principle before it to actualize it. The creature, then, differs from God by being in potency. Yet, since its existence is from God, it is like him, so that it too has some causal power. Hence, the second creature (the third being) is even more potential than the first creature (the second being), since it receives from both the first being (God) and the second. Likewise, the fourth being is more potential than the third, and so on. Thus, not only do creatures differ from God, but they also differ from each other, since they are related to God in diverse ways, according to the various grades of potentiality.[17]

Albert expresses this order in yet another way, through the example of art flowing from the artisan's mind into his vital spirits, hands, tools, and raw materials (see pp. 15–16 above). Just as the form of art takes on new and ever more material modes of existence as it emanates, so too the form whereby God flows becomes ever more determinate as it flows into intelligence, from one intelligence to the next, from each intelligence into its own sphere, from the last celestial sphere into the sublunary realm, and from that realm into the center of each being.[18]

Albert even describes a sort of triple contemplation, not entirely unlike that propounded by Ibn Sīnā. Underlying his remarks once more is an elaborate comparison of intelligence with art. God, the universally acting intellect, constitutes things by contemplating himself. As the first intellect, he produces the first intelligence. Now, just as art produces artificial forms by understanding, so too an intelligence produces intelligences and intelligible things by knowing. Again, art may be considered in three ways: considered as from an intellect, art is an intellectual light; considered in itself, as a form, it constitutes its image, an artificial form; considered as something made (by the mind) and potential (in its future inventor or its learner), it requires the potency of raw materials in which to constitute its image. Likewise, intelligence has a threefold consideration. When the first intelligence considers itself as from the first intellect, then it sees that it has necessary being. When it considers itself just as such, that is a lesser consideration—as Albert puts it, the light (*lumen*, not *lux*) of the first intellect sets in the first intelligence;[19] this results in the constitution of an inferior, namely, the form of the outermost sphere or *primum mobile*.[20] And when the first intelligence considers itself as having been potential before it was made, then the matter of the outermost sphere arises. But that is not all: the light of the first intellect, having emanated into the first intelligence, superabounds, and the first intelligence, considering itself as from the first intellect, considers this superabundance in the same way, thus constituting the second intelligence. This second intelligence, considering itself as such and as potential, constitutes the form and the matter of the circle of the signs; moreover, considering itself as from the first intellect and the first intelligence, it knows itself in superabundant light, thus constituting the third intelligence. In like manner are produced the intelligences, forms, and matters of the spheres of the fixed stars, Saturn, Jupiter, Mars, the sun, Venus, Mercury, and the moon. And after the intelligence of the moon comes the intelligence governing the terrestrial sphere, within which causes exert their influence as detailed in the many branches of natural philosophy (*De causis et proc. univ.* 1.4.8 [55.65–57.64]).

Many things need to be said about this scheme. To begin with, given Albert's recognition that, according to the *Liber de causis*, God alone creates, what do celestial intelligences accomplish by their triple contemplation? In accord with what he has already said in the tractate on flowing (see above, p. 18) and his explanation why secondary causes are needed (p. 55), they determine the creative efflux. But he makes this clearest in his *Metaphysica* (knowledge of which he presupposes in *De causis et processu universitatis*). In *De causis et processu universitatis*, he has carefully pointed out that the light received by the first intelligence shines on, so that the second intelligence receives from God and the first intelligence both, but this does not mean that the second intelligence is more lightsome than God alone could make it; on the contrary, in *Metaphysica*, he states that the doubling of the irradiation results in a contraction—the contraction and determination of the second intelligence:

> Prout est lumen causatum a causa prima, irradiat ab ea [i.e., intelligentia primi ordinis sub causa prima] lumen intelligentiae, cui iungitur irradiatio causae primae, et quod sic fit duplici irradiatione, magis est determinatum et contractum, quam quod fit ab uno lumine simplici.[21]

Then the doubled irradiation is tripled and quadrupled, resulting in the contraction of the third and fourth intelligences, until finally the irradiation reaches maximal contraction, the contraction of things here below:

> Et iste sic duplicatus radius iungitur inferiori et iterum magis determinatur, et sic fit processus descendendo usque ad materiam generabilium, in qua per qualitates et formas materiales maximam recipit determinationem. (*Metaph.* 11.2.20 [C16.2:509.12–16]; see also 11.3.6 [540.45–56])

Indeed, the intelligences are related to each other somewhat as more and less universal concepts, not that they *are* more or less universal concepts,[22] but that their power encompasses more or less:

> Quod dicitur una universalis et alia particularis, non est ideo dictum, quod universalium et particularium sint receptivi intellectus isti, sed potius dicitur universalis sicut virtus plus ambiens, sicut est virtus sphaerae superioris ad inferiorem, et dicitur particularis sicut virtus sphaerae magis determinatae ad materiam. In talibus enim habent se in similitudine quadam formarum ad invicem. . . . Omnes enim movent ad esse, sed sicut ordinantur esse, vita, sensus et ratio et intellectuale mortale, ita ordinantur formae illae. (Ibid., 11.2.19 [507.14–33]; see also 11.2.21 [509.43–50])

And since, far from adding anything to the causal power flowing from God, the intelligences contract it, the stream of emanation eventually gives out:

> Nullum sequentium virtutem agendi habet a seipso. A sequentibus ergo contrahentibus et determinantibus nullam accipit virtutem causandi. Quo autem plura conveniunt non augentia causandi virtutem, eo plus diminuitur causandi virtus. Constat igitur, quod quanto aliquid in consequentibus remotius est, tanto minorem habet agendi virtutem et debiliorem, ita quod in ultimo sic deficit causandi virtus, quod ipsum ulterius nihil causat. . . . (*De causis et proc. univ.* 2.2.15 [108.81–89])

As Albert explains it, several principles underlie this scheme. One is that contemplation is an irradiation of light; another that this light is of itself a cause of being (*ens*);[23] another that reception is according to the mode of the recipient and, consequently, that the causality of the first cause reaches the last effects only through prior effects. For, lesser beings cannot attain to the purity of divine light, so that, if God's gifts remained in that purity, lesser beings would not desire them, since nature desires nothing in vain.[24] Given these principles, the fewer the mediators between God and a given intelligence, the more lightsome that intelligence, and the greater its effects; and each intelligence has both greater and lesser effects, according to the greater and lesser nobility of its three contemplations.

Besides firmly rejecting any suggestion that creatures create, Albert makes another notable departure from the Avicennian scheme when he inserts a "circle of the signs" between the outermost sphere and the sphere of the fixed stars, thus pushing the latter into third place, whereas Ibn Sīnā puts it second. According to Albert's preferred astronomical theory, explaining the motions of the fixed stars requires two starless spheres: the starless outermost sphere revolves on the poles of the equator and gives all stars a westward motion, while the starless circle of the signs revolves on the poles of the ecliptic and gives all stars an oblique, eastward motion; the (zodiacal) signs themselves are found, among other constellations, in the sphere of the fixed stars.[25] As a consequence of positing two starless spheres, Albert has ten, not nine, mobile heavens, so that the agent intellect governing the terrestrial sphere is not the tenth, but an eleventh intelligence—unless, of course, God himself moves the outermost sphere. That second alternative was the position Albert advanced in his *Metaphysica*. Why did he say that?

More correctly, the question should be why Ibn Sīnā did not, since Aristotle's God is nothing if not a mover. Apparently, "ab uno unum" kept Ibn Sīnā from following Aristotle here. For if God can make only the first thing, that thing must be an intelligence, not a mobile body. After all, intelligence is nobler and more truly one than is body. Furthermore, if God can make only the first thing, and if that first thing is a body, where do intelligences come from? Not from God, who has already made the only thing he can make. And not from the body either, again because intelligence is nobler than body. Now, if God does not create the first body, then the intelligence which he does create must produce it. And surely God himself would not move the creature of his creature. By this reasoning, while the intelligences move the bodies they produce, God is beyond the movers: he is an efficient cause, yes, but an efficient cause of existence, not a mover. Or rather, he is indeed a mover, in the manner of a final cause, but he is the ultimate cause of all motions, not the proper or proximate cause of any one motion.[26]

In his *Metaphysica*, Albert attributes Ibn Sīnā's position to Plato and reports that Peripatetics find these "Platonic" arguments merely probable and perhaps even sophistical. For how could one demonstrate the existence of a separate substance if it were idle? And if some such idle substance did exist, would something occasionally rouse it from idleness to activity? Or would it remain always as though asleep? In that case, one could hardly call it the best. So Aristotle argued in the final book of his *Physics* (251ª22–28; see also *Metaph.* 1074ª19–24). Perhaps someone may come to Ibn Sīnā's defense, objecting that God does indeed keep busy, though at giving forms, not at moving spheres. But this will not do, since only composites come to be (Aristotle *Metaph.* 1033ª23–b9, 1069b35–1070ª3), so that matter must be moved as forms are given. Plainly, concludes Albert, according to philosophical reasoning, God does move the outermost sphere. And, although an intelligence as such may seem more like God than any body could be, nonetheless, the intelligence proportioned to the second sphere resembles him less than does the outermost sphere, which is proportioned to the prime mover as his instrument (Albert *Metaph.* 11.2.17 and 11.3.7 [C16.2:505.3–48 and 541.19–89]). What of the thesis that intelligence is God's first effect? It *is* the first effect of God as what Aristotle calls the sempiternal and most noble animal,[27] that is, of God as composite with the first sphere, for, the first intelligence is what God constitutes through his act in that sphere:

> Lux primae causae simplex est et pura. Et ideo cum attingit materiam, non recipit obumbrationem, sed vincit eam et vincendo terminat ad esse instrumenti sui, quod est caelum primum. Cum autem irradiat ad constitutionem intelligentiae primi ordinis, hoc fit per actum, qui est compositi, et est actus primae causae in orbe primo. (Ibid., 11.2.20 [508.85–91])

Thus, God constitutes both the sphere he moves and, through it, the intelligence which moves the next sphere. Nor does this violate "ab uno unum," as long as he causes only one effect immediately and the second through the first.

There are numerous other variations in Albert's accounts of the celestial movers.[28] Whence the inconsistencies of Albert's several descriptions of Peripatetic cosmogony? From the Peripatetic tradition itself. To begin with, although Aristotle, in his *Physics*, *De caelo*, and *Metaphysics*, clearly means that God moves the outermost sphere, yet, as noted above, the writings of such prominent Peripatetics as al-Fārābī and Ibn Sīnā are equally clear in placing God beyond the movers. Furthermore, the *Liber de causis* itself conflicts with

Aristotle's *De caelo*—or so it would seem to one who, like Albert, read *De caelo* in Gerard of Cremona's version. For, where Aristotle says simply that the first moves the first (*Cael.* 288ᵇ3–5: τὸ γὰρ πρῶτον τοῦ πρώτου . . . κινητικόν), Gerard's translation states that the first cause moves the first effect ("causa enim prima est, quae movet causatum primum").[29] And, in the *Liber*, *esse* and *intelligentia*, not the outermost sphere, are the first effect.

Albert could not consult the Greek text of *De caelo*, but he could see that the disagreement between Aristotle and his oriental disciples was no accident, and he did not try to smooth it over. Rather, when paraphrasing Aristotle's *Metaphysics*, he makes God the mover of the outermost sphere, his instrument in generation and corruption;[30] when paraphrasing the *Liber*—which he thinks excerpted from the writings of al-Fārābī and Ibn Sīnā as well as Aristotle—he presents approximations of the Avicennian scheme, so that intelligences mediate in all generation and move the spheres as their instruments.[31] Why does he not side decisively with either Aristotle or Ibn Sīnā? Perhaps neither is entirely believable, though each has something to recommend his position. Consider the argument against Ibn Sīnā's non-moving giver of forms. Albert cannot really accept the refutation he formulates—that forms are ingenerable—"quia non est idem aliquid esse ingenerabile et aliquid esse increabile" (*Phys.* 8.1.14 [C4.2:577.66–68]). Indeed, Ibn Sīnā's "Platonic" position, though merely probable, echoes revelation and sparks a theologian's interest by suggesting the possibility of an illumination quite apart from the motions of stars and planets:

> Hoc autem ideo non est dictum, quod aliqua sit influentia superioris super inferiorem nisi per motum corporis animati secundum Peripateticos. . . . Si autem est aliqua alia irradiatio superioris super inferiora, sicut dixit Plato et sicut dicunt theologi, illa per rationem investigari non potest, sed oportet, quod ad illam investigandam ponantur alia principia ex revelatione spiritus et fide religionis. (*Metaph.* 11.2.21 [C16.2:509.87–510.3])

> Non suscepimus in hoc negotio explanare nisi viam Peripateticorum. Quaecumque autem Plato dixit, habeant firmitatem, quam possunt, donec forte ab aliquo explanentur. (Ibid., 11.3.7 [542.23–25])

In favor of the Aristotelian alternative to Ibn Sīnā's theory, one can say that it refrains from positing indemonstrable things:

> Peripateticorum autem consuetudo fuit nihil penitus dicere, quod certa ratione probare non poterant. Et quia ante primi caeli motorem per rationem

nihil investigari poterat, ideo ante primum motorem nihil esse ponebant. Adhuc autem, quia in omni natura motor eorum quae per se moventur, proportionatus et coniunctus est mobili, ideo dicebant primum motorem et proportionatum et coniunctum esse primo mobili et ex his esse unum, quod per se movetur. (Ibid., 11.2.12 [500.5–14]; see also 11.3.7 [541.65–542.6])

Still, Albert distances himself from it; his paraphrases convey the meaning of Aristotle's *Metaphysics*, *On the Heavens*, and *Physics*, but Aristotle and the Peripatetics may have erred:

Et sive hoc verum sit sive falsum, hic pro certo est intellectus verborum Aristotelis et in prima philosophia sua et in caelo et mundo et in viii suorum physicorum. (Ibid., 11.2.12 [500.14–17])

Et bene potest esse, quod erraverunt in hoc, tamen sic dicunt, et haec quam diximus, est ratio ipsorum. (Ibid., 11.2.17 [505.48–50])

The reasons for his reserve become clearer upon inspection of the merely probable premises supporting the Platonic-Avicennian position: that the incorporeal precedes the corporeal, and the simple the composite; and that the first principle of all *esse* is the first being, pure unity and goodness, not conjoined to a body and not falling under the same genus as any effect.

Platonis autem via fundatur super propositiones probabiles, non necessarias, quod videlicet incorporeum sit ante corporeum et simplex ante compositum; et quod primum principium universi esse sit ens primum, non coniunctum corpori nec in genere existens cum aliquo entium causatorum; . . . et quod hoc numerus non sit, sed potius unitas pura et bonitas et causa esse omnium. . . . (Ibid., 11.3.7 [541.21–30])

Surprisingly, these are premises which appear in one or another form throughout the allegedly Peripatetic *Liber de causis*. Is that only because, as Albert supposed, David the Jew used texts by Ibn Sīnā, "who claims to be a Peripatetic" (*De causis et proc. univ.* 1.4.7 [53.3]), but whom Albert finds somewhat Platonic at times? Perhaps not. Albert recognizes that the identification of God with the mover of the outermost sphere "is certainly the meaning of Aristotle's words in his *Metaphysics* and in *On the Heavens* and in the eight books of his *Physics*," but Aristotle wrote other books too. Is that identification the meaning of "Aristotle's" *Epistula de principio universi esse* also? Its very title, recalling as it does the probable premises, would suggest not.

Moreover, in *De causis et processu universitatis*, Albert no longer calls the distinction of God from the mover of the outermost sphere "Platonic"; rather, he adopts it, without mentioning the controversy surrounding it, and attributes more or less Avicennian schemes to "Aristotle and all who followed Aristotle" and to "the ancient Peripatetics" (ibid., 2.1.6 [66.66–91]). Once again Albert's statement of the relationship between the *Metaphysics* and the *Liber* comes to mind: "Since the business of the metaphysician concerns separate substances, about which Aristotle and Plato reached determinations in diverse ways, here a determination about separate substances is made according to the full truth" (see p. 4 above). Now, Albert says nothing explicit about the divergence between the *Metaphysics* and the *Liber* on the question who moves the outermost sphere, so that one probably cannot ascertain whether he believes that Aristotle eventually adopted the Platonic view; nonetheless, it seems likely that he does and, what is more, his disciple Ulrich proposes exactly that.[32]

The *Epistula* and other pseudo-Aristotelian texts account for the delicacy with which Albert as expositor of Peripatetic thought must handle celestial movers. As for his personal opinion, Albert reveals it in several texts, among them some digressions in his *Physics* (where he challenges heretical theses in Aristotle's *Physics*), his *Problemata determinata* (a letter to the Dominican master general on questions of the day), and his theological works (where he speaks in his own name, not as an expositor of Peripatetic thought[33]). Like the Aristotle of the *Physics*, *De caelo*, and *Metaphysics*, he holds that God moves the outermost sphere; like the Aristotle of the *Liber*, he denies that God is naturally conjoined to that sphere—in which case, his power would not be infinite, but proportioned to the sphere. For, a conjoined mover is proportioned to the body it moves, so that it has just as much power to move as the body has power to be moved; God, however, moves the sphere by his all-powerful command. Indeed, he moves everything, not just the sphere, because he gives everything its form, upon which follows its motion.[34] What becomes of the intelligences, then? Unlike the philosophers, Albert has no use for them, much less for celestial souls, although he cannot demonstrate his position any more than the philosophers can theirs:

> Et differunt opiniones nostrae in tanto, quod ipsi dicunt caelos fluere a causa prima mediantibus intelligentiis, quae sunt primae in ordine eorum quae sunt, nos autem dicimus, quod absolute fluunt a prima causa secundum electionem suae voluntatis; et neutrum horum probari potest nisi persuasionibus probabilibus. (*Phys.* 8.1.15 [C4.2:580.45–51])

Someone may think to buttress the philosophical doctrine of celestial intelligences with revelation; after all, Ibn Sīnā, al-Ġazālī, Isaac Israeli, and Maimonides explain that intelligences are what theologians and ordinary people call "angels." Albert, however, rejects that identification, not only in his theological works, but even in *De causis et processu universitatis*. Both angels and intelligences are separate substances, to be sure, but beyond that, what revelation teaches about angels is not what philosophy says about intelligences. Philosophy distinguishes ten intelligences in the manner explained above, but revelation distinguishes the orders of angels according to their illuminations and theophanies, of which philosophy knows nothing. Likewise, philosophy assigns astronomical functions to intelligences and has nothing to say about the kingdom of heaven, for which angels exist. And Peripatetic philosophy claims that intelligences are always and everywhere—Albert, as Peripatetic expositor, mentions but cannot concern himself with localized Platonic demons—while revelation records that angels are sent here and there with messages; at any rate, the motions and places Scripture describes are not rotations and stars. Of course, God may entrust some angels with the execution of his commands about celestial motion; still, angels have other and better functions too, and this motion of obedience would not be the philosophers' motion of desire.[35]

All of this leaves Albert's readers in some perplexity: if he himself does not believe in these celestial intelligences and souls, why his vigorous defense of "ab uno unum" against the "uncomprehending theologians"?

SIX

God's Immediacy to the Procession of Creatures

While Albert maintains that only one effect proceeds immediately from the one God, he delights in describing the evident multiplicity and diversity of things. Indeed, this diversity teaches him about God, as does unity. For if God's unity produces unity, his self-sufficiency produces diversity. The *Liber de causis* has it that "primum est diues per se ipsum et est diues maius,"[1] from which Albert concludes that God's self-communication would remain incomplete had he made but one creature and filled only its capacity:

> Nisi enim omnium capacitates impleret, non esset *dives maius* omnibus.... superdives non esset, si uno modo tantum communicaretur. Sed superdives est, quando secundum omnem possibilitatem recipientium communicatur. (*De causis et proc. univ.* 2.4.12 [165.36–37, 166.44–47])

> Tanta est enim largitas primi et tanta nobilitas et tanta amplitudo bonitatum eius, quod nihil secundorum capere posset eas, secundum quod in ipso sunt.[2]

The reason for this is God's incommunicability, that is, the impossibility of a creature equal to the Creator. To borrow the language of *Liber de causis* 19 (for which see pp. 28–29 above),

> in secundo autem non plene manifestatur eo quod inter secundum et ipsam [i.e., causam primam] mediator non est continuans utrumque. (Ibid., 2.4.7 [161.10–12])

Or, in more accessible language,

nihil eorum quae sunt, suscipere potest actionem eius secundum infinitatem eius, qua est in ipso. (Ibid., 1.1.6 [14.60–62])

The manifestation of God's abundant goodness therefore requires a diversity of receptive capacities, of essences. Now, *esse* is the one *creatum* from the one Creator (see p. 50 above), while the diverse essences receiving *esse* are from themselves (pp. 17–18 above); furthermore, what is received is received according to the mode of the recipient (p. 9 above). Apparently, then, the Creator bears no responsibility for the diverse modes in which *esse* may be found; rather, the one God causes one thing, and the many things cause their own multiplicity.

The author of the *Liber* seems to hold just that, claiming as he does that God's creative efflux is single, diversified only by its recipients, whose diverse capacities result from their self-formation, if they rank among the self-constituted substances, or from information by secondary causes, if they are generated (pp. 9–11 and 12–13 above). And Albert himself sometimes speaks the same way. To cite only a few instances,

> primus fons . . . uno et eodem modo se habens ad omnia, quamvis non uno et eodem modo se habeant omnia ad ipsum. (Ibid., 1.4.1 [42.69–74])

> Continentia autem secundorum est et non primi, ex parte illa qua terminatae sunt possibilitates. Primum autem, cum nullo modo sit in potentia, nullo modo terminatum est. Et ideo fluxus suus est in copia et universaliter et non restrictus ad aliquam particularem capacitatem vel emanationem. (Ibid., 1.4.2 [44.61–66])

> Secundum enim differentiam receptibilium differunt actus receptorum. Quae tamen differentia ex recipientibus est et non est ex causa prima. (Ibid., 2.4.1 [156.53–56])

But, however true that recipients cause diversity, Albert seeks a fuller answer to the problem of its origin. Indeed, he must, given his understanding of the relation between received and recipient, between *esse* and *id quod est*, between existence and essence. That there is more than one *id quod est* allows for a fuller manifestation of God's super-sufficiency, yes, but whence comes more than one *id quod est*? To reply that an *id quod est* or essence is from itself hardly closes the question when it is not from itself as from an efficient cause.[3] What, then, is the efficient cause of essence, and of many and diverse essences? Evidently, he who pours existence into them, namely, God. But how can that be?

Certainly, if he is to have some responsibility for diversity, then God cannot cause as a nature causes, since nature is determined to one (ibid., 1.2.8 [34.28–50]). But if his power does extend to all sorts of things, how is it that he comes to produce this and not that? Ibn Gabirol gave this question some attention and, as Albert reports, answered that God's action is determined to this or that effect by the mediation of his will (ibid., 1.1.5, 1.3.4 [12.43–65, 39.16–53]).

At first sight, this looks like an answer Albert would have to applaud: rooted in Jewish piety,[4] it seems to make philosophical sense, too, if God is a universally acting intellect, since intellectual beings have will. However, Albert pronounces it "against all philosophy" and attacks it vigorously, even proffering the opinion that *Fons vitae* was a hoax circulating under Ibn Gabirol's name. For, by definition, the first cause causes *per se*, but this theory has God act through another, through something determining him to act.[5] Again, the will is variously disposed in willing various things, whereas God's simplicity cannot admit varied dispositions. Should anyone insist that God does act through something, better to say that he acts through intellect than through will, because intellect has the power of acting first and foremost, while will merely commands that the action be done (*De causis et proc. univ.* 1.1.6 and 1.3.4 [13.63–67, 14.6–11, and 39.54–73]). This last point becomes most obvious in cases where the will and the know-how are separate: when a wealthy but unmusical man commissions a symphony, he does indeed cause the writing of a symphony, yet no one questions that the power to cause symphonies belongs in a truer sense to the musician.

Ibn Gabirol speaks so much of God's will and so little of his wisdom that readers may wonder whether divine decrees are arbitrary. Such voluntarism is not the Peripatetic way. Rather, Peripatetics recognize two principles of action, namely, nature and intellect.[6] And, although natures are determined to one, a rational power extends even to opposites (Aristotle *Metaph.* 1046^{b}5–24). Therefore, only intellect can cause diversity. Which intellect causes the diversity of the universe? That becomes evident from the sort of diversity the universe exhibits, because diversity may be ordered or disordered, and ordering characterizes the wise (ibid., 982^{a}17–19). Since, then, the universe consists of an ordered diversity, it must arise from a wise intellect. More particularly, it must come from God, for, planetary intelligences, however wise, are themselves ordered and so cannot be the universal cause of order (*De causis et proc. univ.* 1.2.8 [34.28–35.6]).

Maimonides, too, teaches that God's wisdom produces the universe; however, unlike Albert, Maimonides teaches it as an alternative to "ab uno unum," which he rejects.[7] As had Ibn Gabirol, Maimonides is setting bib-

God's Immediacy to the Procession of Creatures 69

lical themes against the sort of emanationism found in much Islamic philosophy. In response, Albert, although approving Maimonides' assertion that God's wisdom predetermines the grades and order of things (ibid., 2.4.2 and 12 [157.41–43 and 165.34–36]), criticizes his understanding of that truth (ibid., 2.1.6 [66.92–67.27]). To Albert's mind, those who find in divine wisdom escape from "ab uno unum" must think of this wisdom as multiple. But when Aristotle says that ordering marks the wise, he is speaking of wise men, whose wisdom is not like God's. For, human knowledge derives from the things known, with the result that it has many concepts by which to know the many things; and the wise set these concepts in order. God, on the other hand, knows all things by knowing himself; he has no real multiplicity of Ideas to be ordered.[8] Though wise, then, God is still utterly one, and the problem remains how multiplicity and order come from his oneness.

Divine and human wisdom are dissimilar in other ways as well, among them that, while man's knowledge is particular or universal, God's is neither. This too follows from God's knowing all things by knowing himself, since neither he nor the Ideas are predicable universals, whether in their universality or diffused in particulars.[9] And if God's knowledge transcends these modes, then he can know what remains inaccessible to human minds, namely, the materiality of material things and the individuality of individuals.[10] Indeed, he does know these things, Albert says: God does not understand things in part only, for he contains the Ideas of what he makes, and he does not make things in part only. Rather, their formal aspect comes from his light, and he produces their materiate aspect under the shadow of their form.

> Nec intelligit secundum partem id quod intelligit. Formale enim sui intelligibilis stat in actuali luce ipsius. Materiale autem, quod suppositum est illi, ab eodem producitur sub umbra eius, quod procedit ab ipso. . . .[11]

> Non enim possunt esse nisi ea quorum species sunt in ipso. (Ibid., 1.2.3 [28.72–73])

The case is similar when the individuating factor is *hyliatin* (see pp. 26–27 above) rather than ὕλη; the *esse* of an intellectual being proceeds from God, who produces, under the shadow of that *esse*, its supposit:

> Quamvis enim in intellectuali sit 'id quod est' et suppositum, tamen hoc materia non est. Sed est id quod sub umbra esse intellectualis a primo procedentis producitur a primo ente, in quo sistit et diffunditur lumen et esse a primo intellectu universaliter agente procedens. . . .[12]

Likewise, Albert speaks of essence, of receptive capacity, as produced by God under the act received:

> Causa enim prima non tantum producens est res, sed gradus et ordinem rerum praedeterminat, ut dicit Moyses Aegyptius. Nisi enim omnium capacitates impleret, non esset *dives maius* omnibus nec esset causa universalis. Et ideo sub actu producto producit potentiam susceptivam. (Ibid., 2.4.12 [165.34–39])

In fact, Albert seems to mean that God produces all essences, and the lesser under the shadow of the greater. For, immediately after explaining the production of supposits, he mentions the

> intellectus possibilis, qui in umbra intellectus animae nobilis accipitur et producitur.... unum, ut dicit Isaac, in umbra alterius creatur. (Ibid., 2.5.2 [170.72–171.12])

And, after commending Maimonides and declaring that God produces the receptive potencies of things, he describes the ever increasing shadow under which they are produced:

> Sub actu producto producit potentiam susceptivam. Quae quia sub umbra actus producitur, necesse est, quod imperfecta sit.... Adhuc autem, non eadem est umbra secundi et tertii, et sic deinceps. Imperfectius enim est, quod sub duobus imperfectis est, quam quod sub uno. Et iterum imperfectius, quod sub tribus, et sic deinceps usque ad ultimum, quod sub omnibus est.[13]

Before turning to the question how Albert can maintain both that God is a one from whom comes only one and that God wisely predetermines the grades of things, we must feel its full force. Albert denies that God acts through wisdom as through something distinct from him. Were that the case, then God would not be entirely one, nor would the multiplicity of the universe pose a problem. As it is, God's causing by wisdom must be the same as his causing by his very being, since, did he not act by his very being, he would not be a primary cause.[14]

The same must hold for God's will, since Albert does argue that God acts willingly, though not in the manner Ibn Gabirol imagined. For, Ibn Gabirol denied that God's will was altogether identical with his essence and admitted the proposition that God has more than one immediate effect.[15] In fact, the difficulty of understanding how a will could be identical with God's essence led many other philosophers—Albert mentions Theophrastus, Porphyry, Ibn Sīnā, Ibn Rušd, and even Aristotle himself—to refuse him one.

Their objections, all based on God's simplicity, may be reduced to three: that will is an appetite, whereas God lacks nothing; that the diversity of things willed would diversify God's will; and that willing presupposes knowing, so that God would have at least two faculties. In response, Albert agrees that God has no deliberative will for the satisfaction of a needy appetite and really distinct from his essence; the ancients, Albert claims, practiced negative theology and meant only this when they denied God a will. Instead of such a faculty, God has the noblest will, one which takes unchanging pleasure in the supreme end, God himself, and which acts with that freedom from necessity enjoyed only by an absolutely uncaused cause.[16]

Now, the *Liber de causis* mentions God's will once and briefly, stating that "vult ut faciat recipere bonitatem suam [simul] omnes res" (22 [164.83]); but its nineteenth chapter, explaining that the first cause acts by its being alone, suggests necessary emanation (see p. 10 above). And Dionysius suggests it more strongly, likening the Good to the sun, which shines without choice upon whatever lies in the path of its beams:

> Etenim sicut noster sol, non ratiocinans aut praeeligens, sed per ipsum esse illuminat omnia participare lumine ipsius secundum propriam rationem valentia, ita quidem et bonum, super solem sicut super obscuram imaginem segregate archetypum, per ipsam essentiam omnibus existentibus proportionaliter immittit totius bonitatis radios. (*Div. nom.* 4.1 [PG3:693B], trans. John Sarrazin)

Albert, however, denies that these texts must be read that way. After all, to say that an agent acts by its essence does not prove that it acts by necessity, unless its essence is subject to necessity (*De causis et proc. univ.* 1.3.1 [36.13–15]).

Apparently, some of Albert's contemporaries disagreed, asserting that for an agent to act by its essence is for it to act necessarily, not freely; in their eyes, philosophers who think that God acts by his essence must conclude that he is a one from whom only one proceeds, whereas Christians who believe that God acts by his will may say that all things proceed from him. Albert considers this attempt to evade "ab uno unum" futile, since God's will is his essence, so that his acting by his will is an acting by essence. Besides, God's will, like his wisdom, is one, an immutable one.[17] Still, the very language Albert employs, the language of flowing and irradiating, suggests automatic and unwilled activity: springs do not deliberate whether to flow, nor stars whether to shine. Why, then, does Albert favor such terms? Because God's goodness is such that, although bound by no necessity to create, he will create as a matter of course. The case, Albert says, parallels that of a virtuous man: his virtue gives him the power to act virtuously even while he retains the possibility of acting otherwise; however, if he truly has the virtue, he will not act otherwise.[18]

God, then, always acts in self-communicative goodness. And since he is immutable and is his wisdom and his will, his action entails no change in them; rather, he knows and wills even temporal things by eternally knowing and willing himself as the principle of all things.[19] Therefore, all diversity must be on the side of his effects, as the *Liber de causis* teaches and Albert often repeats.[20] Indeed, that is the whole burden of *Liber de causis* 23, and much of the burden of *Liber* 19. In the words of the latter chapter, "diversificantur bonitates et dona ex concursu recipientis" (158.82). Albert, reading this line, remembers the etymology of "concourse" and thinks of running, of running distances, and of running greater or lesser distances; he comments: "Cuius [i.e., eius quod fluit a deo] diversitas in recipientibus causatur ex cursu sive distantia processionis ab ipso, sicut dictum est. Currunt enim aliqua propinque, quaedam vero longinque" (*De causis et proc. univ.* 2.4.2 [157.36–39]).

Even spatial distance causes diversity: because the planets circulate where they do, and because things sublunary occupy the places they do, planets influence things variously.[21] Yet, in *De causis et processu universitatis*, distance usually means unlikeness (see above, chap. 2 n. 18), and the causal role of non-spatial distance requires careful interpretation. For, such distance is but privation of likeness, and privation cannot give being. Instead, whatever a thing has of being and power comes from the first cause; that the thing receives only as much being and power as it does results from the distance implied in procession.[22]

Of course, that all diversity resides in creatures need not mean that creatures are the chief cause of diversity. Rather, if God produces their receptive capacities, he must be the chief cause. Albert adds that point as he finishes explaining "diversificantur bonitates et dona ex concursu recipientis":

> Cuius diversitas in recipientibus causatur ex cursu sive distantia processionis ab ipso. . . . Cuius ordinis et graduum, ut dicit Moyses Aegyptius, sapientia lumine suo praedeterminans universa et reductionem eorum in unum potissima causa est. (Ibid., 2.4.2 [157.36–43])

Again,

> Sapientia enim activi intellectus in hoc est quod scit et sapit se emittere et lumine suo constituere intellecta secundum numerum et gradum eorum. . . . Cum autem agens per sapientiam constituit ea et causat, quae sapit, processus causatorum ex consequenti efficitur causa numeri et ordinis a primo usque ad ultimum. (Ibid., 2.1.6 [67.13–27]; see also *De XV probl.* 13 [C17.1:43.36–47])

And when the *Liber* says that "diversitas quidem receptionis non fit ex causa prima sed propter recipiens" (LC 23 [166.78–79]), Albert quietly supplements its teaching by introducing divine wisdom as the ultimate cause of diversity:

> Et huius quidem diversitatis causa est diversitas recipientium, in quorum quolibet id quod recipitur, est secundum modum et facultatem recipientis et non secundum modum et facultatem recepti. Diversitas autem recipientium, sicut prius diximus, a sapientia determinatur primi determinantis. . . .[23]

But how can Albert maintain, while still insisting on "ab uno unum," that God causes the diversity of things? What can "ab uno unum" mean if not that God, like nature, is determined to one effect?

The answer must be that God produces all things by producing one thing. How this can be begins to emerge when, in his tractate on emanation, Albert asks whence accidents flow. Among other difficulties, he notes that, while God is the source of all being, Aristotle calls accidents not so much beings as things which happen to beings; are accidents, then, things of which God is not the source? Albert replies that, insofar as they are beings, accidents are from God, because he is the principle of their principle, namely, substance.[24] Theologians will recognize in this solution the notion of concreation.[25] And, apparently, concreation is what Albert means by God's producing matter under the shadow of form, supposit under the shadow of nature, essence under the shadow of existence, and, generally, potency under the shadow of act.

The word "concreare" appears only once in *De causis et processu universitatis*, during an aside on the Platonists: the *Timaeus*, according to Albert, teaches that the forms whereby secondary gods know and act are concreated with them (2.2.33 [127.48]). Most often, rather than distinguishing creation from concreation, *De causis et processu universitatis* employs a related distinction taken from the *Liber de causis* itself—that between creation and information. Albert anticipated this distinction when explaining the fourth chapter of the *Liber* (see p. 50 above), but it does not appear until the seventeenth chapter. Commenting on the latter, Albert reminds his readers once again that creation is from nothing and that only being has nothing before it, so that only being is created. Life and intelligence, on the other hand, are from being, not from nothing, so that, strictly speaking, they cannot be the outcome of creation; since they give being this or that determination, they are said to come about by information.[26] Now, Aristotle teaches that, for living things, to be is to live (*De An.* 415b13); if so, then, in creating the *unum* which is *esse*, God produces the being of beings and, by that very fact, the living of living things. Nothing is to prevent Albert from extending this: sensing is the being of the sensitive, and reasoning of the rational. To put it generally, only nonbeing is other than being; determinate perfections are not. The reason for this may be gathered from *Liber de causis* 1, which portrays *esse* as a primary, universal cause with respect to living, sensing, and reasoning; these latter, then, are the being of living, sensitive, and rational things because they have received an influx of the power of being.[27] Consequently, God, from whom *esse* flows, is not absent from the process of information. When *Liber* 17 proposes that the first Being gives all things being by way of creation, whereas, by way of form, the first Life makes all living things self-moving and the first Intellect gives all intellectual things knowledge, the anonymous author means that God creates and that Intellect informs. But when Albert reads the text, he takes being, life, and intelligence to be three divine names,[28] with the result that God both creates being and informs it with life and intelligence.[29]

Given that God establishes the grades of being under the shadow of *esse*, the meaning of "esse creatum primum" requires reconsideration. To recall our earlier considerations, Albert points out that the *Liber de causis* calls the first created thing *esse*, not *ens* or *entitas*, and he explains that the infinitive refers to an indeterminate concept answering the question whether a thing is (p. 43 above); he identifies this first created thing with the subject of Aristotle's *Metaphysics* in his commentary thereon; and his opinion that the *Liber de causis* brings the *Metaphysics* to its theological completion obliges him to retain this identification. Yet, the *ens* in which Aristotle finds the subject of metaphysics is said of all, especially of essence, not just of the answer to the question whether a thing is (p. 47). What, then, is *esse*, and why is it described somewhat differently than was Aristotle's "being as being"?

Albert does not specify, but one possible answer suggests itself, an answer based on the relation between the earlier parts of metaphysics and its final, theological part. Completing this science involves a change of direction:

whereas the parts covered in Aristotle's *Metaphysics* ascend from the beings with which we are familiar toward separated beings, students of the part represented by the *Liber de causis*, having acquired considerable knowledge of separate substances, are in a position to adopt something of the divine viewpoint, observing the descent of effects from their causes. Now, the beings familiar to us are sensible substances; certainly, we never encounter *esse* except in an *ens*. Accordingly, Aristotle starts with being in its vaguest sense and gradually works out which things have the strongest claim to the name "being." But having accomplished that and begun to adopt the divine viewpoint, the "Aristotle" of the *Liber* moves, no longer from the beings first known to us up toward the really first beings, but from the really first being down toward what comes from it. And what first comes from it is the proper term of its proper act, that is, existence, the term of creation. From there "Aristotle" can descend toward existence as we encounter it, that is, as informed or determined. For, information is posterior to creation: essences are the recipients of the influx of existence, yes, but recipients which exist only by virtue of their receiving.

To summarize what Albert makes of the proposition that from the One only one immediately proceeds, he defends it in two senses, based on several assertions in the *Liber de causis:* that the first created thing is *esse*, that *esse* is intelligence, and that the first created thing is intelligence. According to one sense, "ab uno unum" means that the first and only created thing is the *intelligentia* or concept of *esse*. And since, according to the opening chapter of the *Liber, esse* is a primary cause precontaining whatever comes after it, then the one God, by creating this one thing, produces all things.

Admittedly, *esse* is not always one thing: the many creatures have each their own *esse*. But God is an artisan, whose Ideas flow into his works. The Idea of *esse*, as still in God, is one but uncreated; as received in creatures, it is created but not one, whether numerically or even generically. However, as flowing from God to creatures, as on the way between them, it is no longer identical with God, nor is it yet multiplied in particulars; instead, it is one, analogically common idea about to be received diversely in the many diverse beings. Not that it exists extramentally somewhere between God and things: *esse* as on the way from God to creatures is only a mental consideration of the Idea, but the consideration allows Albert to say that what emanates from the one God is one.

In the other, complementary sense Albert gives "ab uno unum," *intelligentia*, now meaning a separate, intellective nature rather than a concept, is God's proximate effect. Within each creature, *esse* is the first and indeed the only created thing; among creatures, intelligences are first because most like God. Their likeness to him consists, in part, of their unity and simplicity, so that each intelligence is an "unum ab uno" and a "simplex a simplici." And among intelligences, the mover of the outermost sphere is simplest and most one.

This elaborate defense of "ab uno unum" reveals the workings of a very clever exegete. Yet why should Albert have bothered constructing it when so many of his Christian contemporaries gave the Peripatetic dictum short shrift? His student Thomas, for instance, was capable of dismissing it in two sentences:

> Causa agens non est in illis substantiis superioribus sicut in rebus materialibus, ut necesse sit ex uno tantum unum causari, quia causa et causatum in eis sunt secundum esse intelligibile. Unde secundum plura quae possunt intelligi ab uno, possunt ab uno plura causari. (*Metaph.* 12.9, §2560)

But for Albert, however careful the attention Aristotle's opinions generally deserved, "ab uno unum" was not just Aristotle's view, but that of Dionysius as well, as we saw when Albert announced his intention to defend it:

> Nec hoc est contra theologum, quia Dionysius dicit, quod ea quae sunt a primo, per distantiam ab ipso accipiunt differentiam. Relata autem ad ipsum et in ipsum unum sunt et idem. (*De causis et proc. univ.* 1.1.10 [22.9–15])

Again,

> dicendum est secundum Dionysii determinationem, quod distantia a primo facit diversitatem, sicut distantia a primo puncto lucis radiorum facit diversitatem. Et eadem distantia facit, quod in secundo non uniuntur nisi per compositionem, quae in primo sunt ut unum. Esse enim et vita et ratio in primo sunt ut unum. In sequentibus autem non uniuntur nisi per modum compositionis potentiae et actus. (Ibid., 2.1.21 [86.32–39], alluding to *Div. nom.* 5.6 [PG3:821A])

In this matter, Albert believed, the Peripatetic theology of the *Liber de causis* amounted to Dionysian theology.[30]

Nor was his belief wholly unfounded. Though Albert knew nothing of it, Dionysius and the author of the *Liber* shared dependence on Proclus,[31] so that reading the *Liber* can lead one in Dionysian directions. Albert's path must have run somewhat as follows. The *Liber* says both that God has a single efflux (19) and that the first being gives all things being (17); what, then, could the single efflux be if not created being? And how could created being be single except conceptually? Since the *Liber* adopted Plotinus' identification of Being with Intellect and his treatment of Intellect as both knower and Idea, Albert found no insurmountable obstacle to interpreting God's single efflux as the *ante rem* concept of being. On the contrary, parts of *Liber de causis* 4 make sense only when understood of a concept (pp. 38–41 above). And that this concept of being is God's one immediate effect does indeed recall Dionysius' teaching that the intelligible procession of Being is the first of God's gifts, the gift in which Life and Wisdom and all other processions participate (*Div. nom.* 5.5 [PG3:820A–C]).

Afterword

By interpreting the *unum ab uno* as created being, in which all creatures share according to their analogy, Albert removes any supposed opposition between emanation and creation; as he understands it, emanation expresses God's omnipresence even while implying creatures' ever increasing distance from God along the scale of being (LC 23). For, secondary causes add nothing to the power of God, from whom they receive their power (LC 1); God works through mediators because distance diminishes our receptive capacity, not his active power. Whatever the distance, God's power extends to the very center of each creature, to the existence under the shadow of which arises the creature's every aspect.

A sublime conclusion, but what of the convoluted way Albert arrives at it? Compared to Thomas' collation of the *Liber de causis* with Proclus' *Elements of Theology*, or to contemporary Arabists' discoveries about the text or about intellectual life in ninth-century Baghdad, Albert's account of the *Liber* may seem unworthy of our attention. Striving to join Platonic to Aristotelian wisdom is all well and good, but can we, with our historical sophistication, find coherence and cogency in a Peripateticism which claims the *Liber de causis* as its own? Even after Albert gained access to the *Elements of Theology*, he seems never to have recognized the revisions it required of him.

Or are we, perhaps, the ones who need to revise our views? I suggest no weakness in the case for early ninth-century, Neoplatonic, Baghdadi authorship of the *Liber*. What I do suggest is that we not lose sight of how carefully Albert qualifies his thesis about the origins of the *Liber*.

The thesis—that the Jew David excerpted the propositions from "Aristotle's" *Epistula de principio universi esse* and from Ibn Sīnā, al-Ġazālī, and al-Fārābī, writing the proofs himself—leads Albert to search the works of these philosophers for exegetical clues, yet he remains sensitive to their differences. To recall but two crucial instances, while many of his contemporaries took the *Liber de causis* to promote the same mediate creation as Ibn Sīnā, Albert sees, despite the inadequacies of the Latin version, that the *Liber* reserves creation to God alone. And where mediation does occur, Albert argues that Aristotle finds the need for it with creatures, and Ibn Sīnā with the Creator; the Jew David does not simply present his readers with conflicting views from his four sources, but rather selects carefully among them and, in this case, sides with Aristotle (see p. 55 above).

Still, for all the qualifications Albert feels compelled to introduce, he does consider al-Fārābī and Ibn Sīnā major sources for the author of the *Liber*. But that was not a bad guess, since all three underwent Plotinian influence (see chap. 1 nn. 12, 32–33, 35–36, and 54). As for Albert's allying Dionysius with the *Liber*, historical-critical research has added to the reasons for doing so. What such research disinclines us to entertain is his allying the combination of Dionysius and the *Liber* with Aristotle.

Here too, though, Albert himself shows some awareness of their dissimilarities, as when he notes the Platonic origin of the threefold universal (see chap. 4 n. 19), without which he cannot construe Dionysius' writings, or when he distinguishes the analogy of imitation from the analogy explained in *Metaphysics* Γ (see pp. 32–33). Nonetheless, by finding the key to the *Liber de causis* in Dionysius and deeming the *Liber* the completion of Aristotle's corpus, Albert makes Dionysius the key to Peripatetic thought as well. Can we, knowing what we do, take that proposal seriously?

In earlier days, many a philosopher would indeed have weighed it with the utmost seriousness, in that they, too, located Aristotle's achievements within a Platonic framework. Even the *Enneads* of Plotinus himself "are full of concealed Stoic and Peripatetic doctrines. Aristotle's *Metaphysics*, in particular, is concentrated in them."[1] And such a path remains open to us today, despite our wealth of historical information, because the issue is not for history to determine: whatever we may find out about which thoughts explicitly crossed Aristotle's mind, there remains the philosophical question of which philosophical developments are compatible with and even demanded by his basic principles. The same, of course, holds for the intentions of the anonymous author of the *Liber de causis*.

Notes

A Note on Editions and Transliterations

1. In *Opera Omnia*, ed. Institutum Alberti Magni Coloniense, 17.2 (Münster: Aschendorff, 1993). Paul Hoßfeld, in his "Der 'Liber de causis'-Kommentar Alberts und seine naturphilosophischen Kommentare" (*Documenti e studi sulla tradizione filosofica medievale* 6 [1995]: 39–105), suggests many additions to the apparatus.

Titles of Albert's works are abbreviated as in the Cologne editions (for a complete key to that system, see *Albertus Magnus — Doctor Universalis: 1280/1980*, ed. G. Meyer and A. Zimmermann, Walberberger Studien: Philosophische Reihe, 6 [Mainz: Matthias-Grünewald, 1980], 517–19). After a work's internal divisions, references include C for Cologne or B for Borgnet, the volume and, if applicable, the part, and the page and column (for Borgnet editions) or page and line (for Cologne editions); "C17.2" is assumed in references to *De causis et proc. univ.* The Cologne editions italicize phrases Albert takes from the text he is paraphrasing; in *De causis et proc. univ.* 1.1.10, phrases from al-Ġazālī's *Metaphysics* are also italicized, since that chapter amounts to a commentary thereon.

2. In *Opera Omnia*, 10:361–619 (Paris: Vivès, 1891).

3. In his *Die pseudo-aristotelische Schrift "Ueber das reine Gute" bekannt unter dem Namen "Liber de causis"* (Freiburg im Breisgau: Herder'sche Verlagshandlung, 1882; reprint, Frankfurt am Main: Minerva, [1961]), 58–118.

4. Bibliotheek de Rijksuniversiteit, MS Oriental 209.

5. In his *Al-Aflāṭūniyya al-muḥdaṯa ʿinda al-ʿarab*, Dirāsāt Islāmiyya, 19 (Cairo: Maktaba al-nahḍa al-miṣriyya, 1955; reprint, Kuwait: Wakāla al-maṭbūʿāt, 1977), 1–33.

6. In his "The *Liber de causis (Kalām fī maḥḍ al-khair)*: A Study of Medieval Neoplatonism" (Ph.D. diss., University of Toronto, 1981), 135–279.

7. Istanbul, Süleymaniye Kütüphanesi, Haci Mahmud 5683 was discovered by Franz Rosenthal, and Ankara Üniversitesi Dil ve Tarih-Coğrafya Fakültesi Kütüphanesi, Ismail Saib I 1696 by Fuat Sezgin. For detailed descriptions, see Richard Taylor, "Neoplatonic Texts in Turkey: Two Manuscripts Containing Ibn Ṭufayl's *Ḥayy Ibn Yaqẓān*, Ibn al-Sīd's *Kitāb al-Ḥadāʾiq*, Ibn Bājja's *Ittiṣāl al-ʿAql bi-l-Insān*, the *Liber de causis*, and an Anonymous Neoplatonic Treatise on Motion," *Mélanges de l'Institut Dominicain d'Etudes Orientales du Caire* 15 (1982): 251–64.

8. Bardenhewer, 163–91.

9. "Le *Liber de causis*," ed. Adriaan Pattin, *Tijdschrift voor Filosofie* 28 (1966): 90–203.

10. With Pattin's edition, see "De *Proclus Arabus* en het *Liber de causis*," *Tijdschrift voor Filosofie* 38 (1976): 468–73, where he offers such additions and revisions as listing more manuscript references to Avendauth and dropping his claim that the *Liber de causis* (henceforth, LC) cannot predate the twelfth century. Pattin is reporting advances made by Arabists, not comparing the Arabic and the Latin himself; consequently, many errors remain. For detailed critiques of his edition, see C. Vansteenkiste, "Intorno al testo latino del *Liber de causis*," *Angelicum* 44 (1967): 60–83, and Richard C. Taylor, "Remarks on the Latin Text and the Translator of the *Kalām fī maḥḍ al-khair / Liber de causis*," *Bulletin de philosophie médiévale* 31 (1989): 75–102. Pattin's reply to Taylor ("Autour du *Liber de causis*: Quelques réflexions sur la récente littérature," *Freiburger Zeitschrift für Philosophie und Theologie* 41 [1994]: 370–88) is unsatisfactory, amounting to a claim that, when establishing the Latin text, its Arabic original is less revealing than Proclus' thought and what seems intelligible in Latin. He adds a most unlikely suggestion that the Istanbul and Ankara MSS, which ground much of Taylor's critique, count for less than the Leiden MS and perhaps depend upon the Latin.

11. References to LC are by chapter, page, and line in this edition, unless otherwise stated. Whereas many Latin manuscripts and editions halve LC 4—wrongly, as Aquinas suspected on stylistic grounds (*In Librum de causis expositio* lectio 5, §130)—, thus producing thirty-two chapters, I use the Arabic numeration only. For Albert's practice, see below, pp. 5–6.

1. Introduction

1. See Ruedi Imbach, "Le (néo-)platonisme médiéval, Proclus latin et l'école dominicaine allemande," *Revue de théologie et de philosophie* 110 (1978): 427,

and Fernand Brunner, "Création et émanation: Fragment de philosophie comparée," *Studia Philosophica* 33 (1973): 33–63.

2. In "Emanation: Ein unphilosophisches Wort im spätantiken Denken" (in *Parusia: Studien zur Philosophie Platons und zur Problemgeschichte des Platonismus*, ed. K. Flasch [Frankfurt: Minerva, 1965], 119–41), Heinrich Dörrie argues—a bit too strongly: see Stephen Gersh, "Metaphors of Emanation," in *From Iamblichus to Eriugena: An Investigation of the Prehistory and Evolution of the Pseudo-Dionysian Tradition*, Studien zur Problemgeschichte der antiken und mittelalterlichen Philosophie, 8 (Leiden: E. J. Brill, 1978)—that ἀπόρροια is quite rare among ancient Neoplatonists, and mostly confined to physical rather than metaphysical contexts.

3. See Harry A. Wolfson, "The Meaning of *Ex Nihilo* in the Church Fathers, Arab and Hebrew Philosophy, and St. Thomas," in *Mediaeval Studies in Honor of Jeremiah Denis Matthias Ford*, ed. Urban T. Holmes, Jr., and Alexander J. Denomy (Cambridge: Harvard University Press, 1948), 353–70; idem, "The Meaning of *Ex Nihilo* in Isaac Israeli," *Jewish Quarterly Review*, n.s., 50 (1959–60): 1–12; idem, "The Identification of *Ex Nihilo* with Emanation in Gregory of Nyssa," *Harvard Theological Review* 63 (1970): 53–60; Thérèse-Anne Druart, "Al-Farabi and Emanationism," in *Studies in Medieval Philosophy*, ed. John F. Wippel, Studies in Philosophy and the History of Philosophy, 17 (Washington D.C.: Catholic University of America Press, 1987), 23–43; idem, "Al-Fārābī, Emanation, and Metaphysics," in *Neoplatonism and Islamic Thought*, ed. Parviz Morewedge, Studies in Neoplatonism: Ancient and Modern, 5 (Albany: State University of New York Press, 1992), 127–48; and Barry Sherman Kogan, "Averroës and the Theory of Emanation," *Mediaeval Studies* 43 (1981): 384–404. Jules Janssens, in "Creation and Emanation in Ibn Sīnā" (*Documenti e studi sulla tradizione filosofica medievale* 8 [1997]: 455–77), presents useful information but assumes—unlike Ibn Sīnā—that emanation is pantheistic.

4. In psychology, for instance, John of Jandun notes that Albert speaks more than anyone else of powers flowing from the soul's essence: "potentie anime fluunt ab anima, et hoc modo loquendi precipue utitur Albertus" (*Questiones super tres libros de anima* 2.10 [Venice, 1519, 23va], quoted by Katharine Park, "Albert's Influence on Late Medieval Psychology," in *Albertus Magnus and the Sciences: Commemorative Essays, 1980*, ed. James A. Weisheipl, Studies and Texts, 49 [Toronto: Pontifical Institute of Mediaeval Studies, 1980], 514).

5. *Plotinus*, The Arguments of the Philosophers (London: Routledge, 1994), 27–36. See also Jean Trouillard's vigorous defense of emanation, "Procession néoplatonicienne et création judéo-chrétienne," in *Néoplatonisme: Mélanges offerts à Jean Trouillard*, Les Cahiers de Fontenay, 19–22 (Fontenay aux Roses: E.N.S., 1981), 1–30.

6. Amato Masnovo, *Da Guglielmo d'Auvergne a S. Tommaso d'Aquino*, vol. 3, *L'Uomo*, Pubblicazioni dell'Università Cattolica del Sacro Cuore, n.s., 10 (Milan: Società editrice "Vita e Pensiero," 1945), 42–47.

7. Albert describes his intention and method in *Phys.* 1.1.1 (C4.1:1.9–49).

8. It appears thirty-third in the list by Gerard's *socii* of his translations, as *De expositione bonitatis pure*, which renders the Arabic title. (The title "Liber de causis" arose in the thirteenth century.) For an annotated version of the list, see *Dictionary of Scientific Biography*, s.v. "Gerard of Cremona," by Richard Lemay. Pattin's arguments for a revision of Gerard's translation by Gundisalvi ("Le Liber," 98–101) are weak, as shown by Taylor ("Remarks," 78–81); Pattin attempts to reinforce them in "Autour du *Liber*," 355–58, 360, and 387.

9. *De intell. et int.* 1.1.2 (B9:479b) indicates that Albert knew of this text from Ibn Sīnā's *Liber de philosophia prima* 9.2, where an error in the Latin translation creates the impression that Aristotle wrote it. The Arabs actually attributed it to Alexander of Aphrodisias. ʿAbd al-Raḥmān Badawī gives a French translation of the *Epistula* in his *La transmission de la philosophie grecque au monde arabe* (Paris: J. Vrin, 1968), 121–39.

10. *De causis et proc. univ.* 2.1.1 (59.9–18 and 61.65–68). For attributions Albert makes elsewhere, see Fauser's notes and the texts collected by Adriaan Pattin in "Over de schrijver en de vertaler van het *Liber de causis:* Studie over de vijf eerste proposities," *Tijdschrift voor Philosophie* 23 (1961): 512–13, noting that "commentum Alpharabi" refers to the proofs of the propositions, not to a commentary by al-Fārābī on LC, as has sometimes been said. At least some of these attributions may be, not distinct opinions, but shorthand for the opinion in *De causis et proc. univ.*: even *Problemata determinata*, a reply to a letter received in April of 1271, speaks of "Aristoteles in Libro de causis" (1 [C17.1:47.7–9]), while *De caelo et mundo*, dated by its editors to the early 1250s, invokes "Avendaud" ["the son of David"] in Libro de causis" (1.3.8 [C5.1:73.31; B4:86a reads "Avicennae" for "Avendaud," and is so quoted by Pattin]).

11. See Manuel Alonso, "Las fuentes literarias del *Liber de Causis*," *Al-Andalus* 10 (1945): 355–57, for a collection of passages in which Albert mentions the *Epistula*, and add *Probl. determ.* 10 (C17.1:53.6–8), bringing the total to eight references. For speculation as to how Albert arrived at his conjectures about the *Epistula*, see Enrique Alarcón, "S. Alberto Magno y la *Epistola Aristotelis de Principio Universi Esse*," in *Actas del I Congreso Nacional de Filosofía Medieval*, ed. Jorge M. Ayala Martínez (Zaragoza: Sociedad de Filosofía Medieval, 1992), 181–92.

12. Like most of his contemporaries who read no Arabic, Albert was unaware that al-Ġazālī's *Intentions of the Philosophers* (largely a translation of one of Ibn Sīnā's Persian works; see Jules Janssens, "Le *Dānesh-Nāmeh* d'Ibn Sīnā: Un texte à revoir?" *Bulletin de philosophie médiévale* 28 [1986]: 163–77) was

directed toward the refutation of some Neoplatonic tenets. The other doctrinal affinities are real: Ibn Sīnā studied both al-Fārābī's works and the *Theology of Aristotle* (see Georges Vajda, "Les Notes d'Avicenne sur la *Théologie d'Aristote*," *Revue Thomiste* 51 [1951]: 346–406), whose relation to LC will be suggested below; al-Fārābī himself knew the *Theology of Aristotle* (see Paul Kraus, "Plotin chez les Arabes: Remarques sur un nouveau fragment de la paraphrase arabe des Ennéades," *Bulletin de l'Institut d'Egypte* 23 [1940–41]: 269–71).

13. For a sampling of such notes, see Pattin, "Le *Liber*," 101–20.

14. Many scholars believed Albert's account, especially once Moritz Steinschneider identified Albert's "David Judaeus quidam" with "Johannes Avendauth," in turn identified with Johannes Hispalensis. Bardenhewer (53–54 and 125–35) analyzed Albert's claims and criticized the many misinterpretations of them, but some—including Pattin ("Le *Liber*," 93 and, most recently, "Autour du *Liber*," 358–70 and 388)—have continued to defend variations on Albert's view. Certain of Bardenhewer's criticisms were too hasty: Albert does seem to have had Avendauth in mind when he mentioned the Jew David (see nn. 10 and 17). Nevertheless, Albert's source was unreliable, and Arabists situate LC in early ninth-century Baghdad or thereabouts. For their latest evidence, see Richard Taylor's important article, "The Kalām fī maḥḍ al-khair (*Liber de causis*) in the Islamic Philosophical Milieu," in *Pseudo-Aristotle in the Middle Ages: The "Theology" and Other Texts*, ed. J. Kraye, W. F. Ryan, and C. B. Schmitt, Warburg Institute Surveys and Texts, 11 (London: Warburg Institute, University of London, 1986), 37–52. Cristina D'Ancona Costa has weighed the merits of the more particular proposition that al-Kindī himself authored LC; see her *Recherches sur le Liber de Causis*, Etudes de Philosophie Médiévale, 72 (Paris: J. Vrin, 1995), 155–94.

15. Even John of Dacia, who knew all fourteen books, wrote, "Plures autem libros methaphysice non habemus translatos, quamuis in Greco, ut dicitur, bene sunt vsque ad viginti duos" (*Diuisio scientie*, in *Johannis Daci Opera*, ed. A. Otto, Corpus Philosophorum Danicorum Medii Aevi [Copenhagen, 1955], vol. 1, part 1, p. 26, lines 5–6). Thomas Aquinas, in *De unitate intellectus contra Averroistas* 5, was more specific about what was lacking: "illam partem Methaphisice non habemus quam fecit de substantiis separatis" (Leonine 43:313.335–37); see also 1 (299.705–10), where he reports having seen ten books which had yet to be translated, with §38c of the editor's preface; for the centuries-long debate whether these ten books could have been the *Theology of Aristotle*, see Jill Kraye, "The Pseudo-Aristotelian *Theology* in Sixteenth- and Seventeenth-Century Europe," in *Pseudo-Aristotle in the Middle Ages*, 266 with notes. If and when Albert wrote the *Speculum astronomiae*, he also missed the part about separate substances: "[Albumasar] dicat Aristotelem hoc dixisse, licet non inveniatur in universis libris Aristotelis quos habemus, et forte illud est in duodecimo aut in decimo tertio

Metaphysicae, qui nondum sunt translati et loquuntur de intelligentiis, sicut ipse promittit" (ed. S. Caroti et al., *Quaderni di storia e critica della scienza*, n.s., 10 [Pisa: Domus Galilaeana, 1977], 12 [35.32–36]). However, by the time Albert completed his paraphrase of *Metaph.*, he had all but book eleven.

The Arabs and the late antique Greeks had also found *Metaph.* theologically lacking and collected supplementary materials.

16. §10: "Et hec scientia habet tres libros. Vnus appellatur *Vetus methaphisica*. . . . Et in hoc libro determinatur de rebus in ratione qua sunt entes et habent reduci ad primum ens. Alius liber est qui dicitur *Methaphisica noua*. . . . In *Noua* vero *methaphisica* agitur de rebus diuinis et de primis principiis rerum secundum quodlibet sui esse. Tertius liber est *De causis*; et ibi agitur de substantiis diuinis in quantum sunt principia essendi uel influendi unam in alteram secundum quod ibidem habetur quod 'omnis substantia superior influit in suum causatum.'" The text has been edited by Claude Lafleur with the collaboration of Joanne Carrier in *Le "Guide de l'étudiant" d'un maître anonyme de la Faculté des arts de Paris au XIIIe siècle: Edition critique provisoire du ms. Barcelona, Arxiu de la Corona d'Aragó, Ripoll 109, ff. 134ra–158va*, Publications du laboratoire de philosophie ancienne et médiévale de la Faculté de philosophie de l'Université Laval, 1 (Quebec: Faculté de philosophie, Université Laval, 1992); their definitive edition will appear in the "Continuatio Mediaevalis" of "Corpus Christianorum." For the dating of the guide, see Claude Lafleur, "Les 'guides de l'étudiant' de la Faculté des arts de l'Université de Paris au XIIIe siècle," in *Philosophy and Learning: Universities in the Middle Ages*, ed. Maarten J. F. M. Hoenen, J. H. Josef Schneider, and Georg Wieland, Education and Society in the Middle Ages and Renaissance, 6 (Leiden: E. J. Brill, 1995), 144.

Henri-Dominique Saffrey calculates that 22.5 percent of LC MSS couple LC with *Metaph.* ("L'état actuel des recherches sur le *Liber de causis* comme source de la métaphysique au moyen âge," in *Die Metaphysik im Mittelalter: Ihr Ursprung und ihre Bedeutung*, ed. Paul Wilpert, Miscellanea Mediaevalia, 2 [Berlin: Walter de Gruyter, 1963], 275). Not that medieval thinkers were unanimous: however much John of Dacia may have wanted twenty-two books, he argued against the "quidam" who added LC to *Metaph.*, on the grounds that metaphysics does not consider substances according as one has causal influence upon another (vol. 1, part 1, p. 26, lines 7–12).

17. *De causis et proc. univ.* 2.1.1 (59.31–60.5). These, Albert says, are the third and fourth reasons why the Jew David called his work *Metaphysics* (59.20–22: "istum librum 'Metaphysicam' nominavit, tituli eiusdem quattuor subiungens rationes"). Is he perhaps reporting reasons he read in the margin of a manuscript? If so, he seems to agree, judging from the next quotation. For the title, see Pattin, "Le *Liber*," 203, apparatus for l. 16: Selden sup. 24, which Pattin takes to

have been written by an English hand of the early thirteenth century, concludes "Explicit metaphisica avendauth."

The title *Flos divinorum*, discussed by Albert at 60.51–61.8, belongs, not to LC, but to "huiusmodi tractatus," namely, tract. 5 in the metaphysical part of al-Ġazālī's *Intentions of the Philosophers*, which opens, "Tractatus iste quasi flos divinorum" (*Algazel's Metaphysics: A Mediaeval Translation* [ed. T. J. Muckle, St. Michael's Mediaeval Studies (Toronto: St. Michael's College, 1933), 119.6]); it is "huiusmodi," because, as we shall see, Albert finds similar emanative schemes there and in LC. As for the title *De causis causarum*, to which Albert turns at 61.39–64, see the closing words of Ibn Sīnā's *Liber De Anima seu Sextus De Naturalibus:* "Et post hunc sequitur liber de causa causarum" (ed. S. Van Riet, *Avicenna Latinus* [Louvain: E. Peeters, and Leiden: E. J. Brill, 1968–72], 5.8 [2:185.32–33]).

18. *De causis et proc. univ.* 2.5.24 (191.18–23). Albert had translations of *Metaph.* A-I and Λ (one through ten and twelve), but not of *Metaph.* K (eleven); consequently, his *Metaph.* XI, XII, and XIII are our *Metaph.* XII, XIII (M), and XIV (N). "Quando adiuncta fuerint XI Primae philosophiae" does not indicate, as G. Meersseman hypothesized (*Introductio in Opera Omnia B. Alberti Magni O.P.* [Bruges: Beyaert, 1931], 65, 137), that Albert knew only eleven books of Aristotle's *Metaph.* while writing *De causis et proc. univ.*, and acquired M and N later, whereupon he wrote the last two books of his own *Metaph.* For, the passage quoted from *De causis et proc. univ.* 2.1.1 mentions the "twelfth" and "thirteenth," without complaining that these are unavailable. If Albert places LC after book "eleven" and not after book "thirteen," that is simply because "eleven" (Λ) contains Aristotle's most detailed teaching on the first causes, about which LC speaks at greater length; given his nuanced opinion about the authorship of LC, he cannot be suggesting that the sequence A-I, Λ, and *Liber de causis* constitutes a literary unit. For more information about the translations available to Albert, see the prolegomena to his *Metaph.* (C16.1:vii and x–xiii).

19. For samples and discussions of these disclaimers, see Fernand Van Steenberghen, "La filosofia di Alberto Magno," *Sapienza* (Naples) 18 (1965): 381–93; idem, "Albert le Grand avait-il une philosophie personelle?" *Académie royale de Belgique: Bulletin de la Classe des Lettres*, 5th ser., 52 (1966): 15–30 (reprinted in his *La philosophie au XIIIe siècle*, Philosophes médiévaux, 9 [Louvain: Publications Universitaires de Louvain, 1966], 292–306); Rudolf Kaiser, "Zur Frage der eigenen Anschauung Alberts d. Gr. in seinen philosophischen Kommentaren: Eine grundsätzliche Betrachtung," *Freiburger Zeitschrift für Philosophie und Theologie* 9 (1962): 53–62; and James Weisheipl, "Albert's Disclaimers in the Aristotelian Paraphrases," *Proceedings of the PMR Conference* 5 (1980): 1–27.

20. See Aristotle *Metaph.* 1076^a10–16 and Albert *Metaph.* 1.5.15 (C16.1:89.63–64). Since Albert believes some of LC's propositions to be from

a work by Aristotle, it seems incorrect to render "secundum opinionem" "entsprechend [seiner eigenen] Ansicht" and take this passage as criticizing Aristotle (Ingrid Craemer-Ruegenberg, *Albertus Magnus*, Große Denker: Leben, Werk, Wirkung; Beck'sche Schwarze Reihe, 501 [Munich: C. H. Beck, 1980], 77).

21. While little certainty is attainable in such matters, Rudolf Kaiser's detailed arguments in "Versuch einer Datierung der Schrift Alberts des Grossen *De causis et processu universitatis*" (*Archiv für Geschichte der Philosophie* 45 [1963]: 125–36) are, for the most part, persuasive, and he provides a valuable review of earlier literature on the dating of Albert's paraphrases. For the *terminus ad quem*, see *Probl. determ.* 1, 2, and 22 (C17.1:47.22–23; 50.31–32; 56.64–65). Making *De causis et proc. univ.* approximately contemporary with Thomas' *In librum de causis expositio* (written shortly after Moerbeke's translation) explains why neither work shows knowledge of the other, and why *De causis et proc. univ.* uses no Proclus, whereas Albert's *Summa* cites *Inst.* — at least its opening propositions — lavishly. It is unclear why Fauser (v.55–62) sets the *terminus ad quem* at 1268; though Moerbeke did finish his version of Proclus then, some time may have elapsed before Albert acquired and began reading a copy (so Kaiser, "Die Benutzung proklischer Schriften durch Albert den Großen," *Archiv für Geschichte der Philosophie* 45 [1963]: 20–21).

In "Welches sind die Beziehungen Alberts des Grossen *Liber de causis et processu universitatis* zur στοιχείωσις θεολογική des Neuplatonikers Proclus, und was lehren uns dieselben?" (Ph.D. diss., Ludwig-Maximilians-Universität zu München, 1902), Ernst Degen argued that Albert used *Inst.* — the parts excerpted in LC and the other parts as well — throughout *De causis et proc. univ.*, whether in Moerbeke's translation or in another, now unknown translation from an Arabic version. Kaiser ("Die Benutzung," 1–22) refutes this: whereas Albert cites Proclus by name, frequently, and according to Moerbeke's version in his *Summa*, he never mentions Proclus in *De causis et proc. univ.*; the parallels Degen alleges have none of the vocabulary of Moerbeke's Proclus; and the doctrinal similarities are easily accounted for by Proclus' and Albert's common use of Aristotle, and by Albert's use of Pseudo-Dionysius and LC, both dependent on Proclus. Maria Feigl also criticizes Degen, pointing out that Albert's Arabisms come from LC, not from some hypothetic Arabo-Latin version of *Inst.* ("Albert der Grosse und die arabische Philosophie: Eine Studie zu den Quellen seines Kommentars zum *Liber de causis*," *Philosophisches Jahrbuch* 63 [1955]: 131–50).

22. For examples of Albert's use of various translations and commentaries in the physical treatises, see Paul Hoßfeld, "Die Arbeitsweise des Albertus Magnus in seinen naturphilosophischen Schriften," in *Albertus Magnus — Doctor Universalis*, 195–204; idem, *Albertus Magnus als Naturphilosoph und Naturwissenschaftler* (Bonn: Albertus-Magnus-Institut, 1983); idem, "Die Physik des

Albertus Magnus (Teil I, die Bucher 1–4) Quellen und Charakter," *Archivum Fratrum Praedicatorum* 55 (1985): 49–65.

23. For a survey of the first book, see Maria Feigl, "Albert der Grosse und die arabische Philosophie: Eine Studie zu den Quellen seines Kommentars zum *Liber de causis*," *Philosophisches Jahrbuch* 63 (1955): 139–46. The whole of *De causis et proc. univ.*, in abstraction from its nature as an explication of LC, is summarized by Philalethes in "Ueber Kosmologie und Kosmogenie nach den Ansichten der Scholastiker in Dante's Zeit, zu Gesang I des Paradieses," note in *Dante Alighieri's Goettliche Comoedie*, dritter Theil, *Das Paradies* (Dresden and Leipzig: Arnoldische Buchhandlung, 1849; 2d ed., 1865–66; reprint of 2d ed., Leipzig: B. G. Teubner, 1904), 12–18.

24. There are no apparent grounds for asserting that "si les *propositions* (supposées aristotéliciennes) ont droit à d'amples développements, le *commentum* (supposé non-aristotélicien) ne reçoit que quelques lignes et n'a manifestement d'autre fonction que celle d'un récapitulé (annoncé par une formule technique, telle que *capitulariter* ou *summatim restringendo dicendum quod*)" (Alain de Libera, "Albert le Grand et le platonisme: De la doctrine des idées à la théorie des trois états de l'universel," in *On Proclus and His Influence in Medieval Philosophy*, ed. E. P. Bos and P. A. Meijer, Philosophia Antiqua, 53 [Leiden: E. J. Brill, 1992], 91). For one thing, Albert's position is that even the propositions are not all by Aristotle (*De causis et proc. univ.* 2.1.1 [59.11–13]). And, in point of fact, his explanatory chapters take up each part of the LC chapters sequentially from beginning to end, spending more or less time on the various sections according to their obscurity or importance, whether they come from the proposition or the proof; both propositions and proofs are included in the paraphrasing, "capitulariter" chapters. Chapter 3 below will reveal how important material from the *commenta* can be.

25. To facilitate future research on *De causis et proc. univ.*, I note obscurities and errors relevant to the study of Albert's interpretation as a whole, not just to his thoughts on creation and emanation. For still more details on the linguistic difficulties, see Taylor's notes in St. Thomas' *Commentary on the Book of Causes*, translated and annotated by Vincent A. Guagliardo, Charles R. Hess, and Richard C. Taylor, Thomas Aquinas in Translation (Washington, D.C.: Catholic University of America Press, 1996). Present purposes do not require demonstration of LC's monotheistic revision of *Inst.*; what is perhaps the most detailed and explicit comparison of the two texts may be found in the introductions to the individual lessons in *Tommaso d'Aquino, Commento al "Libro delle cause,"* ed. Cristina D'Ancona Costa (Milan: Rusconi, 1986).

26. Compare Aristotle *Ph.* 195^{b}26–27.

27. Note that LC makes the first cause a real being. When Proclus (88) posits true Being prior to Eternity, he is thinking of the Being within Intellect, which is

divided into Being, Life/Eternity, and Intellect/the-participant-of-Eternity; for him, the first cause is above Being, in the sense of determinate being. LC 8 will clarify the sense in which LC's first cause may be called being. For detailed exegesis of LC 2, see D'Ancona Costa, *Recherches*, 53–72 (previously published in *Archives d'histoire doctrinale et littéraire du moyen âge* 59 [1992]: 41–62).

28. The one word *corpora* translates two Arabic words, *ǧirm* and *ǧism*, usually synonymous but sometimes reserved for heavenly bodies and for bodies here below, respectively.

29. "Causa prima creavit esse animae mediante intelligentia" (79.77). *De causis et proc. univ.* 2.1.13 and 16 (76.11–33 and 80.12–19) would seem to indicate that Albert's copy read "mediante intelligentia et alatyr." Bardenhewer (248–50) speculates that "et alachir" (as Jammy and Borgnet spelled it) was a corruption from "id est alachili" (*alachili* being Gerard's transliteration in LC 4 and 11 of *al-ʿaql*, the standard Arabic rendition for νοῦς); "intelligentia *et* alachir" suggested that *alachir* was something other than intelligence, whereupon Albert sought a second entity which might figure in the determination of noble soul, and hit upon the celestial circle which it is proportioned to move. Bardenhewer's theory is economical and attractive, even more so since Pattin recorded the variant "alachhir" from Selden sup. 24. Still, Albert's path may perhaps have been more complex. *Alatyr* appears in the critical edition of Albert's *De caelo et mundo* 2.3.15 (C5.1:178.59); and C. Vansteenkiste, in his review thereof ("Il nono volume del nuovo Alberto Magno," *Angelicum* 50 [1973]: 252), points to the Arabic root ʾṭr, whose basic meaning is enclosure; Albert, in *De fato* 2 (C17.1:70.23–24), attributes the notion to Māšāʾallāh. I have yet to find *alatyr* in the Latin Māšāʾallāh or in other astronomers Albert could have read, but the facts remain curious. Incidentally, Albert does not comment on *alachili* in his paraphrase of LC 4 and 11; his copy was probably among the many MSS which omitted it.

30. "Sicut stramentum" ("like bedding") and the Arabic *ka-bisāṭ* ("like a carpet") correspond to Proclus' ὑπεστρωμέναι (201), from ὑποστόρνυμι, "to spread out under," used especially of bedclothes. In East and West alike, the metaphor met with scribal incomprehension, and many Latin manuscripts read "sicut instrumentum." Albert knows both readings, and makes good sense of both in his various works.

31. The Arabic verb *dabbara*, meaning to organize, regulate or prepare (whence the Latin), translates Proclus' προνοοῦσι (201); it will reappear in LC 8, 19, and 22.

32. As Taylor points out in Thomas Aquinas, *Commentary* (28 n. 1), this is Plotinian; see *Enn.* 5.4.2 and 5.9.5–8, with the fuller description on p. 38 below. Proclus, too, identifies Being and Intellect, although he more often distinguishes them as members of his triadic analysis of νοῦς (compare, for instance, *Inst.* 129 and 138).

33. The word rendered "declines" or "declives" (*māʾila*) defies translation. Taylor, in his dissertation (370), suggests that forms are declining if they "have an inclination for eventual corruption." However, "declines" seems to be said of souls in general, not just of lesser souls, and LC 10 will explain that all intellects have lasting effects. Perhaps, then, another interpretation would be preferable, such as one contrasting soul's discursive thought with intellect's intuition. Compare the text in Franz Rosenthal, "Aš-Šayḫ al-Yūnānī and the Arabic Plotinus Source," *Orientalia*, n.s., 21 [1952]: 490, where the same word describes the slight "inclination" in soul's motion, a deviation from the perfection of intellect's motion, on account of which soul thinks. The word also occurs in the Plotinian *Theology of Aristotle* 2.29 (F. Dieterici, ed., *Die sogenannte Theologie des Aristoteles* [Leipzig, 1882; reprint, Amsterdam: Rodopi, 1965], 20; see Paul Henry and Hans-Rudolf Schwyzer, eds., *Plotini Opera* [Paris: Desclée de Brouwer, Brussels: L'Edition Universelle, and Leiden: E. J. Brill, 1951–73], 2:67 and 69 for an English translation), to describe the soul's "deviating motion," i.e., its looking to the things it wants to know and then returning to itself. For *māʾila* in other authors, see C. Vansteenkiste, "Intorno al testo latino del *Liber de causis*," 82. "Separabiles" (*mutazāyila*) perhaps refers to the descent of particular souls into bodies.

34. As Bardenhewer explains (196), "per modum qui est causa eius" (106.65) ought to have been "per modum secundum quem est," but, in Arabic, "its cause" and "according to it" differ only by diacritical marks. (The mistake recurs in LC 11 [124.79].) Fortunately, "scilicet per modum suae substantiae" (106.65–66) sets readers back on the right track.

35. "Yliathim" (*ḥilya*), a rare word which translates μορφή in the Plotinian material of Bodleian MS or. Marsh 539, al-Sijistānī, and al-Šahrastānī (see Rosenthal, 21 [1952]: 469–70 for a discussion, and 478–81, 486–87, and 22 [1953]: 390–93 for texts with translation), seems to have puzzled Gerard of Cremona, who simply transliterated it. Albert was hardly alone in guessing that it had something to do with ὕλη, "matter"—not a bad guess, since the Arabs did imitate ὕλη with their *hayūlā*; more recently, scholars following a "correction" in the Leiden MS thought the word was *kullīya*, although Gerard successfully rendered this "universitas" and "universalitas," without transliteration, in LC 27 and 29. In point of fact, the Istanbul and Ankara MSS confirm the first Leiden hand and the Latin, reading *ḥilya*. Josef van Ess announced the reading of the Ankara MS in "Jüngere orientalistische Literatur zur neuplatonischen Überlieferung im Bereich des Islam" (*Parusia*, 340). For some reason, Bardenhewer and Badawī both adopted *kullīya* without comment; Giuseppe Serra noted the original Leiden reading in "Alcune osservazioni sulle traduzioni dall'arabo in ebraico e in latino del *De generatione et corruptione* di Aristotele e dello pseudo-aristotelico *Liber de causis*," in *Scritti in onore de Carlo Diano* (Bologna: Pàtron, 1975), 423–27.

As Taylor ("Islamic Milieu," 39 and 45 n. 26; Thomas Aquinas, *Commentary*, 64 n. 1) points out, the whole chapter derives from Plotinian, not Procline, material. D'Ancona Costa, *Recherches*, 97–119 (which readers of Italian may find in *Documenti e studi sulla tradizione filosofica medievale* 1 [1990]: 327–51), develops this insight; indeed, throughout her book she notes passages in which LC sides with Plotinus against Proclus by modifying even what is Procline material.

36. This last idea parallels what Plotinus says of Intellect and the One (see 5.3.11 and 6.7.15, noting the reference to power and unity in lines 21–22 of the latter text; see also Rosenthal, 484). There seems to be no source for it in *Inst*.

37. In light of Taylor's edition (187), "intelligit rem per esse suum" (121.81–82) ought to have been "facit rem per esse suum"; the roots *fʿl* ("to do") and *ʿql* ("to know") are often confused in MSS. This error has not destroyed the argument, for, one need only supply some such premise as that Intellect's knowing is causative, thus: since Intellect is immobile and knows through its immobile being, its knowing is immobile, and since its immobile knowing is causative, its effects are sempiternal.

38. The Arabic and the Latin have "two beings," "two lives," and "two intellects" instead of Proclus' adverbs. It is just possible that the Arabic originally had adverbial accusatives, which would have sounded much like duals dictated quickly in pausal form. I am indebted to Prof. Joel Kraemer for this suggestion.

39. The Arabic passive participle has the same ambiguity as the Greek verbal adjective in -τός; thus, *maʿqūl* (νοητός), rendered "intellectum" by Gerard of Cremona, can mean either "intellected" or "intelligible."

40. The Arabic letters *ʿlm*, depending how they are vowelled, are either the noun "image" or the verb "to know." As is apparent from *Inst*. 195, Gerard's "quia scit eas" (134.78) was a mistake.

41. Bardenhewer (197) notes that *mutawassiṭa* ("intermediate") and *mabsūṭa* ("stretched," *expansa* [134.78]) are rather similar in Arabic script; Taylor, in choosing *mutawassiṭa*, follows Proclus' μέση and the Leiden MS against the Latin translation and the Istanbul and Ankara MSS. Either way, the sense is preserved; but students of Albert's psychology will note the interesting reflections occasioned by *expansa* (*De causis et proc. univ.* 2.2.38).

42. For "substantia eius est rediens ad essentiam ipsius" (138.71–72), Albert apparently reads "scientia eius est rediens ad essentiam ipsius," and for "reditionem substantiae ad essentiam suam" (138.72), he reads "reditionem scientiae ad essentiam suam" (see *De causis et proc. univ.* 2.2.45 [138.42, 46]; Pattin and Fauser do not note these variants, but Bardenhewer finds them in the *editio princeps* of LC). These readings make LC 14 seem more or less a repetition of LC 12.

43. The Arabic words are graphically similar. See the apparatus to Taylor's edition, where he suggests emendations based on *Inst*. 92.

Several errors make the Latin even more difficult. First, as Aquinas surmised by comparing *Inst.* 92, "non quia ipsae sunt acquisitae, fixae, stantes in rebus entibus, immo sunt virtus rebus entibus habentibus fixionem" (144.64) ought to have been "non quia ipsa est adquisita, fixa, stans in rebus entibus, immo est virtus rebus entibus, habentibus fixionem"; Gerard simply misjudged the referent of a pronoun. Second, at 144.70, where the Latin has "entia," the Arabic means "infinite" (Pattin and Fauser note some MSS with "entia infinita," which Albert reads). Third, in light of Taylor's edition (208–9), Gerard's "infinitum est a causa prima et causatum primum est causa omnis vitae et similiter reliquae bonitates descendentes a causa prima" (144.76–77) should have been "infinitas est quod est inter causam primam et causatum primum, et est causa omnis vitae et similiter reliquarum bonitatum descendentium a causa prima."

44. See n. 45 for a tentative suggestion how this bit of Proclus can be reconciled with LC 16 and with LC's monotheistic world, where nothing can come between the Creator and the first created thing.

45. Proclus uses the triad Being (determinate being), Life, and Intellect to analyze νοῦς, but LC makes the first cause Being (no longer determinate). As for the Life which causes life, the first motion from the One should be Intellect in its potential, as yet indeterminate, aspect (see Plotinus 2.4.5.29ff. and 5.2.1); still, LC 15 has just called the infinite the cause of life (see n. 43 above). Is LC 15's triadic group of the first cause, the infinite, and Intellect to be identified with LC 17's Being, Life, and Intellect? And, if so, is the infinite/Life the indeterminate aspect of Intellect (compare 144.71–72 with 147.73–74)? For, LC 4 placed created Being (Intellect as indeterminate) before Intellect and after the One, just as LC 15 locates the infinite between the first cause and Intellect. Compare n. 27 and LC 2, where another of Proclus' triadic analyses of νοῦς is applied to all three hypostases, the first cause, Intellect, and Soul; compare also LC 11, where Being, Life, and Intellect give way to the first cause, Intellect, Soul, and Sense. Cristina D'Ancona Costa offers another possible interpretation in her *Recherches*, 129–33.

46. In 155.64–66, *expositio* is a mistranslation of *šarḥ*, which usually does mean "commentary" but here has a rare, technical meaning, "order" or "series." See Bardenhewer, 94; Badawī, *Al-Aflāṭūniyya*, 20 n. 2; Gerhard Endress, *Proclus Arabus: Zwanzig Abschnitte aus der "Institutio theologica" in arabischer Übersetzung*, Beiruter Texte und Studien, 10 (Beirut: Imprimerie Catholique in Kommission bei Franz Steiner, Wiesbaden, 1973), 131–33; and Taylor's edition, 314 and 400–401. The Arabic sentence means, "And this is the case because neither the whole intellectual order nor the whole psychic order nor the whole bodily order depends on the cause above it, but only the perfect and complete of each order, for, that is what depends on the cause above it."

47. The awkward phrase "propter magnitudinem suae largitatis" (158.82–84) should have restated this point but fails to convey it. Grammatically, "suae" should refer to the "quaedam" which receive more than others; yet why would LC, which pertains to metaphysics and not to ethics, assert that recipients receive more because of their own generosity? Unless we assign "largitatis" some unusual meaning, we seem forced to disregard grammar and, with Albert, to understand the phrase of God's generosity rather than the recipients' (see below, p. 139 n. 2); Bardenhewer did likewise when attempting to reconstruct the Arabic phrase (missing in the Leiden MS) from the Latin, and paraphrased the result "hat dies seinen Grund in der grossen Fülle des Guten" (96). However, not only do inequalities caused by divine generosity run counter to the notion of a single outpouring, but the Arabic as edited by Taylor (225) is unambiguous: the attached pronoun -*hi* must refer to *baʿḍ*, that is, to "some" (recipients), and the phrase must be rendered "because of the greatness of their (the recipients') nobility." Oddly, Taylor's translation—"this is owing to the grandeur of His liberality" (316)—fits Bardenhewer's reconstruction better than his own text.

48. The Latin in 158.80–82 ("quia non . . . communi una") obscures the sense of the Arabic (ed. Taylor, 223–24), which says: "because it is good, in its existence and its being and its power, only because it is good, and the good and the being are one thing. So just as the first being is being and good in one way, it pours goodnesses forth on things by one, common outpouring, and it does not flow out on some things less and on others more."

49. "Continuator" and "continuatio" translate *wuṣla*, which appears where *Inst.* has σχέσις, "relation." *Iḍāfa* was the usual Arabic term for relation, whereas *wuṣla*, from the same root as *ittiṣāl* ("continuousness" or "contiguity"), meant the link or bond which ensured continuity. Here as elsewhere, LC seems to represent an early "translationese," not all of which was retained once philosophical Arabic became standardized; Gerard's "continuator" and "continuatio" reflect familiarity with the meanings of *ittiṣāl* and *wuṣla* in later authors.

50. "Quando agens et factum sunt per instrumentum et non facit per esse suum et sunt composita" (159.71–72) ought to have been "quando agens agit per instrumentum, non facit per esse suum, et esse suum est compositum."

51. This is missing from the Latin. Also, the Arabic is much clearer than the Latin that the first cause causes its effects by its being, not by any action which would link it to its effects. For, "factum" translates both *mafʿūl* ("thing done") and *fiʿl* ("act of doing" or "deed done"; this word appears at 159.73, 74, and 75).

52. "Rich" was indeed the original meaning of the word translated "dives," but it came to mean self-sufficiency. Since the Arabic elative is used for both comparative and superlative degrees of comparison, "et est diues maius" (Bardenhewer 182.16) should not have a "non" added to it, as in Pattin/Fauser (160.72); rather, Gerard ought to have used "divitissimum." (Gerard makes the opposite

mistake at 91.58, where "primam" should have been "priorem.") The positive degree at 160.74 is also elative in Arabic.

53. This last point has been lost in Latin: "res, quae recipiunt regimen intelligentiae" (164.82) should have been negative.

54. Here and in LC 25, "comparatio" and "relatio" suggest that Gerard's copy of the Arabic read *naẓīr*, which the Leiden MS too has for *naẓar*. At first glance, *naẓar* seems not to render anything in the corresponding Procline text, *Inst.* 45; as in LC 9, where second intellects look toward Forms in the first intellects, the inspiration seems Plotinian (see Rosenthal, 474–75 for a transcription and translation of Marsh 539, ff. 17b–18a, about the Being which, after its emanation, looked [*naẓara*] at its cause and became Intellect). On the other hand, in his dissertation (412–14), Taylor argues that, although *naẓar* means "contemplation" in later texts, Arabic philosophical vocabulary was still in flux while Proclus was being translated, so that *naẓar* may have been used to express "relation" here; Taylor reasons that the chapter's Procline source explains self-constitution in terms of conjunction with, not contemplation of, the cause. Perhaps this is the case; still, Taylor himself has shown how LC elsewhere incorporates Plotinian elements.

55. For the author of LC as for all Neoplatonists, the self-constituted do have a cause. Various representatives of the tradition explain this variously; for LC, to deny that the self-constituted are generated from anything is not to deny their creation from nothing (LC 28 [181.80]). Throughout, the author chooses his words carefully: the second form of *kāna* is used for generation, as in Arabic versions of Aristotle's works, while Arab philosophers used *abda'a* for creation *ex nihilo*. See Isaac Israeli, *Liber de definitionibus* §42, with the commentary of A. Altmann and S. M. Stern, *Isaac Israeli, a Neoplatonic Philosopher of the Early Tenth Century*, Scripta Judaica, 1 (Oxford: Oxford University, 1958; reprint, Westport, Conn.: Greenwood, 1979), 68–74.

It is just possible that "relationem suam ad causam suam semper" (172.79) refers to the same cause as "causa formationis suae" (172.78 and 78–79), i.e., that the gazing is self-reversion. Still, the rest of LC makes it abundantly clear that intellect and soul do have a cause besides themselves, and self-reversion does not preclude reversion upon the higher (see S. Gersh, Κίνησις ἀκίνητος: *A Study of Spiritual Motion in the Philosophy of Proclus*, Philosophia Antiqua, 26 [Leiden: E. J. Brill, 1973], app. 2). At any rate, one suspects that, had this complex doctrine been intended, the vocabulary of LC 14 would have been employed here too.

56. "Possibile est ut essentia (*qiyām*) partis eius sit per essentiam eius (*bi-ḏātihi*) iterum sicut essentia (*qiyām*) totius" (180.68–69). Gerard renders *qiyām* (subsistence) *essentia*, although it is from the same root as *qāʾim* (subsistent, stans), and *bi-ḏātihi* sometimes *per se* (180.68) and sometimes *per essentiam eius* (180.69).

57. The argument in LC diverges from its source, *Inst.* 47, and thereby obscures the difficulty: that a self-constituted *whole* must proceed from itself as a whole, and revert upon itself as a whole. For if a whole proceeds from its parts, it is constituted by them, not by itself, even if they constitute themselves. Compare the argumentation in *Inst.* 15 and 17.

58. *Ġayr mustafīd* ("not acquiring") appears where Proclus has ἀμέθεκτον ("unparticipated"). Throughout, LC replaces Proclus' threefold division of τὸ ἀμέθεκτον, τὸ μετεχόμενον ("the thing participated in"), and τὸ μετέχον ("the participant") with a twofold division between what is acquired from another and what is unacquired. (Similarly, LC 11 replaces the threefold division of κατ᾽ αἰτίαν, καθ᾽ ὕπαρξιν, and κατὰ μέθεξιν with the twofold division between *per modum causae* and *per modum causati*.) Perhaps τὸ μετεχόμενον was too tied up with the polytheistic doctrine of henads (see *Inst.* 116). Here LC comes closer to Plotinus than to Proclus, but Albert, through Dionysius, will turn it back in a Procline direction (see chap. 4 below).

59. For other instances of using self-constitution to explain the origin of otherness, see Gersh, *From Iamblichus*, 48–55, especially the discussion of Damascius on p. 53. So far, LC seems to have more or less the view Gerson attributes to Plotinus (p. 2 above).

60. John of Dacia links the two texts most explicitly: "Oppositum arguitur, quia ab vno non procedit nisi vnum, vt habetur in secundo de generatione et libro de causis" (*Summa grammatica*, in *Opera*, vol. 1, part 2, p. 289, lines 10–11).

61. See Bardenhewer, 238 for texts from Bonaventure, and 260–61 for Thomas Aquinas (who, when he came to write his commentary on LC, recognized this as a misreading).

62. "Die Lehre des Heiligen Albertus Magnus vom Grunde der Vielheit der Dinge und der Lateinische Averroismus," *Divus Thomas* (Freiburg) 10 (1932): 203–230; reprinted as a chap. in *Mittelalterliches Geistesleben: Abhandlung zur Geschichte der Scholastik und Mystik* (Munich: Max Hueber, 1936), 2:287–312.

63. *Le système du monde: Histoire de doctrines cosmologiques de Platon à Copernic* (Paris: Hermann, 1913–54), 5:428–40.

64. Ibid., 440.

2. Emanation and Causation

1. Despite the great success emanation terminology enjoyed among medieval writers, Albert's analysis is unusual. To be sure, one finds elaborate emanationist theories in such thinkers as Dionysius and Ibn Sīnā, from both of whom Albert borrows terms and premises; yet their attention is not drawn to the

image itself, unless in passing, and they leave one to guess whether "emanation" merely adds a poetic touch or, in their view, says something which "causation" does not. Roger Bacon and Ps.-Henry of Ghent, in their questions on LC, ask what sorts of causes flow, but not what flowing is. The closest parallels to Albert's focus on the image come from Maimonides and Ibn Gabirol. Maimonides, having mentioned emanation several times, announces a chapter (2.12) explaining the notion. However, his explanation has none of the complexity of Albert's: it is simply that, whereas a body acts only through mediate or immediate contact with its patient, incorporeal causes are not thus localized; our imaginations, boggled by incorporeal action as by incorporeal existence, and unable to find a name adequate to the reality, fasten upon the metaphor (*tašbīh*) "overflow" to express it, the likeness being that springs draw from no particular direction and water all directions, whether near or far. As for Ibn Gabirol, although his remarks about the notion are brief, scattered, and incidental to other discussions, they seem to have been a principal source for Albert's extended analysis; that he refutes aspects of Ibn Gabirol's emanation scheme four times in the present tractate (see chaps. 5 and 6 below) confirms that he had *Fons vitae* on his mind.

William of Auvergne, who considers Ibn Gabirol the noblest philosopher (*De trinitate*, ed. Bruno Switalski, Studies and Texts, 34 [Toronto: Pontifical Institute of Mediaeval Studies, 1976], 12 [77.84–78.85]), shares some of his and Albert's interest in emanation imagery; however, William's understanding of the reality behind it differs vastly from Albert's. (For a sampling of the differences, see nn. 16–17, chap. 3 n. 34, chap. 4 n. 10, chap. 5 n. 8, and chap. 6 n. 15.)

Albert's fondness for this terminology is obvious from the care with which he examines it, from its lavish use throughout his psychological writings, from his paraphrases of LC (e.g., it appears only three times in LC 1, but twelve times in the corresponding *De causis et proc. univ.* 2.1.6 [67.28–68.45]), and from his large emanation vocabulary (including, besides LC's *influxio* and *influere*, such words as *influenter, fluxus, effluxus, fluere, superfluere, fundere, diffusivum, manare, emanare, scaturigo, ebullitio,* and *redundantia*).

2. Albert explains this division at *Metaph.* 5.1.3 (C16.1:214.57–64): "Cum autem causae efficientes duplicis sint effectus, scilicet univoci et aequivoci: univoci, quando in specie una vel genere uno vel secundum proportionem communicant effectus, in eo quod effectus est, et causa, secundum quod causa est, sicut ignis calidus calefacit et ignit; aequivoci autem, quando non communicant dicto modo, sicut motus calefacit et ignit et rarefacit et dissolvit. . . ."

3. "Non enim fluit nisi id quod unius formae est in fluente et in eo a quo fit fluxus. Sicut rivus eiusdem formae est cum fonte, a quo fluit, et aqua in utroque eiusdem est speciei et formae" (*De causis et proc. univ.* 1.4.1 [42.38–41]). Compare Ibn Gabirol, *Avencebrolis (ibn Gebirol) "Fons vitae" ex Arabico in Latinum translatus ab Iohanne Hispano et Dominico Gundissalino*, ed. C. Baeumker,

Beiträge zur Geschichte der Philosophie des Mittelalters, 1.2–4 (Münster: Aschendorff, 1892–94), 3.24 (136.4–5): "quicquid est defluxum ab aliquo, exemplum est eius a quo effluit"; 3.24 (137.23–24): "omne quod fluit ab aliquo, essentia illius et eius a quo fluit una est"; 3.53 (197.17–19): "per se notum est quod quicquid fluit ab aliquo, eiusdem generis est cum eo a quo fluit, quamuis sint diuersa in dispositione"; 3.53 (198.19–20): "omne defluxum simile est ei a quo fluit, et . . . nihil fluit ab aliquo nisi sibi simile."

4. "Similiter non idem est fluere quod univoce causare" (*De causis et proc. univ.* 1.4.1 [42.43–44]), not, as Borgnet had it (B10:410b), "similiter enim idem est fluere quod univoce causare." To the unanimous testimony of the MSS I have consulted and those Fauser has collated, one may add the following considerations. First, after a denial (that flowing is equivocal causing), one would hardly choose *similiter* to introduce an affirmation. Further, Borgnet's reading yields, not an analysis of usage, but a flat contradiction thereof: no one speaks about cats emanating into kittens. Most importantly, the tenor of Albert's argument requires the negative. Finally, his disciple Ulrich of Strasbourg, in a chapter heavily dependent upon this tractate, distinguished flowing from both equivocal and univocal causation (*De summo bono*, Corpus Philosophorum Teutonicorum Medii Aevi [Hamburg: Felix Meiner, 1987–], 4.1.5, lines 17–27), as did the Albertist Jean de Maisonneuve later (*De esse et essentia*, ed. G. Meersseman in his *Geschichte des Albertismus*, Heft 1, *Die Pariser Anfänge des Kölner Albertismus*, Institutum Historicum F.F. Praedicatorum Romae ad S. Sabinae: Dissertationes Historicae, 3 [Paris: R. Haloua, 1933], p. 142, lines 9–12). Unfortunately, some interpreters (e.g., Alain de Libera, *Albert le Grand et la philosophie*, A la recherche de la vérité [Paris: J. Vrin, 1990], 118–19) have accepted Borgnet's reading without question.

5. *De causis et proc. univ.* 1.4.1 (42.44–48). Of course, water is a composite, not a simple form, and it does alter the bed somewhat; as Maimonides says (2.12), one cannot find a perfect image for the reality of emanation. But this image does suggest the bestowal of simple form, because the form and matter come forth as one thing, already composed into the simple element which fills the recipient bed without transmuting it.

6. *De causis et proc. univ.* 1.4.1 (42.48–59); see also 2.2.20 (113.50–62). Albert claims to take his example, which recurs some eighteen times in *De causis et proc. univ.* to illustrate this and related points, from al-Fārābī (2.1.1 [60.39–45]).

7. Ibid., 1.4.1 (42.59–63, 43.8–14); see also 2.5.15 (181.16–21). Albert is thinking of *Metaph.* 1032^{b}11–14, where Aristotle explains how the form with matter comes from art, the form without matter; they are *eiusdem speciei et formae*, and "sic servatur ratio transumptionis huius nominis [fluxus]" (Ulrich 4.1.5, l. 8).

8. See also *Super Ethica* 6.8.522 (C14.2:488.6–20), where Albert indicates that philosophers examining the proximate principles of generation speak of

eduction from matter, whereas metaphysicians bringing things back to first principles speak of emanation.

It is unclear why Alain de Libera (*Albert*, 120) takes Albert to mean that emanation is incompatible with eduction. Of course, emanation and eduction are not always together: Albert considers creation an emanation, and, by definition, creation is not an eduction from matter; neither is the soul's emanation into its faculties.

9. *De causis et proc. univ.* 1.4.1 (43.14–16); see also *Metaph.* 5.3.2 (C16.1:260.66–67). Which of the first Peripatetics does Albert have in mind? Later he speaks of "the Greek philosophers": "'Processum' autem et 'influxum' idem dicimus, quia id quod Arabes 'influentiam' vocant, Graeci philosophi vocant 'processionem'" (*De causis et proc. univ.* 2.1.14 [78.52–55]). Perhaps he takes Pseudo-Dionysius for a Peripatetic, as did the young Thomas, his student (*Sent.* 2.14.1.2 corpus); Ulrich (4.1.5, lines 79–81) attributes the terminology to Dionysius and the first Peripatetics, and explains that the step-by-step descent according to the order of beings resembles processive motion. See further chap. 4 below. Incidentally, *procedere* and *processus* appear with some frequency in the Latin Ibn Gabirol (see especially *Fons vitae* 3.9.51); however, Ibn Gabirol was neither ancient nor Greek, and Albert doubts his Peripatetic credentials (see *De XV probl.* 1 [C17.1:34.20–22]: "Quamvis enim Peripateticum se profiteretur [?], tamen Stoicorum et praecipue Platonis dogma secutus est").

10. *De causis et proc. univ.* 1.4.1 (43.38–43); see also 1.2.2, 2.2.14, and 2.3.10 (27.49–58, 107.66–86, and 147.71–148.29). As Albert notes, that flowing always goes on does not mean that recipients, too, must be always *in fieri*: in the case of some recipients, reception of the continuous flux may well be always complete (*in factum*). The point, of course, is that certain things depend on their causes timelessly. Ulrich gives Albert's brief remarks elaborate development (4.1.5, lines 43–63).

11. "Principium enim primum rei est" (*De causis et proc. univ.* 1.4.1 [42.67]; see also 1.1.11 [24.20–30]).

12. "Influere autem est fluxum talem alicui receptibili immittere. . . . Si quaeritur vero, cum dicitur 'influere,' in quo sit continentia importata per praepositionem, dicendum, quod in possibilitate rei, cui fit influxus. Quae possibilitas rei est ex seipsa" (ibid., 1.4.2 [44.5–40]).

Meister Eckhart, defending his own work, cites Albert for this doctrine: "Ad undecimum, cum dicitur: in omni creato aliud est esse ab alio, aliud essentia, et non ab alio, dicendum quod hoc verum est; et est verbum Avicenne et Alberti in De causis" (G. Théry, "Edition critique des pièces relatives au procès d'Eckhart contenues dans le manuscrit 33 b de la bibliothèque de Soest," *Archives d'histoire doctrinale et littéraire du moyen âge* 1 [1926–27]: 195).

13. Ibn Sīnā *Liber de philosophia prima* 4.1 (ed. S. Van Riet, Avicenna Latinus [Louvain: E. Peeters, and Leiden: E. J. Brill, 1977–83], 3:186.49–50), 5.1

(especially 4:233.37–39), 8.3 (4:397.49), and 9.4 (4:481.53–482.61); al-Ġazālī *Metaphysics* 1.5 (120.14–26). John F. Wippel, "The Latin Avicenna as a Source for Thomas Aquinas's Metaphysics," *Freiburger Zeitschrift für Philosophie und Theologie* 37 (1990): 66 with n. 32, provides guidance where to begin working through the abundant secondary literature on essence and existence in Ibn Sīnā.

14. "Licet enim forma secundum 'id quod est' causam non habeat, tamen secundum esse in effectu causam habet efficientem, et secundum quod fundatur in esse, causam habet materiam" (*De causis et proc. univ.* 1.1.11 [24.38–42]; see also 2.1.24 [89.60–61]).

Siger of Brabant appears to have completely missed or misunderstood this caveat, since he rejects the "opinio Alberti Commentatoris" and "ratio sua ... *Libro de causis*" on the grounds that "quidquid est universaliter in re est effectus Primi Principii ... ; ergo haec distinctio nulla est, scilicet inter essentiam rei et esse per hoc quod unum sit effectus Primi Principii et aliud non" (*Quaestiones in Metaphysicam*, introductio, quaestio 7 [Clm 9559, ed. William Dunphy, Philosophes Médiévaux, 24 (Louvain: Institut Supérieur de Philosophie, 1981), 43.81–44.6; see also Peterhouse 152, ed. Armand Maurer, Philosophes Médiévaux, 25 (1983), 32.67–86]).

15. "Omne id quod de nihilo est, nihil est ex seipso et ex seipso non habet nisi ad esse possibilitatem. Quae possibilitas, cum impletur ab eo quod est causa esse ipsius, continet esse defluxum in ipsam" (*De causis et proc. univ.* 1.4.2 [44.41–45]).

16. Contrast William of Auvergne, who argues against Ibn Sīnā's system on the grounds that the possibility of x's existence is nothing in x if x does not yet exist (*De universo* 2.1.28). Accordingly, William downplays the recipient's role in emanation, with notable consequences for his theology (see chap. 3 n. 34 below).

17. *De causis et proc. univ.* 1.4.4 (46.86–93, 47.27–30 and 36–37): "Terminus est differentia coarctans et terminans, ultra quam fluere non potest. Fluere tamen potest intra ipsam, sicut fluit alveus intra ripas. Ex quo patet, quod si terminos suae diffinitionis non habeat, quod omnibus supereffluit; et in quantum latiores habet terminos, latius fluit; et si strictiores habeat, fluxus eius stringitur et coarctatur.... Termini enim illi colligunt fluxum, usquequo redundat intra ipsos. Et tunc fluit in tertium et sic deinceps, donec in tantum deficit, quod ultra terminos redundare non potest.... Nec redundaret et exuberaret, nisi coarctatum esset." See also 1.4.3 (46.48–60) for light and art used to illustrate the same points. The implication seems to be that secondary causality and its multitude of effects result from the impossibility of one effect having all that the first cause can give; see chap. 6 below.

Again, contrast William of Auvergne, who felt free to speak of God putting a stop to the flow and withholding it as he pleases (*De trinitate* 11 and 12 [77.61–62 and 78.12–13]).

18. Ibid., 1.4.2 (44.58–60). Since the first is incorporeal, this "distance" must not have to do with place; rather, it results from privation of likeness (2.1.14 [77.64–65]). See Augustine *De civitate Dei* 9.17 (CSEL 40.1:434.23–25): "Si ergo deo quanto similior, tanto fit quisque propinquior, nulla est ab illo alia longinquitas quam eius dissimilitudo." Boethius agrees in *De Trinitate* 5 (*The Theological Tractates; The Consolation of Philosophy*, trans. H. F. Stewart, E. K. Rand, and S. J. Tester, Loeb Classical Library, 74 [Cambridge: Harvard University Press, and London: William Heinemann, 1973], 28.40–42): "Omnino enim magna regulae est veritas in rebus incorporalibus distantias effici differentiis non locis." At *De intell. et int.* 1.1.5 (B9:484b), Albert reveals his debt to Augustine by borrowing the expression "regio dissimilitudinis" from *Confessions* 7.10, where it was already a borrowing from Plotinus (1.8.13.16–17; see Augustine, *Confessions*, ed. James J. O'Donnell [Oxford: Clarendon, 1992], 2:443–44), not "théologique et chrétienne" as distinct from "philosophique" (pace Alain de Libera, *Albert*, 218). Dionysius gives a corresponding definition of proximity in *Epist.* 8.2 (PG3:1092B). For more on distance and related themes, see Edward P. Mahoney, "Metaphysical Foundations of the Hierarchy of Being According to Some Late-Medieval and Renaissance Philosophers," in *Philosophies of Existence, Ancient and Medieval*, ed. Parviz Morewedge (New York: Fordham University Press, 1982), 165–257.

Possibly, Albert's desire to use the notion of distance accounts in part for his not repeating Maimonides' explanation of emanation, with its emphasis on non-spatiality.

19. The case may appear otherwise with physical waters (a spring may look quite insignificant compared to the river arising from it) because a river's source is not really one, as Aristotle argues in *Meteorology* 349^{b}3–350^{a}15.

With this step-by-step lessening of the amplitude of fluxion, compare Ibn Gabirol, 3.24 (136.6–137.4): "Quicquid emanat ab aliqua origine, circa originem colligitur, sed procul ab origine dispergitur. . . ."; 3.55 (201.10–13): "Omnis uirtus quae fluit ab aliquo circa illud fortior est. ergo debet ut uirtus quae fluit a factore primo et sancto sit fortior apud eum, quo magis est circa eum, quam est non penes eum et longius ab eo."

20. In Albert's preferred usage, God is *intellectus*; *intelligentia* signifies a sort of creature. (Of course, *intellectus* may refer to a creature too, as when Albert speaks of the possible intellect.) In calling God an intellect, Albert follows Aristotle and his school, not LC, which never terms God an intellect. True, LC 8 (112.73) mentions divine knowledge, but that is naming God through his first effect (LC 5), since intelligence is the first knower (LC 17 [151.73–74]); for the author of LC as for Proclus, God is beyond intellection (LC 8 [112.71–72]).

(In chap. 1 above, I translated LC's *intelligentia* by "intellect" rather than "intelligence" because the corresponding Arabic renders νοῦς, which usually becomes "intellect" when Platonism passes into English; however, now that LC's connection with earlier Platonic texts is plain, I will adopt Albert's distinction between intellect and intelligence.)

21. "Secundo autem modo contingit hoc [sc., fluxum immitti receptibili] secundum umbram luminis fluentis, ex hoc scilicet quod distat a limpiditate primi fontis. Sicut fluit ad animae constitutionem, quae propter dependentiam ad corpus necesse est, quod primae limpiditatis et sinceritatis patiatur adumbrationem" (*De causis et proc. univ.* 1.4.2 [44.14–19]). With this gradual obscuring of light, compare Ibn Gabirol on the clarity and turbidity of water (2.21 [63.10–12]): "aqua decurrens et praeceps, alia superueniens alii, quae, in principio tenuis et limpida, paulatim densatur in stagnum et fit tenebrosa."

The shadow motif comes from Arabic Plotinus material (see F. W. Zimmermann, "The Origins of the So-Called *Theology of Aristotle*," in *Pseudo-Aristotle in the Middle Ages*, 129 and 190–96) by way of Isaac Israeli's *Liber de definitionibus*. As Albert explains, "shadow" is one more way to speak of a thing's possibility or essence limiting flux: "Umbram autem vocamus differentiam, per quam coarctatur et obumbratur amplitudo luminis a priori procedentis" (*De causis et proc. univ.* 1.4.5 [48.42–44]); "umbram vocans [Isaac] diminutionem potestatis" (2.2.35 [128.53–54]; see also *De intell. et int.* 1.1.5 [B9:485a]). The first thing Albert said about flowing was that a flux is of one form with its font, but his remarks about possibilities and shadows have since made plain that emanation always implies a certain degradation. In other words, emanation describes a series of essentially subordinated causes, not the accidental subordination found among purely univocal causes. See chap. 3 below for how Albert saves the unity of font and flux.

22. "Fluit ergo ut distans, ut cadens, ut occumbens et ut oppressum tenebris" (*De causis et proc. univ.* 1.4.2 [44.30–31]). Since distance was mentioned with the second mode, and *casus* with the third, one might suspect that the name for the first mode has dropped out of the list, and that *cadens* and *occumbens* were meant synonymously. However, Ulrich (4.1.5, lines 101–14) connects these four participles with the four modes of influx. Nor does it much matter. For, all procession, even the first, implies distance and, therefore, shading (*De causis et proc. univ.* 2.3.3 and 10 [142.29–33 and 147.61–65]). Consequently, any inferior, however noble, is a shading and setting of its superior (1.4.5 and 8 [48.39–81 and 55.70–72]). Further, one and the same level of being may be variously described in its various activities: according as an intelligence contemplates its essence rather than its origin, "occumbit in ea lumen intellectus primi" (1.4.8 [56.4–5]; see also 2.5.17 [182.47–55]). Thus, while these words may be attached to four grades of being, they may also be detached from them to describe different aspects of a single emanative phase.

23. *De causis et proc. univ.* 1.4.4 (46.70–86): "Ex quo enim fluens non alio movente fluit, sed propria communicabilitate, constat, quod nihil fluit quod est

susceptibile actionis vel passionis. Et sic id quod materiale est, proprie loquendo fluere non habet. Hoc enim quodam agente in materiam et dissolvente eam fluere incipit. Et hoc ex propria virtute fluere non habet, sed per accidens. Fluit ergo, quod secundum seipsum se extendit in sui multiplicationem, quemadmodum Plato dixit de formis per se existentibus. Hoc autem non est nisi primum quidem lumen intellectuale intellectus agentis et secundum lumen corporale, quod luminis intellectualis in corporibus est exemplum. Sicut enim id quod fluidum est, ad sui fluxum non exigit nisi declivitatem, ita quod spiritualiter fluidum est. Adhuc, quod fluat, non exigit nisi non impeditam communicabilitatem nec impediri potest nisi per alieni termini circumpositionem." Corporeal light is the instrument of the stars, and stars in turn are instruments of the celestial intelligences for informing matter with the forms precontained in their intellectual light (*Metaph.* 11.2.26 [C16.2:516.75–78]).

Here Albert speaks of "id quod materiale est"; for prime matter itself, see *De causis et proc. univ.* 2.1.3 (63.50–76), where he denies it a place among the primary causes, because it emanates only in a weakened sense, by providing for the individuation of form through its own division. This is not properly flowing, Albert insists, since flowing is acting and extending oneself as a whole, whereas prime matter, far from acting to extend itself as a whole, is acted upon and extended by its division.

24. See Aristotle *An. Post.* 97^{b}37 and *Topics* 139^{b}34. Albert characterizes metaphor and its scientific inadequacy as follows: "Translatio autem adductio est nominis ad accidentalem similitudinem: et sic translatio aufert genus, sicut similitudo essentialis repugnat accidentali similitudini" (*Top.* 4.1.5 [B2:367b], paraphrasing Aristotle *Top.* 123^{a}33–37). While recognizing a need for metaphor in theology, he faults philosophers who use metaphor rather than syllogistic (*De anima* 1.2.7 [C7.1:36.82–86], *Metaph.* 3.2.10 [C16.1:126.39–49, 70–127.5], *Super Dion. Epist.* 9 [C37.2:529.15–23, 65–70]).

Old catalogs credit Albert with commentaries on Aristotle's *Poetics* and *Rhetoric*; Albert himself refers to what "in poeticis a nobis dictum est" (*Metaph.* 5.5.5 [280.52]), and to his future composition of a *Rhetoric* (*Ethica* 2.2.7.24 [B7:187a]). Unfortunately for those wishing to understand his compositional practice and its rich imagery, these commentaries are unknown today.

25. See *Super Dion. de myst. theol.* 3 (C37.2:468.46–55) and n. 28 below.

26. Augustine writes: "Nec quisquam arbitretur, illud quod dixi de luce spirituali . . . non jam proprie, sed quasi figurate atque allegorice convenire ad intelligendum diem et vesperam et mane: sed aliter quidem quam in hac consuetudine quotidianae lucis hujus et corporalis; non tamen tanquam hic proprie, ibi figurate. Ubi enim melior et certior lux, ibi verior etiam dies: cur ergo non et verior vespera et verius mane? . . . Neque enim et Christus sic dicitur lux, quomodo dicitur lapis: sed illud proprie, hoc utique figurate" (*De Genesi ad litteram* 4.28

[PL34:314–15]). But, for Albert, "per metonymiam in creatione coeli intelligitur creatio Angelorum" (*Summa* 2.11.43 solutio [B32:508b]; see also *De IV coaequ.* 4.72.1 ad sed contra 5 [B34:736a], "allegorice"), and Augustine, in explaining light, morning, evening, day, and night, speaks "metaphorice" (*De IV coaequ.* 4.72.2.2 [B34:744b]). While Augustine insists that his spiritual reading is *ad litteram*, Albert counsels any who "ad litteram magis vellet intelligere" to understand day as the act of illumination proceeding from the first created light, which was naturally borne in a circle (ibid., 4.72.2.1 solutio [742b]). As for light, "cum dicitur in Genesi: *Fiat lux*, intelligitur de luce quae est habitus corporum luminosorum" (ibid., 4.73.2 solutio [749a]). Augustine spoke as he did "quia lumen inter omnes formas corporales magis convenit cum substantia spirituali et intellectuali" (*Summa* 2.11.43 solutio [B32:508b]) or "eo quod lux corporalis a luce spirituali procedit ut causatum a causa" (ibid., 2.11.49 solutio [532a]).

27. *De IV coaequ.* 4.73.2 ad 1 (B34:749a); Borgnet's reading is confirmed by the Lilienfeld MS.

28. "Non cognoscimus deum nisi symbolico vel mystico modo. Symbolico cognoscimus proprietatem dei proportione proprietatis corporeae.... Mystica enim sunt, quae per se et primo deo conveniunt, per aliud autem et secundario creaturis, ut essentia, vita et intellectus, quae nobis non innotescunt, nisi secundum quod sunt in creatis genere vel specie vel numero, et secundum hoc esse non conveniunt deo, sed eminenter" (*Summa* 1.3.13.1 [C34.1:40.56–67]). "Duo sunt attendenda in significationem nominis, scilicet significatum, et modus significandi. Et quantum ad significatum, in mysticis nominibus nomen magis proprie dicitur de Deo quam de creaturis: magis enim proprium est, quod Deus est sapiens, quam quod homo est sapiens: quia magis proprie dicta sapientia sapiens est Deus, quam homo.... Si autem attendatur modus significandi, ... sic nomen translatum in divinam praedicationem, proprietatem suam retinere non potest: sed cum significet substantiam cum qualitate [Priscian *Institutiones grammaticae* 2.4.18], ... negatur haec forma ab ipso, et ponitur supereminentia illius in infinitum" (*Summa* 1.14.58.1.1 ad 1 [B31:583]). See also *Sent.* 1.2.17 solutio (B25:73); *Super Dion. de myst. theol.* 3 and 5 (C37.2:468.46–55 and 473.49–474.6).

29. See chap. 3 below for analogy and what Albert calls "the analogy of imitation." In the case of flowing, his "quamvis materia non proprie fluere habeat, tamen quantum potest, hunc ordinem fluxus imitatur" (*De causis et proc. univ.* 1.4.4 [47.14–15]) suggests the analogy of imitation, with God as prime analogate.

30. For the authenticity of the *Summa*, see the prolegomena to the critical edition and also Robert Wielockx, "Gottfried von Fontaines als Zeuge der Echtheit der Theologischen Summe des Albertus Magnus," in *Studien zur mittelalterlichen Geistesgeschichte und ihrer Quellen*, ed. Albert Zimmermann, Miscellanea Mediaevalia, 15 (Berlin: Walter de Gruyter, 1982), 209–25, and

idem, "Zur *Summa Theologiae* des Albertus Magnus," *Ephemerides Theologicae Lovanienses* 66 (1990): 78–110.

31. For more on the distinction between *actio in genere* and *actio ultra genus*, see the texts reproduced by Barbara Faes de Mottoni in "La distinzione tra causa agente e causa motrice nella *Summa de Summo Bono* di Ulrico di Strasburgo," *Studi Medievali*, 3d ser., 20 (1979): n. 19, pp. 340–41, and n. 74.

32. *Summa* 1.14.56 solutio, ad 1, and ad quaest. 2 (B31:575a, 575b, and 577b); the text at 575b cites Gilbert of Poitiers's *Liber de sex principiis* (PL188:1260D). See also *Super Dion. De div. nom.* 9.19 (C37.1:389.40–59; 390.4–9), where, commenting on the mystical name "motion," which Dionysius takes from the "greatest kinds" of Plato's *Sophist*, Albert states that the motion of a cause to its effects is said properly, not metaphorically, of God. He must maintain that "motion" is mystical and therefore proper because, were it symbolic, Dionysius would have put it in his *Symbolic Theology*, not in *The Divine Names*.

33. His opinion remains far from clear. Contrast Maimonides' unambiguous declaration that emanation is mere metaphor (see n. 1 above); of course, he was generally less sanguine than Albert about the possibilities of theological language (1.58). Perhaps Albert's ambivalence stems from his Platonic tendencies, tendencies which were stronger and more consistent in Augustine and Dionysius. That is, Albert's Aristotelianism should lead him to hold, with Aristotle, that we name things as we know them, and to find the natural order in human learning mirrored in the histories of words; however, his is a Platonizing Aristotelianism and, to the extent that one adopts a Platonic ontology and epistemology, which of a word's meanings comes first becomes more a question. Unfortunately, studies on Albert's theory of language have overlooked these problematic texts and, generally, assimilated his position to that of Aquinas.

34. "Omnis rei lumen forma sit, qua intelligitur" (*De causis et proc. univ.* 2.1.1 [61.25]); "dicit enim Plato, quod forma . . . lumen est rationem et intelligibilitatem praestans ei cuius forma est" (2.1.3 [63.81–83]). See also 1.2.1 (26.17–28) and 2.1.20 (85.33–36). Albert's characteristic concern with the inherent intelligibility of things may be seen in the prominence he gives this imagery.

3. God's Incommunicability to Creatures

1. For a discussion of where in the Dionysian corpus Albert and his contemporaries found this, see Julien Peghaire, "L'axiome 'Bonum est diffusivum sui' dans le néo-platonisme et le thomisme," *Revue de l'Université d'Ottawa* 1 (1932): 6*-8*.

2. For Albert's relation to Hermes, see Loris Sturlese, "Saints et magiciens: Albert le Grand en face d'Hermès Trismégiste," *Archives de Philosophie: Recherches et Documentation* 43 (1980): 615–34. Albert's classing of individuals varies somewhat: at *Summa* 2.9.33.2 (B32:367a), Hermes is a Stoic, not a Peripatetic as here. But, given Albert's view of the history of philosophy, the Peripatetic label could certainly be made to fit Hermes. Albert divides philosophers into Stoics, Epicureans, and Peripatetics. "Omnes Stoici convenerunt in hoc quod principia physicorum ponebant esse non-physica, sicut Epicurei in hoc convenerunt, quod principia physicorum physica corpora esse perhibuerunt" (*Metaph.* 1.4.1 [C16.1:47.8–11]); Peripatetics, hitting the mean between these extremes, recognize both physical and non-physical causes. Albert numbers such pre-Socratics as Thales among the Epicureans (see *De causis et proc. univ.* 1.1.2 [7.20–8.3], where he offers two etymologies of "Epicurean"), while Pythagoras, Socrates, and Plato were the chief Stoics (see *Metaph.* 1.4.1 [48.49–50] and *De causis et proc. univ.* 1.1.3 [8.9–16 and 9.83–10.6], where Albert proposes two etymologies of "Stoic"); Peripatetics may boast of Porphyry, Themistius, Ibn Sīnā, al-Ġazālī, and al-Fārābī (*De causis et proc. univ.* 1.2.7 [32.54–56]). This threefold division recalls Aristotle's remark that most early philosophers looked only for material principles (*Metaph.* 983^{b}6) and his insistence that Ideas explain nothing about the being or becoming of sensible things. As for calling the Platonists Stoics, B. Hauréau (*Histoire de la philosophie scolastique* [Paris: G. Pedone-Lauriel, 1880], 2.1:282 n. 1) suggests that Albert confused Zeno of Elea (mentioned by Aristotle) with Zeno of Citium (mentioned by Seneca and Cicero); see, however, Alain de Libera, "Albert le Grand ou l'antiplatonisme sans Platon," in *Contre Platon*, vol. 1, *Le platonisme dévoilé*, ed. Monique Dixsaut (Paris: J. Vrin, 1993), 247–71, for antecedents to Albert's division.

3. "Modus autem istius fluxus et influxus ab antiquis Peripateticis valde diversus assignatur. Antiquissimi enim, a quibus primo incepit philosophia, sicut Trismegistus et Apollo et Hermes Aegyptius et Asclepius, Trismegisti discipulus, modum hunc fluxus ponebant in hoc quod primum principium penetrat omnia et est omne quod est de esse omnium ita quod quidquid est in universis praeter ipsum, vel est materia vel accidens [*Asclepius* 19c, 40c]. Nec diversificatur in essentia, secundum quod est in omnibus, sed in esse, secundum quod plus et minus occumbit obumbratione materiae in hoc vel in illo. Per hoc enim incipit distare a prima sinceritate et lumine ipsius. Et ideo dicit haec verba Hermes Trismegistus, quod 'deus est omne quod est [*Asclep.* 1a, 2a, 9, 20a, 34c]. . . .' Posteriores autem philosophi Peripatetici fluxum hunc non ponebant nisi in communicabilitate primi et bonitatum eius, quae fluunt ab ipso" (*De causis et proc. univ.* 1.4.3 [45.23–51]). (Trismegistus and Hermes the Egyptian seem distinguished as grandson from grandfather [*Asclep.* 37 and Augustine *De civ. D.* 8.26].)

Note that the very language Albert approves for the order of flowing—*occumbere, obumbratio, distare, sinceritas*—can bear an unacceptable sense.

4. *De causis et proc. univ.* 1.4.3 (45.52–55): "Et opinio quidem antiquorum pessimus error est et destruit omnes gradus entium. Secundum eos enim omne quod est, formatur immediate ab ipsa primi essentia."

5. Lucan *De bello civili* 9.580; Plutarch *De Iside et Osiride* 9; David of Dinant, "Davidis de Dinanto Quaternulorum fragmenta," ed. Marian Kurdziałek, *Studia Mediewistyczne* 3 (1963): 88.9–10; see Kurdziałek's introduction, LI–LII n. 235, for Plutarch and Albert. The passage about Pallas Athene is not among the surviving bits of David's work, but Albert explicitly cites Lucan and Plutarch via David (*Super Dion. De div. nom.* 1.58 [C37.1:36.2–7]; *Sent.* 2.1.5 quaestiuncula, obj. 4 [B27:17a]; *De homine* 5.2 sed contra 8 [B35:71a]; *Summa* 2.1.4.3 obj. 2 [B32:108b–109a]; see also *Metaph.* 1.4.7 [C16.1:56.73–80]).

6. *Phys.* 1.2.10 (C4.1:31.15–16) and *Summa* 1.4.20.2 (C34.1:102.59–62). Albert claims that David's arguments can also be found "in quodam libro antiquo Alexandri cujusdam Graeci" (*De homine* 5.2 [B35:69b]; so too *Sent.* 2.1.5 [B27:17a] and *Metaph.* 1.4.7 [C16.1:55.13–16 and 56.78–80]). Kurdziałek (XXIII–XLIV and LX), discussing these and other texts, speculates that "Alexander's book" was actually part of David's *Quaternuli*.

7. *Quaternulorum fragmenta* 71.4–7: "Substancia uero, ex qua sunt omnia <corpora>, dicitur yle; substancia uero, ex qua sunt omnes anime, dicitur racio siue mens. Manifestum est ergo Deum esse racionem omnium animarum et yle omnium corporum." Compare *De causis et proc. univ.* 1.1.1–2 (3.16–7.19) and 2.4.1 (156.79–88). For a non-pantheistic reading of David, see Enzo Maccagnolo, "David of Dinant and the Beginnings of Aristotelianism in Paris," in *A History of Twelfth-Century Western Philosophy*, ed. Peter Dronke (Cambridge: Cambridge University Press, 1988), 429–42.

Why Albert chose to address pantheism in terms of communicability and incommunicability is not immediately clear. Perhaps he was thinking of the many passages where Ibn Sīnā argues that there is only one God and that nothing can share the necessary being proper to him; the Arabic root *šrk*, "to share," becomes *communicare* in Latin (*Philosophia prima* 1.6, 8.4, 8.5, and 9.1 [3:43.20–23, 54.41, 4:397.55–58, 402.51–54, 406.31–35, 411.34–48, and 434.6–13]). And Albert's commentary on Peter Lombard *Sentences* 1.8.1 ("De proprietate et incommutabilitate et simplicitate Dei essentiae") includes a curious article where he sometimes has "incommunicabilis" for "incommutabilis" (*Sent.* 1.8.2 [B25:222b–223b]); judging from the arguments, the confusion was not Borgnet's, but one cannot decide what to make of this until the critical edition appears. Finally, Albert had access to two translations of Dionysius *Div. nom.* 1.2 (PG3:588C): Eriugena's, according to which "non tamen communicabile est universaliter bonum," and John Sarrazin's, which has it that "non tamen incommunicabile est universaliter bonum."

8. See chap. 1 nn. 47–51.

9. For the near synonymy of *anniyya* and *huwiyya* in LC, see Endress, 81, 95–98; for the many attempts to render forms of and expressions with εἶναι in Arabic, which has no copula, see Soheil M. Afnan, *Philosophical Terminology in Arabic and Persian* (Leiden: E. J. Brill, 1964), 29–30, 89, 94–102, and 117–24. In LC, Gerard's *essentia* represents *māhiyya*, *qiyām*, *qiwām*, or <u>d</u>āt (<u>d</u>āt also appearing as *esse* and, along with certain other words, as the Latin third-person reflexive pronoun); besides <u>d</u>āt and *anniyya*, *esse* represents *wuğūd*.

10. Though Albert judged that the argument of LC 19 rested upon the distinction expressed by the pair *esse* and *id quod est*, he was well aware that *esse* in LC 19 did not always signify that which is contradistinguished from *id quod est*. Albert's consciousness of the differences between his own usage and that of the Latinized LC will become evident when he explains the *continuator* of LC 19 (see pp. 28–29); he seems to have decided, wisely, not to try finding much consistency in LC's use of *esse*, *ens*, and *essentia*.

11. See especially G. Meersseman, *Geschichte des Albertismus*, Heft 1, *Die Pariser Anfänge des Kölner Albertismus* (Paris: R. Haloua, 1933), 48–70; see also Léonard Ducharme, "*Esse* chez saint Albert le Grand: Introduction à la métaphysique de ses premiers écrits," *Revue de l'Université d'Ottawa* 27 (1957): 209*–52*; L.-B. Geiger, "La vie, acte essential de l'âme, l'*esse* acte de l'essence d'après Albert-le-Grand," in *Etudes d'histoire littéraire et doctrinale*, Université de Montréal, Publications de l'Institut d'Etudes Médiévales, 17 (Montreal: Institut d'Etudes Médiévales, and Paris: J. Vrin, 1962), 49–116; Gallus M. Manser, *Das Wesen des Thomismus*, 3d ed., Thomistische Studien, 5 (Fribourg: Paulusverlag, 1949), 530–37; M.-D. Roland-Gosselin, *Le "De Ente et Essentia" de S. Thomas d'Aquin*, Bibliothèque Thomiste, 8 (Kain: Le Saulchoir, 1926), 172–84; Leo Sweeney, "The Meaning of *Esse* in Albert the Great's Texts on Creation in the *Summa de Creaturis* and *Scripta Super Sententias*," in *Albert the Great: Commemorative Essays*, ed. Francis J. Kovach and Robert W. Shahan (Norman: University of Oklahoma Press, 1980), 65–95; and Georg Wieland, *Untersuchungen zum Seinsbegriff im Metaphysikkommentar Alberts des Grossen*, Beiträge zur Geschichte der Philosophie und Theologie des Mittelalters, n.s., 7 (Münster: Aschendorff, 1972).

Our century, like the fifteenth, has witnessed efforts to distinguish Albert's positions from those of Thomas, especially on existence. While readily admitting differences between Albert and Thomas in their handling of the distinction between essence and existence, I find a number of these efforts spoiled through appropriation to Thomas of doctrines predating him by centuries. Thus, some of the aforementioned scholars either do not grant Albert as much concern with existence as I or, if they grant it, judge it disappointing compared to that of Thomas (who, for his part, may have questioned its relevance to some contexts where Albert has been faulted for lacking it).

Justice to Albert and to ourselves as readers demands that we read him in light of his predecessors, not under the shadow of his successors. But here again difficulties beset us, because what our contemporaries make of his sources often differs from what he made of them. The urge to interrupt Albert with complaints that Aristotle drew only a logical distinction between essence and existence is just one instance of this problem. But either we reduce Albert to a historical curiosity, or, if we take him as he wished to be taken, that is, as a teacher of things Peripatetic, we must avoid judgments which assume currently received interpretations and, instead, try to discern what grounds he may have for his interpretation. Perhaps his reading is less indefensible than commonly supposed: according to F.-X. Maquart, in "Aristote n'a-t-il affirmé qu'une distinction logique entre l'essence et l'existence?" (*Revue Thomiste* 31 [1926]: 62–72), when we note that Aristotle's distinction between essence and existence occurs in the *Posterior Analytics* and consequently dismiss it as merely logical and without implications for the real order, we confound his material logic with our modern, purely formal logic. See further Maquart's "Deux autres arguments de M. Rougier" and "Un dernier argument de M. Rougier," on pp. 267–76 and 358–66 of the same volume. As for Plotinus, Gerson (5–14) argues convincingly that he posited a real distinction between essence and existence in all but the One; from Plotinus, the distinction enters the Neoplatonic tradition, including LC, though LC 8 more than LC 19.

12. "Et hoc est quod dicit Boethius in libro de hebdomadibus: '"Quod est" habere aliquid potest praeter "id quod ipsum est." Esse vero nihil habet admixtum'" (*De causis et proc. univ.* 1.1.8 [17.12–15], quoting *De hebdomadibus* 40.35–37 from memory). Ibn Sīnā is duly acknowledged at *De V univ.* 2.8 (B1:38a), where *existentia* appears as equivalent to *esse* ("et ideo dicit Avicenna, quod esse et existentia accidit ei quod est").

Disagreement over the meanings of *esse* and *id quod est* in Boethius continues to this day. Ralph McInerny surveys scholarly interpretations—some aligning Boethius and Ibn Sīnā—in the sixth chapter of his *Boethius and Aquinas* (Washington, D.C.: Catholic University of America Press, 1990).

13. See chap. 1 n. 35. Naturally, the spelling of Gerard's transliteration underwent numerous changes at the hands of puzzled scribes; Bardenhewer's *helyatin*, Pattin's *yliathim*, Borgnet's *hyleachim*, and Fauser's *hyliatin* all reflect the Arabic ḥilya.

14. "Certain philosophers" seems Albert's acknowledgment that Aristotle's own usage differs: although, discussing the objects of mathematics, Aristotle writes that whatever is not simply an essence but a "this something," even an imperceptible "this something," has some matter (*Metaph.* 1036^{b}35–1037^{a}2), he

confines this intelligible matter to the inner workings of the human discursive faculty. That is why Plotinus challenges him with the difficult question how he can posit a multiplicity of separate movers when multiplicity presupposes matter (5.1.9.26–27).

15. Often *esse* is the nature itself: "Similiter esse voco formam compositi quod praedicatur de ipso composito, sicut homo est esse Socratis, et Angelus est esse Raphaelis" (*De IV coaequ.* 4.21.1 [B34:464a]). One cannot always tell exactly which meaning Albert had in mind; sometimes he seems not to care: "*esse autem est essentia ejus vel actus essentiae*" (*Sent.* 1.8.3 solutio [B25:224b]).

16. *De causis et proc. univ.* 2.2.18 (111.2–41): "Suppositum enim sive hypostasis propter hoc suppositum dicitur, quia sub natura communi positum est. . . . hoc caelum, suppositum dicit sub hoc communi, quod est caelum. Et hoc est in unoquoque 'quod ipsum est.' Esse autem ipsius est per naturam, cui substat. Haec autem determinatio naturae fit per esse, quod habet in supposito proprio, quod per proprium accidens, ut Avicenna dicit, individuat et in se subsistere facit naturam. Natura enim secundum se forma communis est. . . . Quod autem subsistere facit et communitatem naturae terminat ad hoc aliquid, hylealis principii habet proprietatem. . . . Ut autem dicit Boethius et Aristoteles, 'in incorporalibus hyle non est.' Est tamen ibi suppositum, quod in sustinendo naturam communem, hyle habet proprietatem. Et propter hoc a quibusdam philosophis *hyliatin* vocatur, quod denominativum est ab hyle. . . . Est enim hoc quod a prima causa productum est ad esse receptionem. Et hoc est quod saepius iam probatum est et quod Boethius dicit, quod 'quidquid citra primum est, est ex "quod est" et esse.' Aliter enim hoc aliquid non esset. Et propter hoc dicit, quod '"id quod est" habere aliquid potest praeter "id quod ipsum est." Esse vero nihil habet admixtum.' 'Id enim quod est' ad hoc quod sit, oportet, quod admisceatur ei esse, quod per seipsum non habet. Esse vero ad hoc quod sit, nihil admixtum habet. Eo ipso enim est esse quo processus est ab esse primo." See also *Super Dion. De div. nom.* 5.22 (C37.1:315.49–57).

At *Sent.* 2.3.4 solutio (B27:68), Albert, discussing the ontological makeup of angels, uses *fundamentum* for what he here calls *hyliatin* or *id quod est*. He explains that, though there is no one matter of corporeal and incorporeal creatures (because they are not potential in the same way), many of them do share the property of substanding and supporting form, and that this common property requires him to posit a common substance in them, namely, *fundamentum*, the "neque quid neque quantum" which Aristotle describes in *Metaph.* 7 (1029^a20–25). In point of fact, what *Metaph.* 7 describes is prime matter, which Aristotle never made underlie intelligences. And Albert seems to know that: his commentary on the text includes nothing unfamiliar to the Peripatetic school. Likewise, in his commentary on the "Peripatetic" LC, although matter is a sort of *fundamentum* to form (1.1.10 [19.22–25]) and prime matter is the *fundamentum* of all corporeal things (2.1.3 [63.50–55]), Albert never calls the supposit of separate substances *fundamentum*, nor does he cite Aristotle to detail the notion of a supposit (indeed, he leaves the notion rather vague, along with the relation of the distinctions between essence and existence on the one hand and supposit and nature on the other).

17. *De causis et proc. univ.* 2.2.18 (111.56–65): "Cum igitur deus ab omnibus distinctus sit, oportet ipsum hoc aliquid esse. Propter quod dicimus, quod si primum principium suppositum habet, quod illud est idem cum esse suo propter nimiam simplicitatem, quae in ipso est. Et ideo *infinitum* est, a nullo retractum sicut et esse. Et est per omnia diffusum essentialiter et praesentialiter et potentialiter sicut et esse. Et nulli est immixtum, sed ab omnibus distinctum non alio quodam distinguente et determinante, sed suiipsius nobilitate et perfectione." When commenting on the "essentialiter," "praesentialiter," and "potentialiter" of Peter Lombard *Sent.* 1.37.1, Albert suggests several possible interpretations for these terms, and attaches no great importance to fixing the differences between them (*Sent.* 1.37.5 and 10).

18. Ibid., 2.2.18 (111.69–77): "Propter hoc autem quod suppositum divinum sic a nullo retractum est per differentiam advenientem, quidam improprie loquentes dicunt divinum *individuum* esse *infinitum*, individuum vocantes suppositum. Et suppositum magis improprie loquentes vocant *hyliatin*. Infinitum proprie enim primum principium nec genus nec species est nec individuum nec quid nec aliquid, quia ad nullum genus reduci potest." See also 1.1.10 (22.17–23.22) and *Metaph.* 11.2.8 (C16.2:492.61–79); compare Eriugena *Periphyseon* 463C and 523D–524D.

19. *De causis et proc. univ.* 2.4.1 (156.21–59): "Illud [primum] igitur agit non per aliquid sui, quod formet ipsum, sed per seipsum secundum 'id quod est'. . . . Hoc autem in nullo sequentium est. Quodlibet enim sequentium in potentia est, et secundum 'id quod est' nihil est et ex nihilo. Nihil autem omnium quae sunt, agit vel format vel regit secundum 'id quod est nihil.' Agit ergo secundum esse suum. Ergo ex actione unitas eius destruitur. Sequitur enim, quod in ipso sit esse et 'quod est.' Sed primum, quod agit secundum 'id quod est,' agit, secundum quod unum est. . . . Ex quo patet, quod omne secundum est compositum, agens autem primum solum simplex est. Compositum autem dico, quia est in eo quod agit et quo agit. Hoc autem in agente primo idem est."

1.2.1 (26.70–78) foreshadows this doctrine as proof that God, the universally acting intellect, is not an agent in the same sense as other agent intellects: "Omnis enim intellectus agens ordinis determinati per illustrationem super se factam agens est et particulariter agens est et non de se secundum 'id quod est' agens est, quia non secundum 'id quod est' agere potest nec in id quod ante se est, sed potius agit secundum id quod se habet ad antecedentem intellectum, et secundum illud esse, quod super ipsum et in ipsum emanat ab intellectu ordinis se antecedentis."

20. See Aristotle *Gen. Corr.* 322ᵇ23–323ᵃ33, to the explanation of which Albert devotes a five-chapter tractate. Aristotle writes that "touch" is said in several ways; Albert distinguishes most proper, proper but common, and metaphorical ways (*De gen. et corr.* 1.4.2 [C5.2:152.28–33]). Only touching in the most proper sense is reciprocal; celestial bodies or non-spatial beings touch their patients "per ultimum virtutis ab essentia sua egredientis, sed non tangunt per ultimum terminum suae quantitatis" (ibid., 1.4.4 [154.10–12]). See also Francis J. Kovach, "The Enduring Question of Action at a Distance in Saint Albert the Great," in *Albert the Great: Commemorative Essays*, 161–235.

21. Here again, *esse* must be form or nature or essence rather than something resulting from it, for, Albert consistently assigns communicability to forms. The text in n. 16 above teaches that "natura enim secundum se forma communis est," and that is precisely why nature is communicable: "cum enim omnis forma sive natura vel essentia de se sit communis, de se habet, quod sit communicabilis" (*Super Dion. De div. nom.* 2.37 [C37:68.23–24]; see also *Metaph.* 7.5.5 [C16.2:381.28–37]; for a related point outside the realm of agent causality, see *Metaph.* 5.6.13 [293.73–89] with 7.5.3 [376.58–377.3]). This receives confirmation at *De causis et proc. univ.* 2.4.3 (157.83–84: "In agentibus autem per se esse et forma agentis efficitur in eo quod agitur") and 1.4.1 (43.61–68: "Propter hanc communicabilitatem Plato formas posuit in lumine datoris formarum existentes. . . . tunc per esse, quod habent in materia, clauditur communicabilitas earum").

22. *De causis et proc. univ.* 2.4.1 (156.60–74): "Omne agens compositum per commixtionem eius quo agit, agit in id quod agit, quamvis non commisceatur ei secundum 'id quod est.' Nisi enim contingeret ipsum et formaliter misceretur ei, non ageret in ipsum. 'Quod enim non tangit, non agit.' Et quod rei non miscetur per penetrationem ad intima, non constituit nec format. Sicut est videre in igne, qui caliditate miscetur his in quae agit et transformat. Et sic est in anima nobili et intelligentia, quas coniungi et misceri oportet luminibus suis his in quae agunt et quae formant. Esse enim sive 'quo est' communicabile est, 'id autem quod est' incommunicabile. Cum igitur *prima causa* agat secundum 'id quod est,' sequitur, quod in omni actione sua incommunicabilis est omnibus quae aguntur ab ipsa."

23. LC 19 clearly describes the "per esse agens" for the sake of its overall argument about God, but its author, like Proclus (*Inst.* 122), may have thought the description applied to a number of spiritual agents; "propter causas primas" in the closing sentence (159.77) leaves matters somewhat unclear. Albert cannot entertain this possibility while making the chapter hinge on the identity of *esse* and *id quod est* in God alone.

24. Albert excludes cases of accidental causation from this discussion (*De causis et proc. univ.* 2.4.3 [157.82–83]).

25. "Quando autem agens omni simplicitate simplex est ita, quod in ipso esse et 'quod est' idem est, sequitur, quod illud agens secundum totum sui a

causato sui seiunctum sit et continuatorem medium non habeat" (ibid., 2.4.3 [158.8–12]).

All of this is an elaborate way of saying that precisely because God *is* his quiddity and does not just *have* a quiddity, his quiddity cannot be shared. Thus, in *De causis et proc. univ.*, Albert says that, because God's *esse* is his *id quod est*, he is utterly incommunicable. However, in theology, where Albert has to deal with revealed truths as well as philosophical wisdom, he seems to reverse this: because God the Father's *id quod est* is his *esse*, he is completely communicable to the Son and the Spirit. The argument runs as follows. Every form is of itself communicable; but there is no mere "-able" in God, who is pure act; therefore, God's nature is actually communicated to several hypostases. For since form is of itself communicable, when it is not actually communicated, this must happen because of that in which the form is, i.e., because of the *id quod est*; but, in God, the *id quod est* is not other than the communicable essence, and therefore cannot impede it (*Sent.* 1.4.3 solutio and ad 6 [B25:159b–160a and 161a]; *Super Dion. De div. nom.* 2.37 [C37:68.23–41]). This theological argument does not contradict the philosophical proof made in *De causis et proc. univ.*: the philosopher argues that the divine essence cannot be multiplied, while the theologian asserts that supposits are multiplied within the essence without multiplication of that essence (see *Sent.* 1.19.14 solutio and 15 ad quaest. [535a and 536b]). See further n. 34 below.

Believers in the Trinity may wonder that *De causis et proc. univ.* speaks of the divine supposit in the singular. Albert defends his practice at *Sent.* 1.8.2 (223a): "Et quod objicitur secundo loco, quod non est quod est in divinis vel suppositum nisi in persona, dicendum quod hoc verum est secundum rem, sed ex modo intelligendi, cum dicitur, *Deus*, significatur divinitas in habente, et illud habens dicitur suppositum non in ratione personae: et gratia illius sequitur substantiam divinam incommunicabilitas." In other words, one need not know about the three supposits in God in order to know that supposit and nature are (logically) distinct in him.

26. Indeed, Albert elsewhere admits that the first cause "metaphorice attingit materiam" and "est potentia activa mixta materiae" (*Metaph.* 11.2.20 [C16.2:508.20–35]; see also *Summa* 1.13.55.1 ad 4 [B31:558a]). In *De causis et proc. univ.*, his anti-pantheistic preoccupation with the uniqueness of the divine essence leads him to avoid the metaphor and to contrast sharply beings whose essence may be multiplied so as to become a *continuator* (point of contact).

27. *De causis et proc. univ.* 1.1.11 (24.80–88): "Et si quis obiciat, quod primum efficiens est efficiens per formam et ultimus finis non est desideratus nisi per hoc quod est forma, et ideo si primum principium est principium ut efficiens et finis, erit etiam principium ut forma: dicimus, quod non negamus primum esse formam, prout forma cadit in intentione efficientis et finis. Sed impossibile est

primum esse principium formale, prout forma est producta ab efficiente et quiescens in materia."

28. Ibid., 2.4.11 (164.50–59): "Quodlibet illorum facit sine mediatore et instrumento per seipsum. Non enim eodem mediatore uti posset ad omnia. Aliter enim omnia in una forma essent univoca. Mediator enim forma est, sicut superius probatum est. Et si unus esset mediator, una esset omnium forma. . . . Et in hoc decepti erant, qui omnia dixerunt esse deum. Putabant enim, quod mediatore operetur. Quod nullo modo esse potest."

Note that LC 19 speaks of a "continuator" and an "instrumentum," while Albert adds a "mediator" (apparently from LC's "non est continuator neque res alia media" [159.70–71]) and makes the three terms synonymous. His denial that God acts by a *mediator* must be read in this context, not as a rejection of secondary causality, which his task as expositor of LC requires him to uphold (see chap. 5 below).

29. *De causis et proc. univ.* 1.2.6 (32.22–25): "Est scientia per id quod est incomparabile et non miscibile et non communicabile his de quibus est, cum tamen sit penetrativum omnium et immediatum cuilibet et proximum"; 2.1.2 (62.15–20): "Et causa quidem prima est, in qua sicut in fonte effectivo et formali et finali sunt omnia. Propter quod essentialiter et praesentia luminis sui et potentia virtutis suae necesse est eam esse extensam per omnia praeter hoc quod nulli est immixta sicut essentialis pars essentiae ipsius"; 2.4.1 (156.84–88): "Deus autem ut causa prima in puritate unitatis consistens nulli communicabilis est vel miscibilis. Virtute tamen operationis et praesentia luminis sui et extensione essentiae nihil deserit eorum quae sunt"; 2.4.11 (164.41–49): "Non enim in alio est sicut aliquid essentiae eorum vel sicut aliquid potentiae ipsorum vel sicut in subjecto, sed est in ipsis sicut extensum per ea, in nullo commixtum eis, quia, sicut iam habitum est, continuatorem non habet ad suum causatum, sed per seipsum ubique essentialiter est et essentias causans et per seipsum ubique praesentialiter est undique illuminans et per seipsum ubique est potentialiter cunctis posse et virtutes ministrans."

Notice Albert's willingness to speak of God penetrating his effects; the text reproduced in n. 3 above condemned such statements only because there they were meant as a claim that God is part of his effects.

30. "Esse suum et 'hoc quod est' omnino et omnimode idem est. . . . Propter quam etiam simplicitatem nullo termino clauditur vel restringitur, sed omnia penetrat, ad omnia extenditur, omnibus adest et in omnibus est. . . . Quod autem omnino simplex est, terminos non habet. Terminans enim et terminatum natura et substantia diversa sunt" (ibid., 1.2.5 [31.64–74]).

Incidentally, when speaking of *esse* and *id quod est*, Albert never uses the expression "realis distinctio," though most scholars take him to have had that and not a merely logical distinction in mind. This passage, with its statement that the limiting and the limited are diverse by nature and by substance, comes as close as can be to an explicit confirmation of that reading. See also *Super Dion. De div. nom.* 2.37 and 5.22 (C37:68.35–38 and 315.54–57), where Albert affirms that God's *esse* and *id quod est* are logically distinct, and presents the fact that they are not also distinct "secundum rem" as something unique to God.

31. See also n. 17 above and *De causis et proc. univ.* 1.3.6 (42.1–2): "Per quodcumque designatur, nihil est diversum a substantia ipsius."

32. "Efficitur unicuique immediatum et magis propinquum quam proxima principia sua. Proxima enim principia non sunt proxima nec immediata nisi virtute primi penetrantis ea. Magis autem proximum est et immediatum, quod per se proximum et immediatum est, quam id quod per alterum" (ibid., 1.2.5 [31.32–37]).

33. "Quod enim de sui natura communicabile est, intellectuali extensione semper extendit se in communicationem. . . . Propter quod etiam dicunt, quod nullo termino coarctatur, maxime fluit, sicut primum, quod nullo termino est diffinibile" (ibid., 1.4.3 [46.33–44]).

If God is most communicable, then the flux can be more or less communicable according as it is closer to or farther from its divine font. Albert uses this to explain the "divine intelligence" of LC 18: "Quaecumque igitur intelligentia largitiones divinas participat sub maxima communicabilitate et simplicitate, . . . haec pro certo prima participatione divinas participat bonitates" (2.3.15 [152.16–22]). Eventually, the stream of emanation gives out: "Per esse, quod habent in materia, clauditur communicabilitas earum [formarum]" (1.4.1 [43.67–68]).

34. Ibid., 1.4.2 (44.45–62): "Hoc proprie vocatur influere, ut influxus sit ex parte primi, receptio autem et continentia ex parte secundi. . . . Continentia autem secundorum est et non primi, ex parte illa qua terminatae sunt possibilitates." Any "measure" in communicability is on the side of creatures, and there must be measure on their side because, were recipients not limited, they would be everything and so would have no need to receive.

Somewhat more clarity may now be obtained on communicability in Trinitarian discussions. In the Trinity, God the Father can indeed communicate his *esse*, which is identical with his *id quod est*, to another *id quod est*, because — and here the mystery lies — that other *id quod est* is also identical with the one *esse*, and so is not a limit determining the reception of that *esse*. Where *esse* and *id quod est* are distinct, that is, in all creatures, this cannot be, but the problem is not on the side of God. See also 1.2.2 (27.36–39).

Incidentally, apart from *communicabilitas* and the unavoidable *processio*, Albert seems hesitant to use his emanation vocabulary of the Trinity. In this he differs from William of Auvergne, who, taking his cue from the scriptural teaching that wisdom is an emanation from God (Wis 7.25), argues that the first emanation must be within the Godhead, according to God's fullness and not according to the capacity of some recipient (*De trinitate* 14 [esp. 82.7–11 and 87.46–59]). Albert also makes Wis 7.25 refer to the generation of the Son (*Dominica in ramis palmarum: Sermo fratris Alberti*, ed. Bernhard Geyer in "Die Universitätspredigten des Albertus Magnus," *Sitzungsberichte: Bayerische Akademie der Wissenschaften: Philosophisch-Historische Klasse* 1966.3: 25.24–26; contrast the probably spurious *Sermo de sanctis* 38 [B13:563a]), but he leaves the theme undeveloped. As emerges from *Summa* 1.9.41.2.3 (C34.1:322.15–28 and 323.17–39), the danger of subordinationism is what keeps him from applying emanationist models to the Trinity.

35. Albert argues this in greatest detail at *Super Dion. De div. nom.* 2.43 and 46 (C37.1:72.23–34 and 74.69–75.11).

36. As he explains in *De homine* 21.1 (B35:184b), he takes this distinction from Ibn Sīnā (*De anima* 3.1 [1:170.7–171.22]). Of course, Albert's sources sometimes keep him from observing the distinction (*Super Ioh.* 1.8 [B24:42b]).

37. See V. Lossky, "La notion des 'analogies' chez Denys le Pseudo Aréopagite," *Archives d'histoire doctrinale et littéraire du moyen âge* 5 (1930): 279–309. Albert cites Dionysius at *De causis et proc. univ.* 2.4.14 (167.60–62).

38. "Peripatetic" rather than "Aristotelian," because Aristotle himself subdivides "equivocals" (ὁμώνυμα) or speaks of "things said in many ways" (πολλαχῶς λεγόμενα) where some of his later followers talk about "analogy."

39. *De causis et proc. univ.* 2.2.19 (112.20–25) provides one among many examples: "*Omne quod est primum et causa rebus* sequentibus . . . *ad formam suam convertat unumquodque secundum uniuscuiusque propriam analogiam.*" Note also the expressions "*analogia suae possibilitatis*" (2.2.20 and 23 [115.3–4 and 117.5–6]), "*secundum uniuscuiusque propriam potestatem et analogiam*" (2.2.37 [130.77–78]) and "*secundum analogiam potestatis uniuscuiusque*" (2.2.39 [133.36–37]); at 2.2.23 (117.23–28), *analogia* parallels *facultas*; and LC 19's "*secundum modum uirtutum earum receptibilium et possibilitatem earum*" (158.77–78) is paraphrased "*secundum modum* analogiae *virtutis rerum receptibilium et possibilitatem earum*," just as its "*secundum modum suae uirtutis et sui esse*" (158.79) becomes "*secundum modum* analogiae *suae et secundum modum capacitatis sui esse*" (2.4.4 [158.51–52 and 55–56]).

40. Ibid., 2.2.44 (138.11–16). See also 2.4.15 (168.28–40), where Albert associates *analogia* with *modus propinquitatis ad causam primam, modus quo res causam primam percipiunt, quantitas proportionis, modus esse, proportio* and *quantitas*.

41. Indeed, proportion is the basic meaning of the Greek "analogy"; Dionysius can refer to orders of being as "analogies" because the proportion of their capacity to God's gifts results in a hierarchy.

42. "*Deus . . . habet convenientiam cum causatis non univocationis, sed analogiae, non tamen talis analogiae, quod aliquid idem participetur a deo per*

prius et a causatis per posterius, quia sic esset aliquid simplicius et prius deo, sed quia deus est secundum substantiam aliquid ut vita vel sapientia vel huiusmodi non per participationem et alia participant illud accedendo ad primum, quantum possunt, sicut est convenientia exemplatorum ad exemplar" (*Super Dion. De div. nom.* 1.57 [C37.1:35.46–56]).

43. See *Super Dion. De div. nom.* 9.14–17, Albert's commentary on PG3:913C–916A, for his elaborate proofs of the one-sidedness of this relation; see also *Metaph.* 5.2.8 (C16.1:245.82–246.12). Dionysius himself would have found this doctrine in Proclus' commentary on Plato *Parmen.* 132D–133A; see Eugenio Corsini, *Il trattato "De Divinis nominibus" dello Pseudo-Dionigi e i commenti neoplatonici al "Parmenide,"* Università di Torino: Pubblicazioni della facoltà di lettere e filosofia, 13.4 (Turin: G. Giappichelli, 1962), 151–53.

44. *De causis et proc. univ.* 2.3.3 (142.14–29): "Cum enim dicitur omnis virtus in communitate virtutis, non distribuitur virtus primi eo quod, sicut in I huius scientiae libro probatum est, primum nec virtus primi in nullo genere continetur cum aliquo. . . . Et si dicatur, quod per analogiam communitatem habet cum alio, haec analogia in sequentibus fundatur et non in ipso. Sequentia enim primo proportionantur secundum modum quo participant ipsum et imitantur. Primum autem non proportionatur alicui nec imitatur aliquid. Quod enim sequentia participant, non est primum nec aliquid primi, sed est aliquid eius vel eorum quae sunt ab ipso, ut magnus ait Areopagita Dionysius."

45. "Neque enim est diligens comparatio causatis et causis; sed habent quidem causata causarum contingentes imagines" (*Div. nom.* 2.8 [PG3:645C], trans. John Sarrazin). As Albert explains, this holds good of the causes which are only causes with respect to an effect, not of causes which are also effects of their effect in a reciprocal relationship (*Super Dion. De div. nom.* 2.66).

46. "Deus proprie non potest connumerari alicui rei, quia non est aliquid sibi commune et creaturis neque per speciem neque per genus neque per analogiam, quia in communitate generis et speciei est aliquid unum in pluribus eodem modo per diversas differentias vel per diversas partes materiae, in communitate autem analogiae est aliquid unum in pluribus diversis modis, sicut ens in substantia et accidente et sanum in homine et urina. Sed non potest aliquid unum esse in deo et in quodam altero, quia oporteret, quod contraheretur in utroque, et sic deus esset compositus et esset in ipso universale et particulare; et ideo non est in deo aliqua dictarum communitatum ad aliquid aliud; sed est tamen aliquis modus analogiae ipsius ad creaturas, non quod idem sit in utroque, sed quia similitudo eius quod est in deo, invenitur in creaturis secundum suam virtutem" (*Super Dion. De div. nom.* 13.22 [C37.1:445.50–66]; see also 4.51 [158.38–46] and *Super Dion. De myst. theol.* 1 and 2 [C37.2:459.3–43 and 467.53–60]).

Though Albert explains none of this in *De causis et proc. univ.*, the analogy of imitation does figure in the text reproduced in n. 44, in *De causis et proc. univ.*

1.3.6 and 2.1.17 (41.53–74 and 82.1–19), and in many fleeting allusions; indeed, throughout *De causis et proc. univ.*, Albert alludes to developments in the doctrine of analogy made in his Dionysian, not his Aristotelian, commentaries. That this particular Aristotelian paraphrase looks somewhat different from the others and shares themes with the Dionysian commentaries should not greatly surprise us, since it deals with the theological culmination of philosophy.

47. "Generatio aequivoca est, quando ratio geniti non est in generante, . . . univoca autem, quando ratio geniti est in generante vel creante. Sed non est aliquid creatum a Deo, cujus ratio propria non sit in ipso. . . ." Of course, this is not to take away what has been said thus far, so as pantheistically to make Creator and creature univocal in a form; rather, God has virtually what he gives, as Albert continues: "Si sit in Deo ratio calidi, non tamen est calidus, vel albus propter rationem albi: haec enim ratio non est diffinitio albi, sed est sicut ratio in causa prima, ex cujus virtute non qualitate procedunt hujusmodi res" (*Sent.* 1.8.30 sed contra and reply [B25:262–63a]; see also *Super Dion. De div. nom.* 1.1 [C37.1:1.27–35] and *De causis et proc. univ.* 2.1.13 [76.68–78]).

For Albert, all causation, even of things coming to be by chance or through putrefaction, can be traced back to univocal causation (*Metaph.* 7.2.10 [C16.2:353.24–35], 11.1.6 [466.69–467.12], and 11.1.8); he explicitly refuses to follow commentators who except God from this proposition (ibid., 11.1.11 [477.2–18]). In general, he holds that every case of equivocity and, *a fortiori*, of analogy, can be reduced to, though not identified with, univocity (*Super Ethica* 1.5.29 [C14.1:24.59–63 and 25.38–47]).

48. "Causa enim universalis non dicitur, quia praedicabilis sit de multis, sed quia universaliter influit omnibus sub se existentibus. . . . causa primaria ad omnia secundaria, in quae causalitate sua extenditur, est in multis. Et in quantum communicat formam et rationem et nomen sicut causa univoca, secundum aliquid est etiam de multis. Et sic accipit universalis nomen et rationem. Dicit enim Aristoteles, quod universale est, quod est unum in multis et de multis. Quia vero universalius est, quod in pluribus est et de pluribus, ideo primaria universalior est quam secundaria" (*De causis et proc. univ.* 2.1.5 [65.47–79], explaining LC 1).

("Aristotle's" definition seems to come from combining the thought of *Metaph.* 1038^{b}11–12 with the formulae of *Cat.* 3^{a}7–21; the latter text only apparently rejects it [*De praedic.* 2.6 (B1:176b)]. De Libera, "L'antiplatonisme," n. 35, points to a similar definition in Ibn Sīnā.)

49. "[Bonum] separatum per seipsum exserit seipsum et multiplicat et indeficienter ex ipso sicut ex quodam sigillo bona per participationem dicta ab ipso procedunt"; "fluit ergo, quod secundum seipsum se extendit in sui multiplicationem, quemadmodum Plato dixit de formis per se existentibus. Hoc autem non est nisi primum quidem lumen intellectuale intellectus agentis et

secundum lumen corporale, quod luminis intellectualis in corporibus est exemplum"; "non per essentiam in omnibus fluit nisi primum, quamvis esse alterum et alterum habeat, secundum quod est in primis et secundis et ultimis. Differentia enim coarctans essentiam non variat, sed esse alterum et alterum facit. Sicut differentia constitutiva addita generi essentiam generis non multiplicat, sed esse generis facit alterum et alterum" (*De causis et proc. univ.* 1.4.2 and 4 [45.17–19, 46.76–81, and 47.52–59]). Albert explains the language of self-multiplication most fully when commenting on Dionysius, his source: "Producit deus res ut efficiens et forma rerum, non quae sit pars compositi, sed sicut forma exemplaris; et ideo ad multiplicationem effectuum dicitur multiplicari, sicut exemplar quodammodo potest dici multiplicari ad multiplicationem exemplatorum, in quibus est sua similitudo" (*Super Dion. De div. nom.* 2.85 [C37.1:99.13–18]).

4. The First Created Thing

1. *De causis et proc. univ.* 1.4.5 (49.12–15): "Videtur nullus gradus esse in entibus secundum speciem vel genus determinatus. Et propter hoc quidam dixerunt omnia esse unum et quod diffusio primi in omnibus est esse eorum." See also *Super Dion. De div. nom.* 4.51 (C37.1:157.48–55).

2. *De causis et proc. univ.* 1.4.5 (48.80–49.5): "Ordinem in gradibus entium non facit nisi casus et occubitus a lumine primi entis. Sed difficile est videre, quae sit causa occubitus in eo quod primo a primo ente procedit. Illud enim ex primo ente nullam potest habere obscuritatem. Propter quod videtur aeque limpidum esse semper et sincerum. Et similiter tertium, quod procedit ab illo ab aeque limpido et sincero, nullam capere potest obscuritatem. Et sic deinceps. Et sic videtur, quod in omnibus entibus aequa sit limpiditas luminis et sinceritas in processione, qua primum procedit a primo."

3. Naturally, we must understand God's "disposition" in a negative way, Albert warns (ibid., 2.4.11 [165.15–18]): "*Primum* igitur et in omnibus est et *in omnibus secundum unam dispositionem* est. Quae dispositio nihil dicit additum super ipsum, sed circumlocutio est simplicissimae suae unitatis et puritatis."

I say "agents produce their like" because, as Oliver Leaman points out (*Averroes and His Philosophy* [Oxford: Clarendon, 1988], 115), it is especially thinking of God as an agent cause which occasions the question how he can create many beings; if God exercises formal and final causality only, why cannot desire and imitation take many forms? But the thesis that Aristotle's God is an agent has fallen out of favor, a situation which may impede Albert's readers from giving its proper weight to the problem he himself takes so seriously. Again, though,

Albert's reading of Aristotle is not at all indefensible; see Jacques Maritain, *Bergsonian Philosophy and Thomism*, trans. Mabelle L. Andison in collaboration with J. Gordon Andison (New York: Philosophical Library, 1955), 357–61, for judicious remarks on the controversy whether Aristotle denies that God produces the world as efficient cause and, indeed, Creator.

4. Siger of Brabant makes a similar point; see J. J. Duin, *La doctrine de la providence dans les écrits de Siger de Brabant: Textes et étude*, Philosophes Médiévaux, 3 (Louvain: Editions de l'Institut Supérieur de Philosophie, 1954), 430–33.

5. *Enn.* 5.3.15.2–7: Ἃ μὴ ἔχει, πῶς παρέσχεν; . . ."Ἓν μὲν γὰρ ἐξ αὐτοῦ ἁπλοῦν τάχ' ἄν τις δοίη . . . πῶς δὲ πολλά; The passage continues with allusions to Plato's *Parmenides*. It is paraphrased in the Arabic *Epistola de scientia divina* §§139–41. See also chap. 5 n. 4 below for Pythagoreanism as a possible source for "ab uno unum."

Albert does find "ab uno unum" in the Platonic texts available to him, although he ordinarily invokes Peripatetic authorities in this matter: "Mundus perfectus est. Et hujus rationem meliorem dicit Plato in *Timaeo* [29E–31B]: quia scilicet a perfecto opifice non dicebat esse nisi perfectum. Aliter enim opus non responderet exemplari artis, quod est in mente artificis, et ideo dicit, quod a perfecto processit perfectum, et ab uno unum" (*Summa* 2.11.66 [B32:622a]).

6. *Philosophia prima* 9.4 (481.50–51); the context is a presentation of his emanationist scheme. Naturally, al-Ġazālī repeats this (*Metaphysics* 4.3.6 and 5 [117–20]), only to refute it in his *Incoherence of the Philosophers*. Ibn Rušd also repeats it, in the course of a critique of Avicennian emanation (large commentary on Aristotle's *Metaph.*, 12.44).

Ibn Rušd points out that "ab uno unum," as usually understood, is not Aristotle's teaching. At one point in his *Incoherence of the Incoherence*, he makes it a peculiarity of later Islamic philosophers, while at another he calls it the speculation of all ancient philosophers except Aristotle, whose difficult doctrine they misunderstood; it is merely dialectical, he says, but they mistakenly thought it demonstrative. Among its proponents, al-Fārābī and Ibn Sīnā are singled out for special abuse as those who reduced metaphysics to conjectures (*Averroes' "Tahafut al-Tahafut (The Incoherence of the Incoherence)*," trans. Simon van den Bergh [London: Luzac, 1954], third metaphysical discussion, 1:104, 106–10, 136, 146–49, 154). However, neither al-Ġazālī's *Incoherence of the Philosophers* nor Ibn Rušd's *Incoherence of the Incoherence* had been translated in Albert's day. See further Herbert A. Davidson, *Alfarabi, Avicenna, and Averroes, on Intellect: Their Cosmologies, Theories of the Active Intellect, and Theories of the Human Intellect* (Oxford: Oxford University Press, 1992), 224–28, for Ibn Rušd's short commentary on the *Metaph.*, also unavailable to Albert, and consult Kogan on Ibn Rušd's doctrinal evolution.

In the Latin West, Siger of Brabant sometimes speaks of "ab uno unum" as what Ibn Sīnā claims Aristotle said; once, Siger even takes issue with Ibn Sīnā's interpretation; see Duin, 394–95 and 429–31.

7. *De causis et proc. univ.* 1.1.6 (13.68–72). See chap. 1 nn. 9 and 11 for the *Epistula;* apart from *De causis et proc. univ.* 2.1.1 (61.66–67), Albert never mentions it without ascribing some doctrine to it, usually one pertaining to creation, and he often lists Ibn Sīnā or al-Fārābī as sources of information about it. For more on these texts, see Alain de Libera, "*Ex uno non fit nisi unum:* La *Lettre sur le Principe de l'univers* et les condamnations parisiennes de 1277," in *Historia philosophiae Medii Aevi: Studien zur Geschichte der Philosophie des Mittelalters,* ed. B. Mojsisch and O. Pluta (Amsterdam: B. R. Grüner, 1991), 1:543–60; see especially 549–55 for a rather complex hypothesis concerning how Albert came to guess at the contents of the *Epistula.*

8. Albert quotes the judgments made by John of Damascus at *De fide orthodoxa* 1.8 and 2.3, and by Augustine at *Trin.* 3.2.13 (*Super Dion. De div. nom.* 4.11 [C37.1:120.62–121.2]; *Summa* 1.13.53.1 [B31:540b–541a]).

9. See Roland Hissette, *Enquête sur les 219 articles condamnés à Paris le 7 mars 1277,* Philosophes Médiévaux, 22 (Louvain: Publications Universitaires, 1977), 66 and 70–72, for the texts and the alleged heretics; Duin, 384–442, analyzes Siger's position in detail. Some unedited commentaries on the *Nicomachean Ethics,* probably written after 1277, argue from "ab uno unum" that God does not bestow human happiness directly: the one and eternal God creates one, eternal intelligence, whereas happy men are many and began to be happy at various times; see Georg Wieland, "The Reception and Interpretation of Aristotle's *Ethics,*" in *The Cambridge History of Later Medieval Philosophy,* ed. Norman Kretzmann et al. (Cambridge: Cambridge University Press, 1982), 664–65, and p. 2 above.

10. William of Auvergne also upholds "ab uno unum" and "ab eodem idem," but within the Godhead, in the course of his argument that the first emanation, the Word, must be consubstantial with its font, God the Father (*De trinitate* 14 [83.34–43 and 86.23–87.45]); that the first creature must be one, he denies at great length (*De universo* 1.1.24–27; 2.1.9 and 25–30). Roland J. Teske examines the various contexts in which William discusses "ab uno unum" in "William of Auvergne's Use of Avicenna's Principle: *'Ex uno, secundum quod unum, non nisi unum,*" *The Modern Schoolman* 71 (1993–94): 1–15.

11. Roger Bacon, for one, makes the equation without noting any difficulty: "Hic notificat esse superius cum eternitate. . . . Dicit ergo 'prima rerum creatarum est esse' ipsius intelligentie" (*Quaestiones supra Librum de causis,* ed. Robert Steele, collaborante Ferdinand M. Delorme, Opera hactenus inedita Rogeri Baconi, 12 [Oxford: Clarendon, 1935], 36.25–31). And, though Aquinas entertains several possible interpretations, he quickly settles upon the right one:

"Videtur tamen non esse eius intentio ut loquatur de aliquo esse separato, sicut Platonici loquebantur; neque de esse participato communiter in omnibus existentibus, sicut loquitur Dionysius; sed de esse participato in primo gradu entis creati, quod est *esse superius*" (*In Librum de causis expositio*, ed. C. Pera [Turin: Marietti, 1955], lectio 4, §102). Ps.-Henry of Ghent (writing ca. 1250) does linger over this seeming discrepancy in the text, ultimately determining that *intelligentia* is the first creature, whereas *esse* is the first thing created *in* creatures, since it is their first substantial form (*Les "Quaestiones in Librum de causis" attribuées à Henri de Gand*, ed. John P. Zwaenepoel, Philosophes Médiévaux, 15 [Louvain: Publications Universitaires, and Paris: Béatrice-Nauwelaerts, 1974], qq. 24–25 [especially 61.44–62.58]).

Unfortunately, most medieval and Renaissance commentaries on LC lie unedited (see the list in Richard C. Taylor, "The *Liber de causis*: A Preliminary List of Extant Manuscripts," *Bulletin de philosophie médiévale* 25 [1983]: 81–84), so that one cannot easily verify how widespread which interpretations were.

12. Their mistake is partly excused by defects in the translation: see chap. 1, p. 10 and nn. 51 and 53.

13. Indeed, in an early, threefold division of *intelligentia*, Albert cites LC for precisely that meaning: "Quandoque vero dicitur natura intellectualis separata, sicut sumitur in libro de causis" (*Super Dion. Epist.* 5 [C37.2:497.31–33]).

14. See also *De causis et proc. univ.* 1.2.2 (27.22–35), where *intelligentia* is the *actio* of an *intellectus*, just as *sensatio* is that of *sensus*, *vegetatio* that of a *vegetativum principium*, and *essentia* that of *ens*. This meaning appears in *Metaph.* 11.2.30 (C16.2:520.55–521.1, 15, and 69–70) as well, because there Albert is paraphrasing the *translatio Media* of 1074ᵇ19–20 (οὐ γάρ ἐστι τοῦτο ὅ ἐστιν αὐτοῦ ἡ οὐσία νόησις, ἀλλὰ δύναμις), which reads: "non enim est hoc quod est sua substantia, *intelligentia*, sed potentia."

15. Neither do the ten categories have differences, but, unlike *esse*, they have something analogous. For instance, substance is not just being; it is also "per se existens" (*De causis et proc. univ.* 1.1.10 and 2.1.18 [22.25–34 and 83.37–40]; see also *Metaph.* 8.1.6 [C16.2:396.41–46]).

16. Here (LC 4 [88.64]), Albert thinks, *intelligentia* must refer to the concept "intellective substance." He seems undisturbed by having to assign the word more than one meaning within a chapter; of course, he himself often shifts between contrasting senses of a word without warning and within a single sentence.

17. LC's Latin version is literal to the point of obscurity here, and Albert rewords it in accord with his overall impression of the chapter. Thus, where LC has "omne quod ex eo sequitur causam primam est *achili* [id est] intelligentia, completa" (88.68–69), which means "whatever of created being is adjacent to the first cause is perfect intelligence," Albert paraphrases: "*Omne* enim ens,

quod sequitur causam primam, efficitur *intelligentia* complexa." And where LC has "et quod ex eo est inferius est intelligentia" (88.70), which means "its lower part is intelligence," Albert paraphrases: "Id autem *quod inferius est* esse procedens ab ipso, *est* etiam *intelligentia* formalis" (*De causis et proc. univ.* 2.1.23 [88.1–2 and 9–10]). Apparently, "ex eo" leads him to think of *esse* coming from the first cause and of lesser intelligences coming from *esse,* whereas, in point of fact, the Arabic idiom is partitive and refers to aspects of the collective hypostasis Intellect.

18. *De causis et proc. univ.* 1.1.3 (9.19–28), 2.1.5 (65.47–54), 2.1.20 (85.17–44), and, especially, 2.2.22 (116.34–62); *Metaph.* 5.6.5 (C16.1:285.57–286.23) gives a somewhat more complicated division. Albert derives this threefold universal from the account of Plato's teaching in Eustratius' commentary on *Eth. Nic.* 1096ª13, where Aristotle begins his critique of the Good (*The Greek Commentaries on the Nicomachean Ethics of Aristotle in the Latin Translation of Robert Grosseteste, Bishop of Lincoln (†1253),* vol. 1, *Eustratius on Book I and the Anonymous Scholia on Books II, III, and IV,* ed. H. Paul F. Mercken, Corpus Latinum Commentariorum in Aristotelem Graecorum, 6.1 [Leiden: E. J. Brill, 1973], 69.85–70.29; Eustratius' terminology differs a bit, but Albert gives sufficient indication that he is the source at *Super Ethica* 1.1.9 and 5.29 [C14.1:7.26–27 and 25.1] and *Super Dion. De div. nom.* 2.84 [C37.1:97.49–50]). The three sorts of universal also appear in the part of Ibn Sīnā's *Kitāb al-Šifā'* dealing with logic (*Opera philosophica* [Venice, 1508; réimpression en fac-similé agrandi, avec un tableau des abréviations, Louvain: Edition de la bibliothèque S.J., 1961], 2rb, 12ra, and 12va), where they are called intellectual, natural, and logical genera and described as before, in, or after the many; see *Encyclopaedia of Islam,* new ed., s.v. "Djins [genus]," by S. van den Bergh. Perhaps Albert's neat division comes from his reading Eustratius' diffuse reflections in light of Ibn Sīnā's succint statement.

19. Ibn Sīnā encourages this when explaining the threefold universal: "Omnium quae sunt comparatio ad deum et ad angelos est: sicut comparatio artificialium quae sunt apud nos ad animam artificem" (*Logica* 12va). Albert notes the "Stoic" (i.e., Platonic; see chap. 3 n. 2) origin of the threefold universal almost every time he refers to it, both in *De causis et proc. univ.* and throughout his works; nevertheless, he seems to consider it part of the Peripatetic heritage as well. For he uses it in many paraphrases, even though these are expositions of Peripatetic philosophy only; indeed, speaking of the *universalia ante rem* in the intellect of the first cause, he writes: "Dixerunt tam Stoici quam Peripatetici huiusmodi causas universalia esse prima" (*Metaph.* 5.6.5 [C16.1:285.65–67]).

Still, Albert does have reservations about the theory as held by Plato, some of which will emerge later (see chap. 5 n. 18 below). For now, suffice it to mention his indecision whether Aristotle or Eustratius gives the more accurate account of Plato's view. To Aristotle, Plato's Ideas are logical universals mistakenly located before rather than after sensible things and given independent existence; to Eustratius, Aristotle's critique misses its target, since the Ideas were neither logical universals nor independent of the divine mind. Aristotle's account found a measure of support among certain ecclesiastical writers, who accused Plato of positing an uncreated exemplar outside of God; Albert sometimes defers to their combined authority. For instance, when Peter Lombard reports that Plato counted three uncreated principles—God, the exemplar, and matter—Albert concurs: "Ipse putabat . . . esse formas in Deo distinctas ab intellectu Dei: quod improbat Aristoteles in XI *primae Philosophiae*" (*Sent.* 2.1.5 [B27:17b]). Again, at *Summa* 2.1.4.1.2, Ambrose, Peter Lombard, and Peter Comestor witness against Plato, and now the charge—at least through most of the article—is that the Ideas are produced from and outside of God, on the grounds that they must be many. Yet, as a Christian with Augustinian and Dionysian leanings, Albert cannot but feel the attraction of Eustratius' reply to Aristotle. Thus, at *Summa* 1.13.55.2.1 (B31:561), he writes that perhaps Plato spoke the truth, that the forms are lights (*lumina*) and emanations proceeding from the divine mind into the intelligences, from the intelligences into the spheres, from the spheres into the elements, and from the elements into the formative powers of seeds; Aristotle never denies this, Albert explains, but only that the forms exist separately, apart from intelligences and spheres and the like. And at *Metaph.* 1.4.12 (64.80–85 and 65.31–37), he affirms that Plato meant that, in God, the Ideas are one simple Idea. Throughout his works, Albert always insists that the errors Aristotle attributes to Plato are indeed errors; his indecision concerns the attribution only (*Super Ethica* 1.5.29 [C14.1:25.64–67]). In *Metaph.*, he tends to be especially generous with Plato (3.2.13 [136.49–61] and 11.1.8 [C16.2:470.68–77]); he even likens Plato's teaching to that of LC 9 (1.5.15; cf. p. 4 above, where he contrasts the "full truth" of LC with the polemic against Plato in *Metaph.* M and N). Regrettably, Albert never paraphrased Plato's philosophy (*Metaph.* 7.5.3 [378.39–42]: "Et forte non omnino dixit [Plato] falsum, sed de hoc pertractare est alterius philosophiae; nunc enim non suscipimus explanare nisi dicta et opiniones Peripateticorum").

20. "Est duplex forma: quaedam exemplaris, et haec quidem communis est non per praedicationem, sed per processum ab ipsa exemplatorum, sicut forma calcificis omnibus calceis, et ideo non oportet, quod univoce participetur ab omnibus, sed ab unoquoque secundum suam possibilitatem, sicut supra dictum est de sigillo; est etiam quaedam forma communis pluribus per praedicationem, quae est forma generis vel speciei, et a tali una forma procedunt plura univoce" (*Super Dion. De div. nom.* 2.83 [C37.1:97.20–29]). "Circumscriptum esse habet, cuius esse est limitatum et terminatum per terminos essentiae, sicut sunt genus et differentia, et huiusmodi circumscribentia non possunt esse in divino esse, quia ipsum est simplex et idea omnis entis, et propter hoc etiam videtur

non valere ratio Aristotelis contra Platonem, quod si homo particularis habet hominem, quod homo ille habet hominem, quia universale, quod posuit, abstractum est exemplar, quod est praehabens rem et non distinguitur per genus et differentiam" (ibid., 5.16 [312.5–15]). See also *Super Ethica* 1.2.9 and 29 (C14.1:7.29–30 and 25.20–27).

Edward Booth, in his *Aristotelian Aporetic Ontology in Islamic and Christian Thinkers* (Cambridge Studies in Medieval Life and Thought, 3d ser., 20 [Cambridge: Cambridge University Press, 1983]), never mentions Eustratius; not surprisingly, then, his study of Albert's ontology (163–204) misses the distinction between logical and intellectual universals, with the result that he considers Albert's thought a "logico-emanationist figure," that is, an "ontologising" of logic or "a conflation of logical structure with real structure" (165). This and several other distortions are magnified in his comparison of Albert with Thomas (209–16, 220, 224, 227–36, 238, 242, 244–45).

21. *De causis et proc. univ.* 2.1.21 [85.86–86.21]: "Intelligentiae autem secundae influunt bonitates magis determinatas et ideo magis declives ad particularia et magis separatas inter se. Propter quod talis processus bonitatum non stat in aliquo mediorum, sed procedit usque ad consecutionem ultimi, quod est esse in materia.... magis et minus declives et magis et minus distantes, secundum quod plus et minus procedunt a primo." Albert intends this as an explanation of LC 4 (89.69): "Intelligentiae autem secundae inprimunt formas declines, separabiles...." For *declines* (or *declives*), see chap. 1 n. 33.

22. *De causis et proc. univ.* 2.1.17 (80.73–81.31); see also *Super Dion. De div. nom.* 5.20 (C37.1:314.4–13). Actually, Albert's argument proves more than that *esse* is the first created thing: if *esse* alone presupposes nothing, then, as he goes on to say, it is the only created thing. This second conclusion will concern us later.

It is as term of resolution that *esse* is finite; when Albert says that it is finite with respect to its Creator (see p. 40 above), he seems to mean that *esse*, which is of itself apt to be divided into an infinity of particular concepts, exists in its generality, and therefore as term of resolution, in the light of God's mind: "Comparatum enim ad id unde est sive a quo est, finitum est, terminatum lumine intellectus primi.... Finitum autem est non ex seipso, sed ex primo principio. Sic enim ut ens finitum stat in lumine intellectus agentis ipsum. Et nisi esset finitum hoc modo, non posset esse terminus resolutionis et principium compositionis universorum" (*De causis et proc. univ.* 2.1.19 [83.75–84.3]). Compare the language at *De XV probl.* 1 (C17.1:32.48–54).

23. *De causis et proc. univ.* 2.1.17 (81.19–56): "*Esse* enim *simplex* mentis conceptus *est* ad nihil formatus vel determinatus, quo quaelibet res esse dicitur, cum de ipsa quaeritur per quaestionem, an sit.... Esse autem vocatur non ens vel entitas. Processus enim *simplex* primus a causa prima procedit ut actus in esse constituens omne quod est. Quia igitur esse processum illum nominat ut

actum entis, propter hoc creatum primum potius est esse quam ens vel entitas. Ex hoc autem quod primum est, sequitur, quod *simplicius sit* omnibus aliis. Simplicissimum enim est, quod in aliud resolvi non potest. Esse autem est, in quo stat resolutio entium."

As noted above (chap. 3 nn. 9–10), characteristics of Arabic and of Gerard's translating prevented Albert from giving such weight to morphology throughout LC. Thus, while explaining LC 17, which proposes that the first Being gives all things being (*ens, huwiyya*) by way of creation, whereas the first Life and the first Intellect give life and knowledge by way of information, Albert is forced to attribute to *ens* what he has said of *esse*; nonetheless, he soon begins substituting his preference, *esse* (2.3.13 [150.44–52]). Elsewhere, while addressing particular objections based on different ontological vocabularies, he sometimes finds *ens* more useful than *esse* (*De IV coaequ.* 1.2.1 ad 2 [B34:321a]). See also p. 47 below.

24. Albert explains such unilateral relations, real in creatures but only logical in God, at *De causis et proc. univ.* 1.1.10 (20.21–34): "Primum, quod *necesse* est *esse*, *non pendet ex alio* per eum modum, quo *illud pendet* ex *ipso*. Multa enim *pendent* ex primo per relationem ad ipsum. Ipsum autem a nullo dependet. Et huius causa est, quod relatio causatur ab aliquo genere motus in eo in quo est. Secunda autem causata per ipsum exitum in esse substantiale vel accidentale aliquid mutationis passa sunt, et sic relatio realis radicari potest in ipsis. Primum autem nihil mutationis pati potest. Sequitur ergo nullam relationem realiter radicari in ipso. Ex quo sequitur ulterius, quod destructis omnibus secundis nihil penitus destruitur in ipso, et deductis in esse omnibus secundis nihil penitus fit vel generatur in ipso." See also *Super Dion. De div. nom.* 4.5 and 177 (C37.1:116.22–35 and 262.66–76) and *Metaph.* 11.2.8 (C16.2:492.80–493.10).

The possibility of these unilateral relations is assumed by LC 19 (following Proclus *Inst.* 122), although Albert does not know that (see above, p. 24), and by Dionysius (see chap. 3 n. 43); Augustine discusses it at length (*Trin.* 5.4). The necessary premises, but not their theological application, already appear in Aristotle *Cat.* 7[b]15–8[a]12 and *Metaph.* 1021[a]27–[b]3.

25. *De causis et proc. univ.* 2.1.18 (82.53–70): "Quamvis enim *esse creatum simplex* conceptus mentis *sit* . . . tamen, ut dictum est, concretum habitudinibus est et ad nihil, ex quo est, et ad potentiam primi, in qua fuit, antequam esset. Sed istae habitudines non faciunt in ipso compositionem essentialem. Non enim sunt diversae essentiae componentes, sed unius et eiusdem habitudines ad diversa, quae magis in ratione sunt quam in natura. Primum enim principium inter omnia magis multiplex est in habitudinibus relationum, quae proveniunt ex multorum comparatione ad ipsum. Sed tamen, quia istae habitudines non fundantur in ipso, sed in aliis, nullam suae simplicitatis faciunt diminutionem. Sed hoc verum est, quod habitudines esse creati in ipso esse creato fundantur.

Et ideo, licet essentialem non inducant compositionem, faciunt tamen simplicitatis aliquam diminutionem." See the parallel texts at *Sent.* 1.2.13 and 1.8.15 ad aliud (B25:68b–69a, 242b). Albert explains how relation is the least real category at *De praedic.* 4.2 (B1:224b–225): relation may have a foundation in things, but its perfection is in reason comparing the things, not in the things related.

26. *De causis et proc. univ.* 2.1.17 (81.68–72): "Secundum autem seipsum nihil est. Propter quod esse suum non est purum in fine puritatis et simplicitatis, sicut est esse primi. Propter quod quidam antiquorum dixerunt, quod esse est proprium primo. Nullum enim sequentium habet esse purum."

27. Ibid., 81.85–82.4: "Primum enim principium non ingreditur essentialiter constitutionem rei alicuius. Propter quod resolutio entium non devenit usque ad primum principium, quando in essentialia fit resolutio. Ex quo sequitur, quod esse dictum de primo principio et esse dictum de secundis non sit univocum. Univocum enim in omnibus his est essentialiter, de quibus praedicatur." At *Super Dion. De div. nom.* 1.62 (C37.1:39.41–48), the same doctrine appears as proof that God's name, "qui est," surpasses human understanding.

28. "Si vero [esse dictum de primo] esset in uno genere cum esse aliorum, sequeretur, quod aliquid esset prius primo principio et simplicius eo, quod absurdum est. Cum ergo primum principium esse dicitur et creata sive causata esse dicuntur, non est ibi communitas nisi per analogiam. Quae communitas in uno est per se et proprie, in aliis autem per imitationem illius" (*De causis et proc. univ.* 2.1.17 [82.11–18]). See the parallel text at *Sent.* 1.8.24 ad 1 (B25:253), and see pp. 32–33 above for analogy through imitation. That procession and this sort of analogy are two ways of putting the same thing is confirmed at *Super Dion. De div. nom.* 4.51 (C37.1:38–45): "Quaedam analoga sunt quorum est respectus ad unum, quod recipitur in eis secundum diversos modos essentiales, sicut ens essentialiter est in substantia et in accidente et medicina in vetula et in sciente artem; sic autem non est respectus rerum ad unum, quod est deus, qui non commiscetur cum eis, sed habent respectum ad ipsum participando aliquid quod est ab ipso. . . ."

29. "Et cum dicitur primum, non habet ad sequentia relationem generis, sed principii. Genus enim omne compositum est, quia aliter ab alio genere non haberet distinctionem. Dictum autem est, quod *esse primum simplex est* et in compositione primum" (*De causis et proc. univ.* 2.1.17 [82.23–27]). See also *Summa* 1.4.19.3 ad 2 (C34.1:95.65–82).

30. *De causis et proc. univ.* 2.1.18 (83.49–53). *Super Dion. De div. nom.* 5.9 (C37.1:308.62–67) specifies that, whereas being is common to God and creature only through the analogy of imitation, created being is common to creatures through the analogy *per prius et posterius*. (Oddly enough, he there contrasts the two sorts of analogy by calling the latter the one "quae consideratur in philosophia"; yet, on his reading of LC, both figure in philosophy.)

31. *Super Dion. De div. nom.* 11.25 (C37.1:423.64–65): "Utrum sit aliqua per-se-vita facta a deo, et similis quaestio est de aliis."

32. *Metaph.* 1.1.2 (C16.1:3.87–4.17): "Simplicia vero sunt prima causata et effluxiones divinae, sicut primum esse, primum subsistere, primum vivere, primum intelligere et huiusmodi, . . . quae Dionysius vocat processiones divinas, eo quod sunt essentiae primae simplices a deo procedentes, in quibus tota mundi fundatur universitas." It begins to look as though Thomas Aquinas had Albert in mind when he rejected "esse participato communiter in omnibus existentibus, sicut loquitur Dionysius" as a possible interpretation of LC's first created thing (see n. 11). Not that Thomas need have known *De causis et proc. univ.*, since he had heard and indeed transcribed Albert's Dionysian lectures in his student days; see C37.1:vi-viii.

33. *Super Dion. De div. nom.* 11.25–26 (C37.1:423.63–69, 424.39–45): "Quaeratur, utrum sit aliqua per-se-vita facta a deo, et similis quaestio est de aliis. Et videtur, quod non. Quod enim nullo modo est nisi in alio, illud non potest dici per se esse; sed vita procedens per creationem a deo non est nisi recepta in rebus viventibus. . . . Ad primum ergo dicendum, quod ipse non intendit ponere, quod natura vitae habeat esse naturale per se separatum ab inferioribus, sicut posuit Plato, sed quod habet per se esse naturae, quae etiam habet aliquod esse destructis omnibus inferioribus, quia accidit sibi habere esse in hoc vel in illo, ut probat Avicenna." See also *Metaph.* 1.1.2 (C16.1:4.89–93): "Talia etiam licet sint causata divina et processiones simplices, non tamen esse habent extra materiam, sicut dixit Plato, et ideo ista sensibilia non fundantur in ipsis per modum illum quem Plato induxit." For Ibn Sīnā's proof, see p. 25 above.

34. *Sufficientia* 1.7 (ed. Venice, 1508, folio 17vb), cited at *Super Dion. De div. nom.* 5.32 (C37.1:322.17–38): "Potest enim esse creatum primum, quam appellat Dionysius processionem unam, considerari tripliciter: aut per comparationem ad principium, a quo fluit, et sic est una; potest etiam considerari secundum propriam rationem, secundum scilicet quod est ut in via egrediendi a principio, antequam suscipiatur in rebus, et sic iterum est una. Sed cum utroque istorum modorum accipiatur ut communis, non faciet esse; non enim constituit aliquid in esse, nisi secundum quod particulatur per receptionem ipsius in aliquo. . . . Et haec erit tertia consideratio ipsius esse, secundum quod hoc modo particulatum est. Non tamen est intelligendum, quod esse creatum sit aliquid unum habens esse, nec in essentia primi principii nec in via veniendi ad res, sicut improbat Avicenna de natura, sed habet esse tantum tertio modo, secundum quod est particulatum in hoc vel illo, et primae duae considerationes sunt tantum secundum rationem." See also *Super Dion. De cael. hier.* 13 (C36.1:193.43–46), where, again appealing to Ibn Sīnā, he concludes: "Deus autem non creavit naturam per se, quia non esset, postquam creata esset, cum esse sit suppositi, nec iterum creavit eam in ratione tantum, sed in rebus, in

quibus habet esse et multitudinem...." If, in *De causis et proc. univ.*, Albert usually discusses created *esse* in its second consideration, that is at least partly because LC 4 demands it.

35. "Nihil idem quaesitum est et subiectum in scientia aliqua; deus autem et divina separata quaeruntur in scientia ista; subiecta igitur esse non possunt.... Ideo cum omnibus Peripateticis vera dicentibus dicendum videtur, quod ens est subiectum inquantum ens et ea quae sequuntur ens, inquantum est ens et non inquantum hoc ens, sunt passiones eius" (*Metaph.* 1.1.2 [C16.1:4.39–42, 51–54]). See also *Phys.* 1.3.18 (C4.1:76.37–51) and Ibn Sīnā *Philosophia prima* 1.1–2.

36. *De causis et proc. univ.* 2.1.18 (83.47–48). At least ca. 1250, when commenting on the first procession from God, Albert thought that Dionysius used "esse" for "ens" (*Super Dion. De div. nom.* 5.20 [C37.1:314.65–81]). See also *De IV coaequ.* 1.2.1 ad 2 (B34:321a): "Cum dicitur, Prima rerum creatarum est esse, ponitur *esse* pro ente, sicut dicit ibi Commentator in expositione illius propositionis. Et idem dicit beatus Dionysius in libro de *Divinis nominibus*." ("Commentator in expositione illius propositionis" perhaps refers to LC 17, since *ens* does not appear in LC 4.)

37. Albert does not usually admit this identification; see p. 65 below.

38. For the likeness of intelligence to God, see LC 22 (163.84–85); for its manifold participations, see LC 6, 8, and 15 (101.79–81, 112.78–79, and 144.77–79), and Dionysius *Div. nom.* 5.3 (PG3:817A–B). Albert makes the contrast between perfection and notional simplicity clearest at *Super Dion. De div. nom.* 7.16 (C37.1:349.62–74): "Tenet in illo quod est primum secundum rationem, in quo stat resolutio intellectus, veniens ex compositis secundum rationem in magis simplex, sicut ens est primum, et non tenet in eo quod est primum secundum esse, quia illud oportet esse perfectissimum, et sic oportet, quod in ipso sint omnes perfectiones, quae sunt in omnibus generibus. Et ideo ... huiusmodi primo propinquiora sunt, quae plures participationes habent, sicut intelligentia ..., quamvis remotiora sint ab eo quod est primum secundum rationem." See also 5.6 (306.49–58, commenting on PG3:817A–B), 5.23 (316.10–16), 6.3 (328.75–79), *De causis et proc. univ.* 2.2.28 (122.61–68), and *Phys.* 8.1.15 (C4.2:579.61–65).

39. Such is the doctrine Albert's disciple Ulrich reports: "Cum autem dicimus esse immediatum et primum causatum primi, loquimur de eo, quod est primum secundum ordinem naturalem fluxus a primo principio, quem supra ostendimus esse tantum ipsarum formarum; et inter illas prima forma est esse, quia ipsa est omnium sequentium fundamentum, per cuius determinationem aliae formae constituuntur.... Si autem loquamur de primo secundum ordinem naturalem eorum, quae hoc fluxu constituta sunt in esse completum et determinatum, sic primum creatum est intelligentia" (4.2.1, lines 16–26). See also

Albert *Summa* 2.1.3.3.1 ad 11 (B32:28b–29a), where the twofold interpretation recurs. This interpretation of the first created thing is not entirely unlike that by Ps.-Henry of Ghent (see n. 11); however, Ps.-Henry's brief *quaestiones* establish a twofold interpretation by distinguishing the creation of complete beings from that of things pertaining to their essences, and among these *essentialia*, he gives *esse* no special claim to the predicate *creatum*.

5. Mediation in the Procession of Creatures

1. "Quod enim causat non causante quodam alio ante se, ex nihilo facit omne quod facit.... Actus igitur primae causae proprie creatio est. Esse autem, 'quo res est,' primum est, quod ante se nihil praesupponit. Esse igitur in omnibus quae sunt, primae causae proprius effectus est" (*De causis et proc. univ.* 2.1.13 [75.57–65]). See also 1.2.8, 2.1.17, 2.2.17, and 2.4.9 (34.3–27, 80.73–81.4, 110.6–15, and 163.56–60). For similar reasoning in Aquinas and for his youthful doubts whether this ruled out a "ministerial creation" by creatures, see Paul Pearson, "Creation Through Instruments in Thomas' Sentence Commentary," in *Philosophy and the God of Abraham: Essays in Memory of James A. Weisheipl, OP*, ed. R. James Long, Papers in Mediaeval Studies, 12 (Toronto: Pontifical Institute of Mediaeval Studies, 1991), 147–60.

Readers of Albert's theological works may find these arguments surprising since there he often contends that philosophers cannot know creation (e.g., *Summa* 1.13.53.1 quaest. ad 4 and 2.1.3.2 ad 5 [B31:544b–545a and B32:21]), though he willingly adds philosophical authorities to his theological arguments for creation. Apparently, he thinks that creation is a truth at which philosophers arrive only late in metaphysics (*Phys.* 8.1.4 and 14 [C4.2:556.62–557.16 and 579.41–47] attribute it to "Aristotle's" *De natura deorum*, for which see Weisheipl, "Disclaimers," n. 54, and de Libera, *Albert le Grand*, 72–76), through probable rather than demonstrative arguments (*Sent.* 2.1.8 [B27:22a]), and that their notion of creation needs refining (e.g., *Summa* 1.13.53.2 quaest. 1 ad 4 [B31:549a]). However, this matter would suffice for a separate monograph. See pp. 62–64 below for a similar and, indeed, related situation.

2. In point of fact, al-Ġazālī rejected the thesis that God made only the first creature, and that the other universal causes were created each by the next above it. But perhaps Albert was not far wrong: al-Ġazālī can be read as having adopted many Avicennian positions, although he is usually portrayed as hostile to them; see Richard M. Frank, *Creation and the Cosmic System: Al-Ghazālī & Avicenna*, Abhandlungen der Heidelberger Akademie der Wissenschaften, Philosophisch-historische Klasse, Jg. 1992, Abh. 1 (Heidelberg: Carl Winter, 1992).

3. *De causis et proc. univ.* 1.3.5 (40, especially lines 59–70): "Dicunt, quod media necessaria sunt ad agendum. Ab uno enim primo non est nisi unum. Secunda autem non constituuntur ex uno simplici. Unum enim simplex nec ad speciem nec ad numerum determinat vel ad utrumque. Et hac ratione dicunt dixisse Aristotelem, quod 'oportet cognoscere principia et causas et usque ad elementa,' quia res non perfecte constituitur sine his. Propter quod primo principio addiderunt intelligentias et orbes caelorum et qualitates elementorum, sine quibus res non perfecte constituitur in esse. Primum ergo principium sine his ad agendum videtur imperfectum."

Whereas Albert contrasts Plato with al-Fārābī and Ibn Sīnā, Ibn Rušd thinks Plato the first to have assumed that plurality comes about only through mediators (*Incoherence of the Incoherence*, third metaphysical discussion, 1:107); presumably, Ibn Rušd is looking to passages in the *Timaeus* where the demiurge produces only the immortal and enlists created gods to produce the mortal (41C, 69C). Albert, however, usually takes *Timaeus* 41C — he had no translation of 69C — to describe God's giving intelligences the forms with which they are to inform matter (*De causis et proc. univ.* 1.1.3 [8.36–42], *Metaph.* 1.4.12 [C16.1:64.7–48]); on this reading, created "gods" have a role in generation, which is quite another thing than creation.

4. See above, pp. 17–18. One glossator on Ibn Sīnā's *Šifāʾ* compares this with the doctrine of those Pythagoreans who had the One generate a monad whence proceeds a dyad; for the text, see Henry Corbin, *Avicenna and the Visionary Recital*, trans. Willard R. Trask, Bollingen Series, 66 (New York: Pantheon Books, 1960), 58–59.

5. Ibn Sīnā prefers Ptolemy's to Aristotle's astronomy, which had required between forty-nine and fifty-five movers. He mistakenly credits Ptolemy with discovering the starless outermost sphere (*Philosophia prima* 9.2); actually, Ṯābit b. Qurra added that to the Ptolemaic scheme. See Duhem, 2:205–6 for the cause of this confusion.

6. *Philosophia prima* 9.4. For parallel passages, with more or less significant variations, see *Al-Naǧāt* (Cairo, 1938), 273–78, *Remarks and Admonitions* 2d part, 6th group, §§39–41; *Dānesh-Nāmeh*, metaphysical part, 38–39, and al-Ġazālī 4.3.6 and 5. Al-Fārābī's theory is similar but recognizes only a double creative contemplation: each intelligence save the last produces an intelligence and a sphere by contemplating God and itself; see *Opinions of the Inhabitants of the Virtuous City* 3 for one of his clearer statements. Ibn Sīnā probably thinks of himself, not as disagreeing with al-Fārābī, but as unfolding what al-Fārābī presents less systematically; that may be why some of the parallel passages make no explicit mention of planetary souls, and why he sometimes writes simply that intelligence produces the sphere by contemplating itself, and that, since the self it contemplates has both materiate and formal aspects, so too does the resulting sphere.

7. For a survey of Albert's positive and negative comments on al-Biṭrūǧī, see Angel Cortabarría Beitia, "El Astrónomo Alpetragio en las obras de S. Alberto Magno," *La Ciudad de Dios* 193 (1980): 503–33; idem, "Deux sources arabes de S. Albert le Grand: Al-Bitrūjī et al-Battānī," *Mélanges de l'Institut Dominicain d'Etudes Orientales du Caire* 15 (1982): 31–52. Al-Biṭrūǧī's theory was more complex than the above description, which follows Albert's, would suggest; for Albert's simplifications and partial misunderstandings, see Duhem, 3:327–33.

8. *De causis et proc. univ.* 2.2.17 (110.54–71): "Sunt autem quidam mirabiles homines, qui hunc ordinem negant dicentes omnia immediate fieri divina virtute. Quorum Alpetragius princeps esse videtur, qui sphaeras omnes caelestes a prima causa moveri dicit. Et contra hunc sequuntur duo inconvenientia. Quorum unum est, quod bonitas, quae fluit a primo, omnibus sequentibus sit aeque proportionata. Quod valde inconveniens est. Tertium enim et secundum non unam possunt habere proportionem capacitatis ad simplicitatem bonitatis a primo procedentis. Et similiter est de quarto et quinto, et sic deinceps. Quod autem actum et factum in forma aliqua proprium non habeat actorem et factorem, penitus absurdum est. Actum enim et factum tunc actum et factum est, quando ad formam actoris et factoris est determinatum. Aliter enim nihil esset agens vel generans univoce." Albert agrees with al-Fārābī and Ibn Sīnā that a thing is only imperfectly known without its proximate causes (see the text reproduced in n. 3); his disagreement is with the conclusion they attempt to support with this premise.

Note also the argument—not expressly addressed to al-Biṭrūǧī—at 2.2.29 (123.67–72): "Si aliquis dicat, quod prima causa sive deus in operando medio non indiget, sed omnia facit per seipsum et medio non utitur, ille dicere videtur, quod caeli propter nihil sint et caeli motus et quod deus in natura naturalia non operatur. Quod dictum stultissimum est et eius qui sensu indiget."

Among the "mirabiles homines" following al-Biṭrūǧī's lead, Albert may have placed William of Auvergne; Masnovo (40–41) argues that William refuted "ab uno unum" in part by contending that God is the only true cause and therefore, all the more so, the only creator.

9. Ibid., 1.3.5 (40.71–41.25): "In posse, scire et velle omnimodam habet [primum principium] perfectionem ad agendum.... Media autem ... nec sunt nec potentiam agendi habent nisi a primo.... Unde primum potens est in se et in omnibus secundis nec secundis indiget propter suiipsius impotentiam eo quod potentiam copiose ministrat omnibus secundis. Sed ultima facta mediis indigent eo quod bonitatum, quae sunt a primo, in simplicitate et puritate, qua in primo sunt, non sunt perceptiva. Indigent ergo mediis et determinantibus et componentibus et incrassantibus bonitates, quae sunt a primo, quibus mediis bonitates dictae determinentur et proportionentur eorum possibilitati. Propter

quod etiam Aristoteles in II de caelo et mundo dicit 'quaedam susceptibilia esse bonitatum primi, quaedam autem non, sed susceptibilia sunt bonitatis alicuius quae citra primum est.' Dicit etiam, quod 'quaedam suscipiunt bonitates illas motu uno simplici, quaedam autem non sunt susceptibilia ipsarum nisi motibus pluribus et motibus compositis.'" See also 2.2.2 (95.22–29).

10. The words in brackets do not belong to LC, but Albert's copy apparently included them; see chap. 1 n. 29 for their source and meaning.

11. "Si ergo anima nobilis formata est in principium motus ad formam intelligentiae, oportet, quod anima nobilis formam participet intelligentiae. Non autem participat formam intelligentiae ut intelligentiae nisi per intellectum vel naturam intellectualem. Forma igitur animae nobilis et esse non deducitur ad perfectam speciem motoris nisi mediante intellectualitate. . . . Non autem principium motus est nisi forma determinante et proportionante ipsam ad mobile. Oportet igitur, quod differentia ultima finiens et determinans esse nobilis animae sit ad mobile circulariter inclinatio et proportio. Caelestis autem circulus apud sapientes Arabum '*alatyr*' vocatur. . . . Et hoc est, quod quidam antiquorum dixerunt, quod *prima causa creat animam mediante intelligentia et alatyr*, non quod intelligentia pro medio prima causa utatur, sed quod forma intelligentiae media sit in esse diffinitionis animae, sicut sensibile medium est in esse diffinitionis hominis, cum dicitur vivum sensibile rationale. Et hoc modo terminus in esse animae nobilis est proportio ad alatyr" (*De causis et proc. univ.* 2.1.13 [76.2–30]). The beginning, middle, and end of form or definition figure in Albert's explanation of LC 11 too.

12. Such was his teaching even in the early *Super Dion. De div. nom.* (7.20 ad 5 [C37.1:353.1–6]): "Deus perfecte tribuit esse rebus, nec tamen aliae causae operantes superfluunt, quia oportet aliquid esse quod transmutet materiam et alteret ipsam per contactum; unde concedo, quod non est de necessitate causarum, sed de necessitate operati."

13. Compare Augustine *De Genesi ad litteram* 2.15.30 (PL34:276): "Si aliquid Deus imperfectum fecisse diceretur, quod deinde ipse perficeret, quid reprehensionis haberet ista sententia? Jure autem displiceret, si id quod ab illo inchoatum esset, ab alio diceretur esse perfectum."

14. *De causis et proc. univ.* 2.1.13 (76.39–85); see also *De intell. et int.* 1.1.4 (B9:482a). The last argument gives Albert another way to explain the wording of LC: "Causa prima . . . intellectus universaliter agens est. Et sic dixerunt antiqui Peripatetici, quod *prima causa creat animam* nobilem intellectualem *mediante intelligentia*, non quod intelligentia, quae est causa secunda, utatur pro medio, sed quia lumine eiusdem intellectus agentis, quo constituit intelligentiam, constituit et nobilem animam et hominis animam, in quantum nobilis est in esse naturae intellectualis." In other words, God creates the soul "by means of" his own intellectuality.

Notice that, while Albert acknowledges LC's noble souls to be celestial (*De causis et proc. univ.* 2.1.2 and 11–12 [62.34–38 and 73.27–75.54]), he insists that human souls also have intellectuality and, therefore, a certain nobility: "... anima inferior, quae ignobilis esse dicitur, quamvis forte in suo genere nobilis sit eo quod in aliquo participat nobilitatem superioris et in hoc sit ad imaginem et similitudinem [Genesis 1.26–27] et causae primae et intelligentiae" (ibid., 2.2.35 [128.76–80]). Consequently, he can extend to human souls some of what LC says about celestial souls; indeed, in his psychological and theological works, he does this habitually, often with no mention at all of celestial souls.

15. Ibid., 2.1.13 (77.5–12): "Antiqui dixerunt, quod *prima causa creans animam* nobilem *posuit eam ut stramentum intelligentiae.* Nisi enim strata esset intellectualitate, naturae suae propriae non esset susceptibilis per influxum luminis intelligentiae. Sicut et anima hominis, nisi strata esset formaliter et naturaliter intellectualitate, susceptibilis non esset influxus intelligentiae." See also 2.1.22 (87.42–49), where Albert again speaks of the human soul: "Nec est contrarium, quod Peripatetici dicunt intelligentias irradiare super animas. Hoc enim non est ad esse constitutionem, sed ad irradiationem et virtutis intellectivae perfectionem, ut limpidiori lumine agat intellectus agens et purior efficiatur intellectus possibilis ad recipiendum. In hoc enim *prima causa creans animam ponit eam ut stramentum intelligentiae*. . . ." Speaking as a theologian, Albert adds an interesting "if": "Si volumus salvare quod dicitur in commento libri *Causarum*, dicemus, quod intelligitur, quod intelligentia non sit causa animae rationalis in esse substantiali, sed tantum in forma illuminationum ad bene esse" (*Summa* 2.12.73.1 ad 3 [B33:54a]; cf. *Sent.* 2.1.7 [B27:21]).

16. *De causis et proc. univ.* 2.2.38 (132.60–64): "*Anima* nobilis ut causa *imprimit* in corpora formas *corporeas* et sit *causa corporum* sive formarum corporalium, cum tamen *causata* et formata sit ab *intelligentia* in hoc quod causa est, quamvis sit in substantia a causa prima." The idea is that intelligences illuminate celestial souls with intelligible forms, and the souls move the heavens in such a way as to bring about the instantiation of those forms.

17. Ibid., 1.4.5 (49.39–57): "Procedens distat ab eo a quo procedit, per hoc quod procedens est et diversae essentiae ab eo a quo procedit. Quae diversitas notatur in hoc quod aliud est in ipso 'quod est' et esse. Et si accipiatur immediatum a primo procedens, non potest dici, quod secundum 'id quod est' aliud ante se habeat principium, ex quo sit, sicut elementale principium, per quod constituatur. Tamen secundum 'id quod est' in potentia est et non in actu, antequam sit. In potentia ergo esse differentiam facit a primo esse. Tertium autem ens, quod a primo et secundo est, similiter in potentia est ad secundum. Et hoc magis est in potentia quam secundum. Et sic est de quarto et de quinto et deinceps. Per gradus ergo 'eius quod est' in potentia esse omnia posteriora differunt a primo, et posteriora non eodem modo se habent ad primum. Constat autem,

quod secundum differentiam potentiae differat esse in actu et essentia, quae est in illis. Differunt ergo omnia posteriora et in esse et in essentia." See also 1.3.6, 2.1.6, and 2.2.5 (42.6–30, 66.66–75, and 98.64–80), with the qualification in chap. 6 n. 22 below.

18. Ibid., 1.4.6 (50.2–21): "Forma, qua fluit primum, magis et magis determinatur et coarctatur, secundum quod fluit in secundo vel tertio vel deinceps. Sicut in exemplo diximus de arte, quae a mente artificis fluit in spiritum, de spiritu in organa membrorum, de organis in instrumenta et de instrumentis in materiam exteriorem. In omnibus enim his idem est quod fluit, licet secundum aliud esse sit in primo et secundum aliud in secundo et secundum aliud in tertio et sic deinceps. Et secundum hunc modum dici oportet, quod bonitas fluens a primo sive lumen ad totius materiae illustrationem a primo fluit in intelligentiam et ab intelligentia primi ordinis fluit in eam quae est ordinis secundi, et sic deinceps, et ab intelligentia qualibet in proprium orbem et ab ultimo orbe in sphaeram activorum et passivorum et a sphaera activorum et passivorum in centrum cuiuslibet entis, in quo sicut virtus formativa materiam format ad speciem. Hic enim est ordo, quem omnes posuerunt Peripatetici." See also 2.2.35 (128.12–31).

When Albert specifies that goodness flows into the *center* of each being, he apparently wants to insure that his readers not reduce the divine artisan and the intelligences to the level of human artisans. For, human artisans confer accidental forms which, as it were, cleave to the outside of things—Antiphon notes that a buried bedstead would sprout twigs, not bedsteads (Aristotle *Ph.* 193a13–17)—whereas the light of an intelligence penetrates the inmost recesses of matter and thoroughly transforms it with substantial form (*De causis et proc. univ.* 2.2.12 [105.77–106.12]; *Super Dion. De div. nom.* 11.19 [C37.1:420.18–37]; *Metaph.* 11.3.2 [C16.2:536.88–94]). According to Albert, Plato and Ibn Sīnā fail to see this, since they describe an impressing of forms on matter from outside, from a "giver of forms," and overlook the preexistence of forms within matter, in its potency; as Albert argues, such induction of form entails no transformation of matter or consequent unity of matter with form, any more than does impressing a gold signet on wax, which remains mere wax (*Metaph.* 11.1.8 [470.31–471.7], alluding to Aristotle *De an.* 424a18–23). Not that Albert has anything against calling God a giver of forms. Rather, his objection is to the view that the emanation of forms from God into matter precludes their eduction from matter (see pp. 15–16 above).

19. Perhaps Augustine's distinction between morning knowledge of a creature in God and evening knowledge of a creature in itself (*De Genesi ad litteram* 4.22.39–4.32.50) has come to Albert's mind.

20. Albert leaves it up to his readers how they want to understand this form. In *De causis et processu universitatis*, he insists only that intelligences themselves,

while they may be proper movers of the spheres, cannot be their proximate movers, because intelligence, as Anaxagoras says, is separate, whereas mover and moved must be together (Aristotle *Ph.* 7.2); furthermore, since the spheres move naturally, not accidentally, their conjoined movers must be naturally conjoined; consequently, these proximate movers must be the forms of the spheres. But, despite Albert's openness to various theories, he makes no secret of his dislike for Ibn Sīnā's suggestion that the forms are souls with faculties of imagination and choice. Apparently, Albert prefers to think of the forms as irradiations of intellectual light from the intelligences; and since form gives being, upon which follows motion, these irradiations give the spheres their circular motion and may be called "souls," though that is stretching the word (*De causis et proc. univ.* 1.4.7, 2.2.1, 2.2.36, and 2.3.2 [53.3–55.61, 92.50–61, 129.30–130.29, and 140.41–50]). The neat distinction between celestial intelligences and celestial souls, which cannot be missed in LC or the writings of Ibn Sīnā, cannot be found in Aristotle's works, so that Albert, when commenting on the *Metaph.*, dismisses it and allows only intellectual souls as celestial movers (*Metaph.* 11.3.6 [C16.2:540.83–84]); see p. 61 below for the notably less transcendent theology which results.

21. *Metaph.* 11.2.20 (C16.2:508.37–41). The same doctrine appears at *De causis et proc. univ.* 2.2.14 (107.36–50, 90–108.19), though obscurely; there it is stated in terms of intelligences receiving power from the first cause, but not in its original purity; rather, the power is mixed with potency and privation, because intelligences are from nothing and in potency to their causes.

22. See above, pp. 38–40. While Albert's account of the intelligences does not exactly match that of the ancient Neoplatonists, it now appears that *intelligentia* as concept and *intelligentia* as separate substance have rather more to do with each other than one might have thought.

23. *Metaph.* 11.3.6 (C16.2:540.41–43, 66–67): "Contemplationem enim dicunt esse luminis irradiationem, et lumen illud dicunt factivum substantiarum.... Contemplatio ista est in lumine universaliter activo, quod per seipsum causa est entis." Intellectual light must be what causes being, since beings are intelligible (*De causis et proc. univ.* 1.2.1 and 1.4.5 [26.17–28 and 48.45–51]).

24. *Probl. determ.* 7 (C17.1:51.36–44): "Philosophia enim ponit in ordine naturae semper superius esse causam inferioris et causalitatem primi ad ultimum non devenire nisi per media, quibus approximatur et contrahitur et determinatur lumen primi, ut proportionetur ultimo, cum expresse probatum sit in Libro de causis ultimum non esse perceptibile bonitatum primi, prout sunt in primo, nisi per media determinentur"; *De causis et proc. univ.* 2.5.18 (184.3–10): "Movere possent [bonitates divinae] modo illo quo desideratum movet desiderium. Quod non fieret, si in simplicitate et puritate luminis divini remanerent. Sic enim excellerent omne desiderium et omnem appetitum. Et nihil secundorum posset ad ipsas. Propter quod etiam nihil secundorum desideraret eas, quia, sicut dicit

Aristoteles in I ethicorum [1094ª21], 'non potest esse inane naturale desiderium.'" Reception according to the mode of the recipient figures throughout LC; the principle of mean terms is clearest in LC 18, 29, and 30. Albert finds the principle of mean terms in Aristotle *Gen. Corr.* 331ª24 and *Hist. An.* 588b4–6, and in Dionysius *Div. nom.* 7.3 and *Epist.* 8.3 (PG3:872B, 1093A) as well; indeed, he repeatedly alludes to Dionysius while explaining LC 18 (*De causis et proc. univ.* 2.3.15, 16, and 18 [152.83–88, 153.73–154.3, and 155.26–28]).

25. See *Sent.* 2.15.3, *Super Dion. De div. nom.* 4.44 (C37.1:150.33–151.8), *De caelo et mundo* 2.3.11 (C5.1:166.77–167.29), and *Metaph.* 11.2.25, with the discussion in Duhem, 3:337–44. Albert mistakenly attributes this theory to Ptolemy and Māšā'allāh. Still, however great their authority, he doubts that any mortal has ever comprehended all celestial motions; the "Ptolemaic" theory, while more reasonable than others, is hardly certain (*Metaph.* 11.2.25 [C16.2:516.7–12]; *De causis et proc. univ.* 1.4.8 [56.84–90]; compare Aristotle *Metaph.* 1073ª10–17).

26. For confirmation that "ab uno unum" was what caused al-Fārābī and Ibn Sīnā to distinguish God from the mover of the outermost sphere, see Ibn Sīnā *Philosophia prima* 9.4 (479.4–481.42); Ibn Rušd *Incoherence*, third metaphysical discussion (1:107–8); idem, short commentary on Aristotle's *Metaph.*, 4.54; idem, large commentary on Aristotle's *Metaph.*, 12.44; Albert *Metaph.* 11.2.17 (C16.2:504.78–505.2); and Thomas Aquinas *In duodecim libros Metaphysicorum Aristotelis expositio* 12.9 (ed. M.-R. Cathala and R. M. Spiazzi [Turin: Marietti, 1977], §2559). Davidson (*Alfarabi, Avicenna, and Averroes*, 224–31) traces the evolution of Ibn Rušd's thought on the issue. See also Davidson's *Proofs for Eternity, Creation and the Existence of God in Medieval Islamic and Jewish Philosophy* (Oxford: Oxford University Press, 1987), 281–83, for ancient authors on the distinction between mover and cause of existence.

Relatively little has been written about Albert's attitude toward it, but see W. B. Dunphy, "St. Albert and the Five Causes," *Archives d'histoire doctrinale et littéraire du moyen âge* 33 (1966): 7–21; Alfredo Franchi, "Alberto Magno e le origini della nozione di causalità efficiente: La teoria delle cinque cause nei *quidam* del V *Metaphysicorum*," *Sapienza* 33 (1980): 178–85; Etienne Gilson, "Avicenne et les origines de la notion de cause efficiente," in *Atti del XII Congresso Internazionale di Filosofia (Venezia, 12–18 Settembre 1958)*, vol. 9, *Aristotelismo padovano e filosofia aristotelica* (Florence: Sansoni, 1960), 121–30; idem, "Notes pour l'histoire de la cause efficiente," *Archives d'histoire doctrinale et littéraire du moyen âge* 29 (1962): 7–31. For the Avicennian background, consult Jean Jolivet, "La répartition des causes chez Aristote et Avicenne: Le sens d'un déplacement," in *Lectionum Varietates: Hommage à Paul Vignaux (1904–1987)*, ed. J. Jolivet, Z. Kaluza, and A. de Libera, Etudes de Philosophie Médiévale, 65 (Paris: J. Vrin, 1991), 49–65; for Albert's influence, see Faes de Mottoni, "Distinzione," and Alain de Libera, "Ulrich de Strasbourg, lecteur d'Albert le Grand," *Freiburger Zeitschrift für Philosophie und Theologie* 32 (1985): 105–36.

27. *Metaph.* 1072^{b}28–29: φαμὲν δὴ τὸν θεὸν εἶναι ζῷον ἀΐδιον ἄριστον. Ulrich, showing somewhat less patience than Albert, calls this sphere-worship idolatry (4.3.1, transcribed in Faes de Mottoni, p. 354, lines 18–26).

28. One particularly interesting instance occurs at *Super Dion. De div. nom.* 2.44 (C37.1:73.9–11), where the tenth intelligence apparently moves both the moon and the terrestrial sphere; this would enable Albert to keep his circle of the signs without needing to introduce an eleventh intelligence. Even when he does posit eleven, he habitually calls the last the tenth.

29. At *Phys.* 8.1.15 (C4.2:579.61–580.1), Albert contrasts the outermost sphere, as the first corporeal effect, with intelligence, which is the first effect according to the order of nature, and with *esse*, which is first as the term of all resolution. He makes a similar division at *De caelo et mundo* 2.2.6 (C5.1:139.11–29).

30. Albert does use the Avicennian scheme at *Metaph.* 1.3.13 (C16.1:43.65–78), but only by way of contrasting how little Anaxagoras made of the intelligence he posited, not as part of a discussion of celestial movers.

31. However, at *De causis et proc. univ.* 1.4.8 (57.10–13), he does make the barest mention of a theory that the first substance is a spherical body.

32. See Ulrich *Summa de bono* 2.2.2 and 4.3.1, transcribed in Faes de Mottoni, "Distinzione," p. 346, lines 32–40, and p. 355, lines 62–66.

Despite Albert's assurance that the identification of God with the mover of the outermost sphere "is certainly the meaning of Aristotle's words . . . in *On the Heavens*," when he comments on *Cael.* 288^{b}3–5 ("causa enim prima est, quae movet causatum primum"), he gives it an Avicennian interpretation by taking "causa prima" to be, not the absolutely first cause (God), but the first of the natural causes, of the causes proportioned to their effects (intelligence; *De caelo et mundo* 2.2.6 [C5.1:138.40–70]). Perhaps Albert's grasp of the differences between Aristotle and his many followers grew firmer with time; or perhaps, when a text to be expounded was not primarily metaphysical, Albert felt free to update it and maximize its intelligibility by introducing what he considered Aristotle's mature opinion. At any rate, indiscriminately mixing texts from Albert's many philosophical works turns out to be potentially as misleading as carelessly combining philosophical with theological passages.

33. *De somno et vig.* 3.1.12 (B9:195b): "Physica enim tantum suscepimus dicenda, plus secundum Peripateticorum sententiam persequentes ea quae intendimus, quam etiam ex nostra scientia aliquid velimus inducere: si quid enim forte propriae opinionis haberemus, in theologicis magis quam in physicis, Deo volente, a nobis proferetur."

34. *Probl. determ.* 1 (C17.1:46.86–48.21) and *Sent.* 2.2.1 and 2.14.6 (B27:45b and 266a). These last two texts claim that, while philosophers posited intelligences to move the heavens, the astronomers—including Ptolemy, al-Battānī, Abū Maʿšar, and Ǧābir b. Aflaḥ—thought like Albert that God's will moved them.

One theological text appears to deny that God moves anything: at *Super Dion. De div. nom.* 7.20 (C37.1:352.38–40), Albert writes, "Dicimus enim, quod causa prima non est motor primus, quia ille est proportionatus suo mobili, sed est causa universi esse." However, earlier in the same work, he approves Aristotle's "causa enim prima est, quae movet causatum primum" (4.44 [150.28–32]). Either Albert is vacillating or—what is more likely given the context—he is somewhat awkwardly denying, not that God is the first mover, but that he is the sort of first mover philosophers had in mind, namely, one who bestows motion and form but not the matter subject to them; see also 8.6 (368.3–5).

35. *De causis et proc. univ.* 1.4.8, 2.2.1, and 2.5.24 (58.19–29, 92.10–34, and 191.30–192.6), *Sent.* 2.2.1 and 2.3.3 (B27:45b and 65), *Probl. determ.* 2–7 (C17.1:48.25–51.45), and *Summa* 2.2.7 (B32:132, 134b–135) and 2.11.53.3 (B32:567–68b). In certain passages from his early works, Albert shows himself less unwilling to identify intelligences with angels; for his evolution, see the prolegomena to his *Summa* (C34.1:viii) and Loris Sturlese, *Die deutsche Philosophie im Mittelalter: Von Bonifatius bis zu Albert dem Großen (748–1280)* (Munich: C. H. Beck, 1993), 350–62. For historical background, see Karl Allgaier, "Engel und Intelligenzen: Zur arabisch-lateinischen Proklos-Rezeption," in *Orientalische Kultur und europäisches Mittelalter*, ed. Albert Zimmermann and Ingrid Craemer-Ruegenberg, Miscellanea Mediaevalia, 17 (Berlin: Walter de Gruyter, 1985), 172–87.

6. God's Immediacy to the Procession of Creatures

1. "The first is self-sufficient and is most sufficient" (LC 20 [Bardenhewer 182.16]). For the linguistic peculiarities, see above, chap. 1 n. 52; despite these, Albert understands the text correctly, paraphrasing "*dives maius vel ditius omnibus*" (*De causis et proc. univ.* 2.4.6 [160.42]) or attaching a Dionysian "super-" to "dives."

2. Ibid., 2.4.2 (157.44–46). Here Albert is trying to explain LC 19 (158.83–84), with its misleading "propter magnitudinem suae largitatis"; LC's author was actually speaking of the recipients' nobility, not of God's generosity (see above, chap. 1 n. 47). How, though, can Albert reconcile talk of divine generosity with the rest of LC 19? Does not the notion of inequalities caused by divine generosity

contradict the teaching that God's efflux is single? Albert would indeed translate 158.83–84 "some receive more than others, and this is on account of the greatness of God's generosity," but he does not say that divine generosity causes inequalities. Notice the final clause of his paraphrase: "*Quaedam enim eorum recipiunt plus quam quaedam alia*, quae minus recipiunt. Huius autem causa *est magnitudo largitatis* eius, ad quam non omnia aequalem habent capacitatem" (2.4.4 [158.65–68]). By the addition of this clause, Albert's interpretation, despite his almost inevitable mistake about "propter magnitudinem suae largitatis," rejoins the anonymous author's intention: the point becomes, not that God is more generous with some than with others, but that his generous outpouring surpasses every capacity and surpasses different capacities to different extents.

3. See p. 18 above. Albert's readers must study his language closely, as when he denies that a thing's essence is *a se*: "Quod autem anima fons vitae sit, non habet a se. . . . Adhuc autem, ab intelligentia habere non potest sicut a prima causa. Intelligere enim est vivere, et agere secundum intellectum est agere vitae actionem. Intelligentia autem non a se habet, quod intelligentia est" (ibid., 2.3.11 [148.36–46]). Compare *Super Dion. De div. nom.* 9.7 and 13.5 (382.9–23 and 434.79–435.3), where Albert distinguishes *per se*, as referring to a thing's intrinsic principles, from *a se*, which has to do with efficient causality.

Siger of Brabant wrongly accuses Albert of equivocating on *ex* and on *per* and so of missing this distinction between intrinsic, formal causes and extrinsic, efficient causes: see Siger's *Quaestiones in Metaphysicam*, introductio, quaestio 7 (Clm 9559, 44.96–6, and Peterhouse 152, 32.80–86), and chap. 2 n. 14 above. His mistake is perhaps excusable, given Albert's fluid terminology: the latter sometimes uses *a se* like *per se*, and sometimes *ex se* like *a se* (*De causis et proc. univ.* 1.1.8 and 2.3.11 [17.1–11 and 148.63–64]).

4. Like his contemporaries in the Latin West, Albert had no information about the man Ibn Gabirol; he thought him an Arab. William of Auvergne, noting Ibn Gabirol's teaching on the *verbum* (in the latter's usage, another name for the divine will; see *Fons vitae* 5.36 [322.23 and 323.17]), took him for a Christian Arab (*De universo* 1.1.26, in *Guilielmi Alverni Opera omnia* [Paris: apud Andraeam Pralard, 1674; reprint, Frankfurt am Main: Minerva, 1963], 621A–C).

5. Ibn Gabirol acknowledges that the divine will, when considered in itself, is infinite and identical with the divine essence; yet he asserts that, when considered as acting, that will is a finite intermediary between God and form (1.7, 3.57, 4.19, 4.37, 4.39 [9.28–10.4; 205.23–206.2; 252.19–253.4; 325.23–24; 328.4]).

6. So *De causis et proc. univ.* 1.2.8 (34.30–31); 1.3.2 (37.38–39) adds appetite, but that, Albert always insists, follows upon cognition.

7. 2.22. See Arthur Hyman, "Maimonides on Creation and Emanation," in *Studies in Medieval Philosophy*, 45–61.

8. Albert's point is that the uncaused cause cannot be caused in respect of his knowledge; in fact, even describing his Ideas as principles of his knowing is speaking loosely. Rather, his Ideas are really one Idea, which is really identical with his absolutely simple essence. Thus, he knows diverse things without diversity in his knowing. If philosophers and theologians commonly speak of his Ideas in the plural, that is because the creatures he knows are really and variously related to him by unilateral relations. Albert explains this at length in *De causis et proc. univ.* 1.2.3–7; see also chap. 4 nn. 19 and 24 above.

9. Ibid., 1.2.6, after Ibn Rušd, large commentary on Aristotle's *Metaph.*, 12.51; Ibn Rušd makes this point against Ibn Sīnā (according to whom God knows particulars universally) in *Incoherence* 13 (1:275–81). See p. 42 above for the distinction between divine Ideas and predicable universals.

10. Human minds grasp only the applicability of universals to individuals; in other words, we know individuals as instances of universals, not as individuals. Thus, when trying to make an individual known, we classify him in various ways. We may narrow the field enough for practical purposes: our friend falls under the groups "residents of Ohio," "professors of mathematics," "amateur pilots," and "members of Dan Quayle's high school class." Still, we find no reason why two individuals cannot share all those characteristics. What causes our ignorance of individuals? We know things by abstracting their form from their matter; the matter, the principle of individuation, we leave behind, which means that we have in our minds no likeness of matter by which to know it; like Aristotle, we can only suggest what matter is by negations and analogies.

11. *De causis et proc. univ.*, 2.2.44 (138.3–7); see also *Super Dion. De div. nom.* 2.79 and 4.62 (C37.1:93.61–63 and 170.74–171.8). At *Super Dion. De div. nom.* 7.3 and 20 (339.1–51 and 352.25–47), Albert denies that the philosophers knew this — as, indeed, many did not; his varying estimate of their achievements corresponds to his judgments that the philosophers knew nothing of creation and that some philosophers reached probable knowledge of it. For "shadow," see chap. 2 n. 21 above; here, the point would be that the substratum is proportioned to the form.

12. *De causis et proc. univ.* 2.5.2 (170.66–71); see also 2.2.14 (107.42–56) and the text reproduced in chap. 3 n. 16 above.

13. Ibid., 2.4.12 (165.38–48). Quite possibly, God's production of one essence under the shadow of another is how Albert understands the emanation of celestial intelligences, souls, and bodies (see above, pp. 58–59); contraction of irradiation, after all, amounts to the same thing as shadow. And how else could Albert understand this emanation? For he denies that creatures can create (p. 53) and even that they constitute in determinate natures the bare existences God creates (p. 56). For these reasons, Ulrich (4.2.9, transcribed in Faes de Mottoni, pp. 348–49, lines 55–86) interprets this emanation in terms of formal causality, just

as Albert interprets God's creation of the soul "mediante intelligentia et alatyr" (pp. 55–56 above), so that celestial intelligences, souls, and bodies have only God for the efficient cause of their constitution. *De causis et proc. univ.* 2.2.14 (107.90–108.19) suggests the correctness of Ulrich's interpretation, although, as usual, Albert's explanations have none of the clarity of Ulrich's.

14. Ibid., 2.1.7 (68.50–51): "Per esse suum causae sunt. Aliter enim non essent primariae."

15. William of Auvergne, his belief in divine simplicity notwithstanding, also seems to envision a somewhat more than logical distinction between two divine attributes when he claims that the divine will invalidates "ab uno unum"; God, he says, creates through his will, not as one: "Quod ergo dicunt, quia ex uno secundum quod est unum, et per id, quod est unum omni modo, et cetera non pertinet ad creatorem in causationibus, et creationibus istis. Non enim operatur creator haec causata, vel causat per id, quod unum, aut inquantum unum sed per voluntatem suam, et prout vult" (*De universo* 1.1.27 [1:624aE]).

16. *De causis et proc. univ.* 1.3.1–2, especially 35.21–49, where Albert distinguishes four kinds of necessity and shows how they come from the four causes, none of which God has.

17. Ibid., 2.4.14 (167.19–38): "Ab uno non est nisi unum. . . . Si enim dicatur, quod hoc est verum in per essentiam agentibus et non in his quae agunt per voluntatem, hoc absurdum est. In primo enim idem est voluntas quod essentia. Et sicut primum invariabile est secundum essentiam, ita invariabile est secundum voluntatem. Sicut ergo adhuc sequitur, quod ab uno non sit nisi unum, sic a voluntate, quae nullo modo diversificatur secundum volita, non est nisi unum. Voluntas enim volens hic et hoc, secundum volita variata est. Similiter voluntas volens hic nunc et volens hoc non nunc, sed tunc, secundum dispositionem volitorum variata est. In eo autem in quo nulla vicissitudo est, talis variatio esse non potest. Quin immo sicut sciens se sicut omnis rei principium scit omne quod est, ita volens se ut omnis rei principium vult omne quod est. Fluxus ergo ille nec a se nec ex parte causae, a qua fluit, potest aliquam habere diversitatem." See also *Metaph.* 3.3.15 and 11.3.7 (C16.1:155.5–12 and C16.2:542.7–29), and *Super Dion. De div. nom.* 4.9 (C37.1:118.15–22): "Inquantum est perfecta, oportet, quod in ipsa secundum veritatem harum rationum sint omnia quae sunt nobilitatis, ut vita, sapientia, voluntas et huiusmodi, inquantum vero habet simplicitatem summam, oportet, quod quidlibet horum idem sit alteri secundum rem. Et ideo agere secundum essentiam in ipso est agere secundum suam voluntatem et secundum suam sapientiam. . . ." Contrast ibid., 9.6 (381.50–62), *Super Dion. De cael. hier.* 1 (C36.1:10.11–36), and *Summa* 2.1.3.3.1 (B32:26), where Albert restricts the application of "ab uno unum" to agents acting from natural necessity; *Metaph.* 11.2.2 (484.72–89) has it that an intellectual *unum* acting by its

essence produces many things but through the simple act of moving the outermost sphere.

Christians sometimes distinguish creation from intra-Trinitarian procession as a work of God's will from a work of his nature (John of Damascus *De fide orthodoxa* 1.8 [PG94:813A]); this distinction between works of will and works of nature comes from human life—the artist wills to paint or sculpt things of various sorts, while his *natura* produces a *natus* like him in species—and cannot be pressed in the case of God, whose nature and will are not really distinct (*De IV coaequ.* 1.1.5 [B34:314]; *Sent.* 2.1.8 ad quaest. [B27:22a]).

18. *De causis et proc. univ.* 1.3.1 (36.20–34): "Per hoc quod dicitur, quod non sit in ipso agere et non agere, nihil probatur. Hoc enim dupliciter dicitur. Non esse enim in aliquo agere et non agere potest esse per obligationem ad unum et impossibilitatem ad alterum. Alio modo potest esse per libertatem ad unum et ad alterum. Sed quia melius est esse unum quam alterum, propter hoc non transponitur de uno in alterum. Sicut in casto est caste agere et non caste et in liberali dare et non dare. Sed quia melius est caste agere et liberaliter dare quam non caste agere et avare retinere, ideo non transponitur castus et liberalis in oppositum suae actionis. Et sic agere et non agere quidem est in primo, sed non potest non agere, quia melius est emittere bonitates quam retinere, et minimum inconveniens in primo impossibile est." See also *Metaph.* 11.2.2 (C16.2:484.98–485.16), as well as *Summa* 1.13.55.1 quaest. 1 (B31:556 and 558), where three of the four objections are from Dionysius.

19. See the first text in n. 17 above, and *De causis et proc. univ.* 2.5.17 (182.20–25): "Nec in opere umquam recipit vicissitudinem per sui transitum de opere in opus. Quin potius sciendo se, ut principium omnium est, facit universa. Et cum de scibili non transeat ad scibile, non vicissitudinatur in opere."

20. Outside of *De causis et proc. univ.*, see *Super Dion. De div. nom.* 2.46 (C37.1:74.28–33): "Quamvis ex parte primi omnia immediate producat, eo quod ex parte ipsius non est accipere aliquam diversitatem, causata tamen ex parte eorum non aeque immediate procedunt ab ipso, immo, sicut dicit Augustinus, aliquid fecit prope se et aliquid prope nihil."

21. *De causis et proc. univ.* 2.2.37 (131.1–29), *De unitate intell.* 3.2 (C17.1:28.40–48), and more clearly, *Super Dion. De div. nom.* 3.7 (C37.1:105.74–82): "Secundum philosophiam loquendo causa diversitatis est materia cum quantitate. Ex quantitate enim materia sortitur diversum situm, et secundum diversum situm partium eius recipit diversas formas; quae enim perfecte proportionatur prope motum caeli, cuius est inflammare et dissolvere, recipit caliditatem et raritatem et formam nobiliorem, quae est forma ignis, et secundum quod plus elongatur, recipit formam minus nobilem."

22. *De causis et proc. univ.* 2.1.14 (77.64–69, 78.31–62), on the question "unde habeat anima, quod anima est" (a question presupposing the distinction

between *a se* and *per se* discussed in n. 3 above): "Distantia enim non est nisi per similitudinis privationem. . . . Et si distantia causa erit esse animae, sequitur necessario, quod privatio sit causa esse alicuius, quod penitus absurdum est. . . . Ad quod dicendum esse videtur, quod effluxus sive processus primae causae forma est, quae ipso processu a causa prima secunda efficitur et per hoc quod secunda est, distans efficitur et in diversitate essentiae a prima causa ponitur, quia nihil distans a prima causa eiusdem essentiae est cum ipsa. Sic autem distans minoris efficitur potentiae ad agendum et maioris potentiae ad fieri sive patiendum, secundum quod communiter omnem receptibilitatem passivam potentiam esse dicimus. Nihilominus quidquid habet esse et virtutis, habet a causa prima. Et tale esse formae sic distantis et in potentialitatem actae causa est esse animae. . . . Processus igitur talis non in quantum distans causat esse animae, sed in quantum virtus primae causae in tali processu procedit in effectum et efficitur operans in ipso. Idem voluerunt dicere, qui potentialitatem causam esse dixerunt, non quod potentialitas causa sit, sed quod causa sit processus sive forma procedens per distantiam subacta potentialitati." See p. 57 above for the differentiation of beings by degree of potentiality.

23. Ibid., 2.4.12 (166.38–44). See also *Super Dion. De div. nom.* 2.46, 3.7, 4.9, 4.63, and 8.18–19 (C37.1:74.51–65, 105.74–85, 118.35–52, 172.13–41, and 374.32–375.24), where Albert distinguishes such causes of diversity as spatial distance, secondary causes, divine wisdom, and in the spiritual life, diversity of nature, of guilt, and of effort. While *sapientia* appears nowhere in LC, Albert includes it in his account of Peripatetic theology, apparently because Aristotle, in *Metaph.* Λ, presents God as the cosmic ruler who is thought thinking thought (ibid., 4.9 [118.20–25]; cf. chap. 2 n. 20 above).

Ulrich (4.1.6) tries to divide the causes of diversity according to Aristotle's four causes; in doing so he goes beyond anything Albert says.

24. *De causis et proc. univ.* 1.4.4 (48.5–26): "Accidens autem, ut probat Aristoteles in VII philosophiae primae, secundum sui naturam potius est esse quam essentia. . . . Et quia per infinitas subiecti occasiones causatur accidens, propter hoc dicit Philosophus, quod id quod per accidens est, . . . reducitur ad unum, quod est subiectum. Et hoc est substantia [*Metaph.* 1028^{a}10–30, 1030^{a}18–^{b}13, 1031^{a}1–14]. Si autem aliquis ex hoc obiceret, quod aliquid est ens, quod non est ab ente primo, patet, quod non sequitur duplici ratione. Una est, quod accidens non simpliciter est ens. Et sic non oportet, quod reducatur ad id quod est principium simpliciter entis. Secunda ratio est, quod accidens, secundum quod est ens, ad primum ens reducitur ut ad principium. 'Quidquid enim est principium principii, est principium principiati.' Diximus autem, quod primum principium est substantiae; substantia autem principium accidentis. Et sic primum ens principium erit accidentis."

25. See, for example, *Sent.* 2.1.6 ad 2 (B27:20). "Concreation" appears as early as Augustine (*Confessions* 13.33, *De Genesi ad litteram* 1.15.29). Ulrich gives it especially clear expression: "Cum accidens non sit essentia absoluta, cuius actus sit esse, sed potius sit esse ipsius substantiae, ipsum proprie non creatur, quia non deducitur ad esse, sed potius substantiae concreatur. . . ." Likewise, when creation is defined as making something from nothing, "nec etiam sumitur 'aliquid' secundum illam communitatem, qua dicit etiam principia substantiae, quae sunt potentia et actus sive materia et forma, et quascumque partes substantiae, quia etiam horum actus non est esse, ad quod creatio terminatur, sed potius dicit substantiam completam et per se existentem, cuius solius actus est esse, ut dicit Philosophus, et omnia praedicta, inquantum pertinent ad hoc esse, sunt huic substantiae concreata" (4.1.7, lines 70–73, 75–81). See also Aquinas *Summa Theol.* 1.45.4 corpus and ad 1.

26. *De causis et proc. univ.* 2.3.13 (150.44–55): "Primum enim in omnibus est ens, quod quia nihil ante se supponit secundum intellectum, necesse est, quod ex nihilo sit. Et ideo in omnibus in quibus est, necesse est ipsum fieri per creationem. Per creationem enim fit, quod ex nihilo fit. Vita autem ante se supponit ens secundum naturam et intellectum et ex esse producitur sicut determinatum ex confuso. Unde vita non dicit simplicem esse conceptum, sed dicit esse formatum ad aliquid. Vita igitur per creationem fieri non potest, quia fit ex aliquo. Relinquitur igitur, quod fiat per informationem. Similiter autem est de intellectivo et scitivo."

While related, the distinctions between creation and concreation and between creation and information are not identical. For one thing, only God creates or concreates, whereas creatures can inform. Again, one may speak of the concreation of matter with a being, but not of the information of a being with matter. Finally, the second distinction is somewhat more abstract: the created is usually distinguished from the concreated as the existent (substance) from what exists in it (its intrinsic principles and its accidents); when distinguishing creation from information, Albert looks, not at the existent, but at the existence whereby it exists, and at the forms whereby it is this or that sort of existent.

27. Ibid., 2.1.17 (81.14–35): "Esse igitur primum est in omnibus illis quae procedunt a primo. . . . Et quia esse virtutem suam influit super omnia sequentia, propter hoc sicut esse actus est entium, ita 'vivere viventibus est esse, et sentire est esse sentientibus, et ratiocinari est esse rationalibus,' ut dicit Aristoteles." See also 2.1.6 (68.29–33), paraphrasing LC 1 (68.77–78): "*Quando secunda causa facit rem* per formam suam, tunc *causa prima . . . influit super rem* eandem esse in quo fundatur formatio causae secundae." The same teaching appears at *Metaph.* 4.1.2 (C16.1:163.9–34).

28. The words "vita est processio procedens ex ente primo quieto, sempiterno, et primus motus" (LC 17 [151.72]) refer, not to God, but to Intellect

before its determination (see p. 10 above); Albert, however, gives them a Dionysian sense: Life is a procession or motion because, besides being three divine names, Being, Life, and Intelligence are three processions from God, though, considered in their divine starting point, they are identical with him.

29. *De causis et proc. univ.* 2.3.10–14. See also 2.1.20 (85.4–8): "Idem ergo principium, quod producit esse ab esse suo increato, per hoc quod vita est, producit esse in vivum; et per hoc quod est sensibilium lux, producit vitam in sensibilibus"; 2.2.17 (110.47–53): "Principium primum *est creans intelligentiam. Et est creans animam* et formans ad intelligentiam. Propter quod dicitur creare animam per intelligentiam. *Et* est creans *naturam* et formans ad animam et intelligentiam. Propter quod dicitur creare naturam per *intelligentiam* et animam. Et sic descendendo creans et formans est usque ad ultimum"; 2.2.28 (122.69–73): "Et est mirabile videre opus primi, quod propter suam perfectionem nihil priorum reliquit, quin deduxerit ipsum in postremum, ut perfectum sit; et nihil posteriorum fecit, quod in primis non incohaverit, ut sic sit et principium et finis." *Super Dion. De div. nom.* 3.4 (C37.1:103.38–39) is particularly interesting, if brief: "Secundum primam productionem eorum [donorum] informatio rei pertineat ad creationem."

30. Contrast Thomas. Both Albert and Thomas find similarities between LC and *Div. nom.*, and both make use of *Div. nom.* when explaining LC, but they justify that procedure differently. Thomas rightly attributes the similarities to the Platonism of both texts, whereas Albert believes that Peripatetic and Dionysian theology converge—a belief reflected in the many parallels between *De causis et proc. univ.* and *Super Dion. De div. nom.*, despite the fifteen or twenty years separating their composition. Not that Albert failed to recognize Platonic traits in Dionysius, but such thinkers as Ibn Sīnā shared them while remaining basically Peripatetic.

31. Cristina D'Ancona Costa, in her *Recherches* (16, 65–72, 124, and 147–52), detects influence, whether direct or indirect, of Dionysius on LC's author. While not impossible, the thesis requires additional evidence. (Readers without access to her *Recherches* may find the material from pp. 65–72 and 147–52 in *Archives d'histoire doctrinale et littéraire du moyen âge* 59 [1992]: 41–62 and *Recherches de théologie ancienne et médiévale* 59 [1992]: 41–85.)

Afterword

1. Porphyry *On the Life of Plotinus and the Order of His Books* 14.4–7, in *Plotinus*, trans. A. H. Armstrong, Loeb Classical Library, 440 (Cambridge: Harvard University Press, and London: William Heinemann, 1966), 1:41.

Selected Bibliography

Primary Sources

Aegidius Romanus. *Super Librum de causis*. Venice: apud Iacobum Zoppinum, 1550. Reprint, Frankfurt am Main: Minerva GmbH, 1968.

Albertus Magnus. *De causis et processu universitatis a prima causa*. Basel, Öffentliche Bibliothek der Universität, MS F.I.21, 140ra–192va [fourteenth century; microfilm]; Lilienfeld, Stiftsbibliothek, MS 209, 1ra–62va [fourteenth century; microfilm]; Paris, MS BN lat. 15449, 2ra–51va [late thirteenth century; microfilm].

——. *Opera Omnia*. Ed. Augustus and Aemilius Borgnet. 38 vols. Paris: Vivès, 1890–99.

——. *Opera Omnia*. Ed. Institutum Alberti Magni Coloniense. Münster: Aschendorff, 1951–.

——. "Die Universitätspredigten des Albertus Magnus." Ed. Bernhard Geyer. *Sitzungsberichte: Bayerische Akademie der Wissenschaften: Philosophisch-Historische Klasse* 1966, Heft 3.

——. *Speculum astronomiae*. Ed. Stefano Caroti, Michela Pereira e Stefano Zamponi sotto la direzione di Paola Zambelli. Quaderni di storia e critica della scienza, n.s., 10. Pisa: Domus Galilaeana, 1977.

——. *Commentaire de la "Théologie mystique" de Denys le pseudo-aréopagite suivi de celui des épîtres I–V*. Introduction, traduction, notes et index par Edouard-Henri Wéber. Sagesses chrétiennes. Paris: Les Editions du Cerf, 1993.

Albertus Magnus and Thomas Aquinas. *Albert & Thomas: Selected Writings*. Ed. and trans. Simon Tugwell, with a preface by Leonard E. Boyle. Classics of Western Spirituality. New York: Paulist Press, 1988.

Apuleius. *Opuscules philosophiques ("Du dieu de Socrate," "Platon et sa doctrine," "Du monde") et fragments [par] Apulée*. Texte établi, traduit et commenté par

Jean Beaujeu. Collection des Universités de France. Paris: Les Belles Lettres, 1973.

Aristotle. *Aristotelis De physico auditu libri octo: Cum Averrois Cordubensis variis in eosdem Commentariis.* Aristotelis Opera cum Averrois Commentariis, 4. Venice: apud Junctas, 1562. Reprint, Frankfurt am Main: Minerva GmbH, 1962.

———. *De anima.* Ed. W. D. Ross. Scriptorum Classicorum Bibliotheca Oxoniensis. Oxford: Oxford University Press, 1956.

———. *Metaphysica.* Ed. W. Jaeger. Scriptorum Classicorum Bibliotheca Oxoniensis. Oxford: Oxford University Press, 1957.

———. *On the Heavens.* Trans. W. K. C. Guthrie. Loeb Classical Library, 338. Cambridge: Harvard University Press, and London: William Heinemann, 1960.

———. *De generatione et corruptione: Translatio vetus.* Ed. Joanna Judycka. Aristoteles Latinus, 9.1. Leiden: E. J. Brill, 1986.

Aristotle, pseudo. *Die sogenannte Theologie des Aristoteles.* Ed. F. Dieterici. Leipzig, 1882. Reprint, Amsterdam: Rodopi, 1965.

———. *Die pseudo-aristotelische Schrift "Ueber das reine Gute" bekannt unter dem Namen "Liber de causis."* Bearbeitet von Otto Bardenhewer. Freiburg im Breisgau: Herder'sche Verlagshandlung, 1882. Reprint, Frankfurt am Main: Minerva GmbH, [1961].

———. *Kitāb al-iyḍāḥ li Arisṭūṭālīs fī al-ḫayr al-maḥḍ.* In *Al-Aflāṭūniyya al-muḥdata ʿinda al-ʿarab,* ed. ʿAbd al-Raḥmān Badawī, 1–33. Dirāsāt Islāmiyya, 19. Cairo: Maktaba al-nahḍa al-miṣriyya, 1955. Reprint, Kuwait: Wakāla al-maṭbūʿāt, 1977.

———. "Le *Liber de causis.*" Edition établie à l'aide de 90 manuscrits avec introduction et notes par Adriaan Pattin. *Tijdschrift voor Filosofie* 28 (1966): 90–203. Also issued separately.

———. *Kalām fī maḥḍ al-khair.* Ed. Richard Charles Taylor in his "The *Liber de causis (Kalām fī maḥḍ al-khair):* A Study of Medieval Neoplatonism," 135–279. Ph.D. diss., University of Toronto, 1981.

———. *La demeure de l'Etre: Autour d'un anonyme: Etude et traduction du "Liber de Causis."* By Pierre Magnard, Olivier Boulnois, Bruno Pinchard, and Jean-Luc Solère. Philologie et Mercure. Paris: Librairie Philosophique J. Vrin, 1990.

Augustine of Hippo. *De Genesi ad litteram.* Ed. J.-P. Migne. Patrologiae cursus completus, Series Latina, 34. Paris, 1841.

———. *De Trinitate libri quindecim.* Ed. J.-P. Migne. Patrologiae cursus completus, Series Latina, 42. Paris, 1845.

———. *De civitate Dei.* Ed. Emanuel Hoffmann. Corpus Scriptorum Ecclesiasticorum Latinorum, 40. Vienna: F. Tempsky, 1899.

———. *S. Aureli Augustini Confessionum libri XIII*. Ed. Martin Skutella, revised by H. Jürgens and W. Schaub. Bibliotheca Teubneriana. Stuttgart: B.G. Teubner, 1981.

———. *Confessions*. Latin text with English commentary by James J. O'Donnell. 3 vols. Oxford: Clarendon Press, 1992.

Bacon, Roger. *Quaestiones supra Librum de causis*. Ed. Robert Steele collaborante Ferdinand M. Delorme. Opera hactenus inedita Rogeri Baconi, 12. Oxford: Clarendon Press, 1935.

Basil of Caesarea. *Homélies sur l'Hexaéméron*. Texte grec, introduction et traduction de Stanislas Giet. 2ᵉ édition revue et augmentée. Sources Chrétiennes, 26 bis. Paris: Les Editions du Cerf, 1968.

al-Biṭrūǧī. *Al-Biṭrūjī: De motibus celorum*. Critical edition of the Latin translation of Michael Scot, by Francis J. Carmody. Berkeley: University of California Press, 1952.

Boethius. *The Theological Tractates; The Consolation of Philosophy*. Trans. H. F. Stewart, E. K. Rand, and S. J. Tester. Loeb Classical Library, 74. Cambridge: Harvard University Press, and London: William Heinemann, 1973.

Calcidius. *"Timaeus" a Calcidio translatus commentarioque instructus*. Ed. J. H. Waszink. 2d ed. Plato Latinus, 4. London: Warburg Institute, 1975.

David of Dinant. "Davidis de Dinanto Quaternulorum fragmenta." Ed. Marian Kurdziałek. *Studia Mediewistyczne* 3 (1963).

Denifle, H., and E. Chatelain, eds. *Chartularium Universitatis Parisiensis*. Paris: Delalain, 1889–97.

Dietrich von Freiburg. *Opera Omnia*. Corpus Philosophorum Teutonicorum Medii Aevi, 2.1–4. Hamburg: Felix Meiner Verlag, 1977–85.

Dionysius, pseudo. *Opera omnia quae existant*. Ed. J.-P. Migne. Patrologiae cursus completus, Series Graeca, 3. Paris: Garnier, 1857.

———. *Dionysiaca*. Ed. P. Chevallier et al. 2 vols. Paris: Desclée de Brouwer, 1937.

———. *De divinis nominibus*. Ed. Beate Regina Suchla. Corpus Dionysiacum, 1, in Patristische Texte und Studien, 33. Berlin: Walter de Gruyter, 1990.

Eriugena. *Johannis Scotti Eriugenae Periphyseon (De divisione naturae)*. Ed. I. P. Sheldon-Williams, with the collaboration of Ludwig Bieler. Scriptores Latini Hiberniae, vols. 7. 9, 11, 13. Dublin: Dublin Institute for Advanced Studies, 1968–.

Eustratius. *In Ethicam Nicomacheam*. In *The Greek Commentaries on the Nicomachean Ethics of Aristotle in the Latin Translation of Robert Grosseteste, Bishop of Lincoln (†1253)*, vol. 1, *Eustratius on Book I and the Anonymous Scholia on Books II, III, and IV*, ed. H. Paul F. Mercken. Corpus Latinum Commentariorum in Aristotelem Graecorum, 6.1. Leiden: E. J. Brill, 1973.

al-Fārābī [?]. "El *Fontes Quaestionum ('Uyūn al-Masā'il)* de Abū Naṣr al-Fārābī." Ed. Miguel Cruz Hernandez. *Archives d'histoire doctrinale et littéraire du moyen âge* 18 (1950–51): 303–23.

   The attribution to al-Fārābī is now generally rejected in favor of Ibn Sīnā.

———. *Al-Farabi on the Perfect State: Abū Naṣr al-Fārābī's Mabādi' ārā' ahl al-madīna al-fāḍila*. A revised text with introduction, translation, and commentary by Richard Walzer. Oxford: Clarendon Press, 1985.

al-Ġazālī. *Algazel's Metaphysics: A Mediaeval Translation*. Ed. T. J. Muckle. St. Michael's Mediaeval Studies. Toronto: St. Michael's College, 1933.

   Despite its title, this edition includes the physical as well as the metaphysical part of al-Ġazālī's *Maqāṣid al-Falāsifa*.

Gilbert of Poitiers. *Liber de sex principiis*. Ed. J.-P. Migne. Patrologiae cursus completus, Series Latina, 188:1247–70. Paris, 1855.

Henry of Ghent, [pseudo]. *Les "Quaestiones in Librum de causis" attribuées à Henri de Gand*. Ed. John P. Zwaenepoel. Philosophes Médiévaux, 15. Louvain: Publications Universitaires, and Paris: Béatrice-Nauwelaerts, 1974.

Hermes Trismegistus. *Asclepius*. In *Hermetica: The Ancient Greek and Latin Writings Which Contain Religious or Philosophic Teachings Ascribed to Hermes Trismegistus*, ed. and trans. Walter Scott, 1:286–377. Oxford: Clarendon Press, 1924.

Ibn Gabirol. *Avencebrolis (ibn Gebirol) "Fons vitae" ex Arabico in Latinum translatus ab Iohanne Hispano et Dominico Gundissalino*. Ed. C. Baeumker. Beiträge zur Geschichte der Philosophie des Mittelalters, 1.2–4. Münster: Aschendorff, 1892–94.

Ibn Rušd. *Aristotelis Metaphysicorum libri XIIII: Cum Averrois Cordubensis in eosdem Commentariis, et Epitome*. Aristotelis Opera cum Averrois Commentariis, 8. Venice: apud Junctas, 1562. Reprint, Frankfurt am Main: Minerva GmbH, 1962.

———. *Averroes' "Tahafut al-Tahafut (The Incoherence of the Incoherence)."* 2 vols. Translated from the Arabic with introduction and notes by Simon van den Bergh. UNESCO Collection of Great Works, Arabic Series. London: Luzac, 1954.

Ibn Sīnā. *Opera philosophica*. Venice, 1508. Réimpression en fac-similé agrandi, avec un tableau des abréviations, Louvain: Edition de la bibliothèque S.J., 1961.

———. *Al-Naǧāt*. Cairo, 1938.

———. *Livre des directives et remarques (Kitāb al-'išārāt wa l-tanbīhāt)*. Traduction avec introduction et notes par A.-M. Goichon. Collection UNESCO d'oeuvres représentatives: Série arabe. Beirut: Commission internationale pour la traduction des chef-d'oeuvres, and Paris: Librairie Philosophique J. Vrin, 1951.

———. *Liber De Anima seu Sextus De Naturalibus.* Ed. S. Van Riet. Avicenna Latinus, 1 and 2. Louvain: E. Peeters, and Leiden: E. J. Brill, 1968–72.

———. *Liber de philosophia prima.* Ed. S. Van Riet. Avicenna Latinus, 3 and 4. Louvain: E. Peeters, and Leiden: E. J. Brill, 1977–83.

———. *Le livre de science.* Traduit par Mohammad Achena et Henri Massé. Deuxième édition revue et corrigée par Mohammad Achena. Collection UNESCO d'oeuvres représentatives: Série persane. Paris: Les Belles Lettres/ UNESCO, 1986.

Isaac Israeli. *Liber de definicionibus.* Ed. J. T. Muckle. In *Archives d'histoire doctrinale et littéraire du moyen âge* 11 (1937–38): 299–340.

John of Dacia. *Johannis Daci Opera.* Ed. Alfredus Otto. Corpus Philosophorum Danicorum Medii Aevi. Copenhagen, 1955.

John of Damascus. *De fide orthodoxa.* Ed. J.-P. Migne. Patrologiae cursus completus, Series Graeca, 94. Paris, 1864.

Le Livre des XXIV Philosophes. Traduit du latin, édité et annoté par Françoise Hudry. Collection Krisis. Grenoble: Jerome Millon, 1989.

Moses Maimonides. *Le guide des égarés: Traité de théologie et de philosophie par Moïse ben Maimoun, dit Maïmonide.* 3 vols. Publié pour la première fois dans l'original arabe et accompagné d'une traduction française et de notes critiques, littéraires et explicatives par S. Munk. Paris: A. Franck, 1856–66.

Plotinus. *Plotini Opera.* Ed. Paul Henry and Hans-Rudolf Schwyzer. Museum Lessianum Series Philosophica, 33–35. Paris: Desclée de Brouwer, Brussels: L'Edition Universelle, S.A., and Leiden: E. J. Brill, 1951–73.

Porphyry. *On the Life of Plotinus and the Order of His Books.* In *Plotinus,* trans. A. H. Armstrong, 1:2–85. Loeb Classical Library, 440. Cambridge: Harvard University Press, and London: William Heinemann, 1966.

Priscian. *Prisciani Caesariensis grammatici Opera.* 2 vols. Ed. A. Krehl. Leipzig: in libraria Weidmannia, 1819–20.

Proclus Diadochus. "Procli *Elementatio theologica* translata a Guilelmo de Moerbeke (textus ineditus)." Ed. C. Vansteenkiste. *Tijdschrift voor Philosophie* 13 (1951): 263–302, 491–531.

———. *The Elements of Theology.* 2d ed. A revised text with translation, introduction and commentary by E. R. Dodds. Oxford: Clarendon Press, 1963.

———. *Proclus Arabus: Zwanzig Abschnitte aus der "Institutio theologica" in arabischer Übersetzung.* Eingeleitet, herausgegeben und erklärt von Gerhard Endress. Beiruter Texte und Studien, 10. Beirut: Imprimerie Catholique in Kommission bei Franz Steiner Verlag, Wiesbaden, 1973.

Siger de Brabant. *Les "Quaestiones super librum de causis" de Siger de Brabant.* Ed. Antonio Marlasca. Philosophes Médiévaux, 12. Louvain: Publications Universitaires, and Paris: Béatrice-Nauwelaerts, 1972.

———. *Quaestiones in Metaphysicam: Edition revue de la reportation de Munich, Texte inédit de la reportation de Vienne.* Ed. William Dunphy. Philosophes Médiévaux, 24. Louvain: Editions de l'Institut Supérieur de Philosophie, 1981.

———. *Quaestiones in Metaphysicam: Texte inédit de la reportation de Cambridge, Edition revue de la reportation de Paris.* Ed. Armand Maurer. Philosophes Médiévaux, 25. Louvain: Editions de l'Institut Supérieur de Philosophie, 1983.

Thomas Aquinas. *Super librum de causis expositio.* Ed. Henri-Dominique Saffrey. Textus Philosophici Friburgenses, 4/5. Fribourg: Société Philosophique, and Louvain: Editions E. Nauwelaerts, 1954.

———. *In Librum de causis expositio.* Cura et studio fr. Ceslai Pera o.p. cum introductione historica Sac. Petri Caramello et praeludio doctrinali Prof. Caroli Mazzantini. Turin: Marietti, 1955.

———. *Tractatus de substantiis separatis.* A newly established Latin text based on 12 mediaeval manuscripts, with Introduction and notes by Francis J. Lescoe. West Hartford, Conn.: Saint Joseph College, 1962.

———. *On the Unity of the Intellect against the Averroists (De Unitate Intellectus Contra Averroistas).* Translated from the Latin with an introduction by Beatrice H. Zedler. Mediaeval Philosophical Texts in Translation, 19. Milwaukee: Marquette University Press, 1968.

———. *De unitate intellectus contra Averroistas.* In *Opera Omnia Iussu Leonis XIII P. M. Edita,* 43. Rome, 1976.

———. *In duodecim libros Metaphysicorum Aristotelis expositio.* 3d ed. Editio iam a M.-R. Cathala, O.P. exarata retractatur cura et studio P. Fr. Raymundi M. Spiazzi, O.P. Turin: Marietti, 1977.

———. *Tommaso d'Aquino, Commento al "Libro delle cause."* A cura di Cristina D'Ancona Costa. Milan: Rusconi, 1986.

———. *Commentary on the Book of Causes.* Translated and annotated by Vincent A. Guagliardo, Charles R. Hess, and Richard C. Taylor. Thomas Aquinas in Translation. Washington, D.C.: Catholic University of America Press, 1996.

Ulrich von Strassburg. *De summo bono.* Corpus Philosophorum Teutonicorum Medii Aevi, 1.1–. Hamburg: Felix Meiner Verlag, 1987–.

William of Auvergne. *Guilielmi Alverni Opera omnia.* 2 vols. Paris: apud Andraeam Pralard, 1674. Reprint, Frankfurt am Main: Minerva GmbH, 1963.

———. *De trinitate.* Ed. Bruno Switalski. Studies and Texts, 34. Toronto: Pontifical Institute of Mediaeval Studies, 1976.

Secondary Literature

Afnan, Soheil M. *Philosophical Terminology in Arabic and Persian*. Leiden: E. J. Brill, 1964.

———. *A Philosophical Lexicon in Persian and Arabic*. Beirut: Dar el-Mashreq Publishers (Imprimerie Catholique), 1969.

Alarcón, Enrique. "S. Alberto Magno y la *Epistola Aristotelis de Principio Universi Esse*." In *Actas del I Congreso Nacional de Filosofía Medieval*, ed. Jorge M. Ayala Martínez, 181–92. Zaragoza: Sociedad de Filosofía Medieval, 1992.

Allgaier, Karl. "Engel und Intelligenzen: Zur arabisch-lateinischen Proklos-Rezeption." In *Orientalische Kultur und europäisches Mittelalter*, ed. Albert Zimmermann and Ingrid Craemer-Ruegenberg, 172–87. Miscellanea Mediaevalia, 17. Berlin: Walter de Gruyter, 1985.

Alonso, Manuel. "El *Liber de causis*." *Al-Andalus* 9 (1944): 43–69.

———. "Las fuentes literarias del *Liber de causis*." *Al-Andalus* 10 (1945): 345–82.

———. "Traducciones del árabe al latín por Juan Hispano (Ibn Dāwūd)." *Al-Andalus* 17 (1952): 129–51.

Altmann, A., and S. M. Stern. *Isaac Israeli, a Neoplatonic Philosopher of the Early Tenth Century*. Scripta Judaica, 1. Oxford: Oxford University Press, 1958. Reprint, Westport, Conn.: Greenwood Press, Inc., 1979.

Anawati, Georges C. "Prolégomènes à une nouvelle édition du *De causis* arabe *(Kitāb al-ḫayr al-maḥḍ)*." In *Mélanges Louis Massignon*, 1:73–110. Damascus, 1956. Reprint in idem, *Etudes de philosophie musulmane*, 117–54. Etudes Musulmanes, 15. Paris: Librairie Philosophique J. Vrin, 1974.

Armstrong, A. Hilary. "'Emanation' in Plotinus." *Mind*, n.s., 46 (1937): 61–66. Reprint in idem, *Plotinian and Christian Studies*. Collected Studies, 102. London: Variorum Reprints, 1979.

Bach, Josef. *Des Albertus Magnus Verhältniss zu der Erkenntnislehre der Griechen, Lateiner, Araber und Juden: Ein Beitrag zur Geschichte der Noetik*. Vienna, 1881. Reprint, Frankfurt am Main: Minerva GmbH, 1966.

Badawī, ʿAbd al-Raḥmān. *La transmission de la philosophie grecque au monde arabe*. Paris: Librairie Philosophique J. Vrin, 1968.

Baeumker, Clemens. *Witelo, ein Philosoph und Naturforscher des XIII. Jahrhunderts*. Beiträge zur Geschichte der Philosophie des Mittelalters, 3.2. Münster: Aschendorff, 1908.

Bédoret, H. "L'auteur et le traducteur du *Liber de causis*." *Revue Néoscolastique de Philosophie* 41 (1938): 519–33.

Bonné, Jacob. "Die Erkenntnislehre Alberts des Grossen mit besonderer Berücksichtigung des arabischen Neoplatonismus." Ph.D. diss., Bonn: Druck von R. Stodieck, 1935.

Booth, Edward. "Conciliazioni ontologiche delle tradizioni platonica e aristotelica in Sant'Alberto e San Tommaso." Trans. Roberto Donatoni. In *Sant'Alberto Magno: L'uomo e il pensatore*, 59–81. Studia Universitatis S. Thomae in Urbe, Serie theologica, 15. Milan: Massimo, 1982.

———. *Aristotelian Aporetic Ontology in Islamic and Christian Thinkers*. Cambridge Studies in Medieval Life and Thought, 3d ser., 20. Cambridge: Cambridge University Press, 1983.

Brunner, Fernand. "Création et émanation: Fragment de philosophie comparée." *Studia Philosophica* 33 (1973): 33–63.

Caroti, Stefano. "Problèmes textuels et lexicographiques dans l'oeuvre scientifique d'Albert le Grand." *Annali dell'Istituto e Museo di Storia della Scienza di Firenze* 6, no. 1 (1981): 187–202.

———. "Alberto Magno e la scienza: Bilancio di un centenario." *Annali dell'Istituto e Museo di Storia della Scienza di Firenze* 6, no. 2 (1981): 17–44.

Corbin, Henry. *Avicenna and the Visionary Recital*. Trans. Willard R. Trask. Bollingen Series, 66. New York: Pantheon Books, 1960.

Corsini, Eugenio. *Il trattato "De Divinis nominibus" dello Pseudo-Dionigi e i commenti neoplatonici al "Parmenide."* Università di Torino: Pubblicazioni della facoltà di lettere e filosofia, 13.4. Turin: G. Giappichelli, 1962.

Cortabarría Beitia, Angel. "Las obras y la filosofía de Alfarabi en los escritos de San Alberto Magno." *La Ciencia Tomista* 77 (1950): 362–87; 78 (1951): 81–104.

———. "Las obras y las doctrinas del filósofo Alkindi en los escritos de San Alberto Magno." *Estudios Filosóficos* 1 (1951–52): 191–209.

———. "Doctrinas Psicológicas de Alfarabi en los escritos de S. Alberto Magno." *La Ciencia Tomista* 79 (1952): 633–56.

———. "Tabla general de las citas de Alkindi y Alfarabi en las obras de San Alberto Magno." *Estudios Filosóficos* 2 (1953): 247–50.

———. *Las obras y la filosofía de Alfarabi y Alkindi en los escritos de S. Alberto Magno*. Estudios Filosóficos, supplementary publication. Las Caldas de Besaya, 1954.

———. "Literatura algazeliana de los escritos de San Alberto Magno." *Estudios Filosóficos* 11 (1962): 255–76.

———. "Al-Kindī vu par Albert le Grand." *Mélanges de l'Institut Dominicain d'Etudes Orientales du Caire* 13 (1977): 117–46.

———. "El filósofo Avempace en los escritos de San Alberto Magno." *Estudios Filosóficos* 27 (1978): 21–61.

———. "El Astrónomo Alpetragio en las obras de S. Alberto Magno." *La Ciudad de Dios* 193 (1980): 503–33.

———. "Fuentes árabes de San Alberto: Albumasar." *Estudios Filosóficos* 29 (1981): 283–99.

———. "Deux sources arabes de S. Albert le Grand: Al-Biṭrūjī et al-Battānī." *Mélanges de l'Institut Dominicain d'Etudes Orientales du Caire* 15 (1982): 31–52.

———. "Fuentes árabes de San Alberto Magno: el astrónomo Mashallah." *Estudios Filosóficos* 34 (1985): 399–415.

———. "Deux sources arabes de S. Albert le Grand: Thābit b. Qurra et al-Farghānī." *Mélanges de l'Institut Dominicain d'Etudes Orientales du Caire* 17 (1986): 37–52.

Craemer-Ruegenberg, Ingrid. *Albertus Magnus.* Große Denker: Leben, Werk, Wirkung; Beck'sche Schwarze Reihe, 501. Munich: C. H. Beck, 1980.

Dähnert, Ulrich. *Die Erkenntnislehre des Albertus Magnus gemessen an den Stufen der 'abstractio.'* Leipzig: S. Hirzel, 1934.

D'Alverny, Marie-Thérèse. "Avendauth?" In *Homenaje a Millás-Vallicrosa*, 1:19–43. Barcelona: Consejo Superior de Investigaciones Científicas, 1954.

———. "Anniyya-anitas." In *Mélanges offerts à Etienne Gilson*, 59–91. Toronto-Paris, 1959.

D'Ancona Costa, Cristina. *Recherches sur le Liber de Causis.* Etudes de Philosophie Médiévale, 72. Paris: Librairie Philosophique J. Vrin, 1995.

Davidson, Herbert A. *Proofs for Eternity, Creation and the Existence of God in Medieval Islamic and Jewish Philosophy.* Oxford: Oxford University Press, 1987.

———. *Alfarabi, Avicenna, and Averroes, on Intellect: Their Cosmologies, Theories of the Active Intellect, and Theories of the Human Intellect.* Oxford: Oxford University Press, 1992.

Degen, Ernst. "Welches sind die Beziehungen Alberts des Grossen *Liber de causis et processu universitatis* zur στοιχείωσις θεολογική des Neuplatonikers Proclus, und was lehren uns dieselben?" Ph.D. diss., Ludwig-Maximilians-Universität zu München, 1902.

De Vogel, Cornelia J. "Some Reflections on the *Liber de causis.*" *Vivarium* 4 (1966): 67–82.

De Wulf, Maurice. *Histoire de la philosophie médiévale.* 6th ed. Louvain: Institut Supérieur de Philosophie, and Paris: Librairie Philosophique J. Vrin, 1934–47.

Dondaine, Hyacinthe F. *Le corpus Dionysien de l'Université de Paris au XIIIe siècle.* Storia e letteratura, 44. Rome: Edizioni di storia e letteratura, 1953.

Doresse, J. "Les sources du *Liber de causis.*" *Revue de l'Histoire des Religions* 131 (1946): 234–38.

Dörrie, Heinrich. "Emanation: Ein unphilosophisches Wort im spätantiken Denken." In *Parusia: Studien zur Philosophie Platons und zur Problemgeschichte des Platonismus: Festgabe für Johannes Hirschberger*, ed. Kurt Flasch, 119–41. Frankfurt am Main: Minerva GmbH, 1965.

Druart, Thérèse-Anne. "Al-Farabi and Emanationism." In *Studies in Medieval Philosophy*, ed. John F. Wippel, 23–43. Studies in Philosophy and the History of Philosophy, 17. Washington: Catholic University of America Press, 1987.

———. Al-Fārābī, Emanation, and Metaphysics." In *Neoplatonism and Islamic Thought*, ed. Parviz Morewedge, 127–48. Studies in Neoplatonism: Ancient and Modern, 5. Albany: State University of New York Press, 1992.

Ducharme, Léonard. "*Esse* chez saint Albert le Grand: Introduction à la métaphysique de ses premiers écrits." *Revue de l'Université d'Ottawa* 27 (1957): 209*–52*.

Duhem, Pierre. *Le système du monde: Histoire de doctrines cosmologiques de Platon à Copernic*. 10 vols. Paris: Hermann, 1913–54.

Duin, J. J. *La doctrine de la providence dans les écrits de Siger de Brabant: Textes et étude*. Philosophes Médiévaux, 3. Louvain: Editions de l'Institut Supérieur de Philosophie, 1954.

Dunphy, W. B. "St. Albert and the Five Causes." *Archives d'histoire doctrinale et littéraire du moyen âge* 33 (1966): 7–21.

Ess, Josef van. "Jüngere orientalistische Literatur zur neuplatonischen Überlieferung im Bereich des Islam." In *Parusia: Studien zur Philosophie Platons und zur Problemgeschichte des Platonismus: Festgabe für Johannes Hirschberger*, ed. Kurt Flasch, 333–50. Frankfurt am Main: Minerva GmbH, 1965.

Faes de Mottoni, Barbara. "La distinzione tra causa agente e causa motrice nella *Summa de Summo Bono* di Ulrico di Strasburgo." *Studi Medievali*, serie terza 20 (1979): 313–55.

Fauser, W. "Albert the Great's Commentary on the *Liber de causis*." *Bulletin de Philosophie Médiévale* 36 (1994): 38–44.

Feigl, Maria. "Quellenstudien zu Alberts des Großen Kommentar zum *Liber de causis*." Ph.D. diss., Cologne, 1951.

———. "Albert der Grosse und die arabische Philosophie: Eine Studie zu den Quellen seines Kommentars zum *Liber de causis*." *Philosophisches Jahrbuch* 63 (1955): 131–50.

Fioravanti, Gianfranco. "L'aristotelismo latino." In *Storia della filosofia*, vol. 2, *Il Medioevo*, ed. Pietro Rossi and Carlo Augusto Viano, 299–323. Roma-Bari: Laterza, 1994.

Flasch, Kurt. *Aufklärung im Mittelalter? Die Verurteilung von 1277*. Excerpta classica, 6. Mainz: Dieterich, 1989.

Franchi, Alfredo. "Alberto Magno e le origini della nozione di causalità efficiente: La teoria delle cinque cause nei *quidam* del V *Metaphysicorum*." *Sapienza* 33 (1980): 178–85.

Frank, Richard M. *Creation and the Cosmic System: Al-Ghazālī & Avicenna*. Abhandlungen der Heidelberger Akademie der Wissenschaften,

Philosophisch-historische Klasse, Jg. 1992, Abh. 1. Heidelberg: Carl Winter Universitätsverlag, 1992.

Gardet, Louis. "En l'honneur du millénaire d'Avicenne: L'importance d'un texte nouvellement traduit: Les gloses d'Avicenne sur la pseudo *Théologie d'Aristote*." *Revue Thomiste* 51 (1951): 333–45.

Gaul, L. *Alberts des Grossen Verhältnis zur Plato: Eine literarische und philosophiegeschichtliche Untersuchung*. Beiträge zur Geschichte der Philosophie des Mittelalters, 12.1. Münster: Aschendorff, 1913.

Geiger, L.-B. "La vie, acte essential de l'âme, l'*esse* acte de l'essence d'après Albert-le-Grand." In *Etudes d'histoire littéraire et doctrinale*, 49–116. Université de Montréal: Publications de l'Institut d'Etudes Médiévales, 17. Montreal: Institut d'Etudes Médiévales, and Paris: Librairie Philosophique J. Vrin, 1962.

Gersh, Stephen E. Κίνησις ἀκίνητος: *A Study of Spiritual Motion in the Philosophy of Proclus*. Philosophia Antiqua, 26. Leiden: E. J. Brill, 1973.

———. *From Iamblichus to Eriugena: An Investigation of the Prehistory and Evolution of the Pseudo-Dionysian Tradition*. Studien zur Problemgeschichte der antiken und mittelalterlichen Philosophie, 8. Leiden: E. J. Brill, 1978.

Gerson, Lloyd P. *Plotinus*. The Arguments of the Philosophers. London: Routledge, 1994.

Geyer, Bernhard. "De aristotelismo B. Alberti Magni." In *Alberto Magno: Atti della Settimana Albertina celebrata in Roma nei giorni 9–14 Nov. 1931*, 63–80. Rome: Federico Pustet, [1932].

———. "Albertus Magnus und die Entwicklung der scholastischen Metaphysik." In *Die Metaphysik im Mittelalter: Ihr Ursprung und ihre Bedeutung*, ed. Paul Wilpert, 3–13. Miscellanea Mediaevalia, 2. Berlin: Walter de Gruyter, 1963.

Gilson, Etienne. "Notes sur le Vocabulaire de l'Etre." *Mediaeval Studies* 8 (1946): 150–58.

———. "Avicenne et les origines de la notion de cause efficiente." In *Atti del XII Congresso Internazionale di Filosofia (Venezia, 12–18 Settembre 1958)*, vol. 9, *Aristotelismo padovano e filosofia aristotelica*, 121–30. Florence: Sansoni Editore, 1960.

———. "Notes pour l'histoire de la cause efficiente." *Archives d'histoire doctrinale et littéraire du moyen âge* 29 (1962): 7–31.

Giocarinis, Kimon. "Eustratius of Nicaea's Defense of the Doctrine of Ideas." *Franciscan Studies*, n.s., 24 (1964): 159–204.

Goichon, A.-M. *La distinction de l'essence et de l'existence d'après Ibn Sīnā (Avicenne)*. Paris: Desclée de Brouwer, 1937.

Grabmann, Martin. "Die Lehre des Heiligen Albertus Magnus vom Grunde der Vielheit der Dinge und der Lateinische Averroismus." *Divus Thomas* (Freiburg)

10 (1932): 203–30. Reprint as a chap. in vol. 2 of idem, *Mittelalterliches Geistesleben: Abhandlung zur Geschichte der Scholastik und Mystik*. Munich: Max Hueber, 1936.

———. "Eine für Examinazwecke abgefasste Quaestionensammlung der Pariser Artistenfakultät aus der ersten Hälfte des 13. Jahrhunderts." *Revue néoscolastique de philosophie* 36 (1934): 211–29. Reprint as a chap. in vol. 2 of idem, *Mittelalterliches Geistesleben: Abhandlung zur Geschichte der Scholastik und Mystik*. Munich: Max Hueber, 1936.

———. "Zur philosophischen und naturwissenschaftlichen Methode in den Aristoteleskommentaren Alberts des Grossen." *Angelicum* 21 (1944): 50–64.

Guttmann, Jacob. *Die Scholastik des 13 Jahrhunderts in ihren Beziehungen zum Judenthum und zur jüdischen Literatur*. Breslau: M. et H. Marcus, 1902.

———. "Der Einfluß der maimonidischen Philosophie auf das christliche Abendland." In *Moses ben Maimon, sein Leben, seine Werke und sein Einfluss: Zur Erinnerung an den siebenhundertsten Todestag des Maimonides*, 1:135–230. Leipzig: G. Fock, 1908. Reprint, New York: Hildesheim, 1971.

Hadot, Pierre. "La distinction de l'être et de l'étant dans le 'De hebdomadibus' de Boèce." In *Die Metaphysik im Mittelalter: Ihr Ursprung und ihre Bedeutung*, ed. Paul Wilpert, 147–53. Miscellanea Mediaevalia, 2. Berlin: Walter de Gruyter, 1963.

———. "*Forma essendi*: Interprétation philologique et interprétation philosophique d'une formule de Boèce." *Les études classiques* 38 (1970): 143–56.

Haneberg, B. "Zur Erkenntnisslehre von Ibn Sina und Albertus Magnus." *Abhandlungen der philosophisch-philologische Classe der koeniglich bayerischen Akademie der Wissenschaften* 11.1 (1866): 189–268.

Hansen, Joseph. "Zur Frage der anfangslosen und zeitlichen Schöpfung bei Albert dem Großen." In *Studia Albertina: Festschrift für Bernhard Geyer zum 70. Geburtstage*, ed. Heinrich Ostlender, 167–88. Beiträge zur Geschichte der Philosophie und Theologie des Mittelalters, Supplementband 4. Münster: Aschendorff, 1952.

Hauréau, B. *Histoire de la philosophie scolastique* 2.1. Paris: G. Pedone-Lauriel, 1880.

Hedwig, Klaus. *Sphaera lucis: Studien zur Intelligibilität des Seienden im Kontext der mittelalterlichen Lichtspekulation*. Beiträge zur Geschichte der Philosophie und Theologie des Mittelalters, neue Folge, 18. Münster: Aschendorff, 1980.

Hertling, Georg von. *Albertus Magnus: Beiträge zu seiner Würdigung*. Beiträge zur Geschichte der Philosophie des Mittelalters, 14.5–6. Münster: Aschendorff, 1914.

Hissette, Roland. *Enquête sur les 219 articles condamnés à Paris le 7 mars 1277*. Philosophes Médiévaux, 22. Louvain: Publications Universitaires, 1977.

Hoßfeld, Paul. "Die Arbeitsweise des Albertus Magnus in seinen naturphilosophischen Schriften." In *Albertus Magnus—Doctor Universalis: 1280/1980*, ed. G. Meyer and A. Zimmermann, 195–204. Walberberger Studien: Philosophische Reihe, 6. Mainz: Matthias-Grünewald-Verlag, 1980.
———. "'Erste Materie' oder 'Materie im allgemeinen' in den Werken des Albertus Magnus." In *Albertus Magnus—Doctor Universalis: 1280/1980*, ed. G. Meyer and A. Zimmermann, 205–34. Walberberger Studien: Philosophische Reihe, 6. Mainz: Matthias-Grünewald-Verlag, 1980.
———. "'Allgemeine und umfassende Natur' nach Albertus Magnus." *Philosophia Naturalis* 18 (1980–81): 479–92.
———. *Albertus Magnus als Naturphilosoph und Naturwissenschaftler*. Bonn: Albertus-Magnus-Institut, 1983.
———. "Die Physik des Albertus Magnus (Teil I, die Bucher 1–4) Quellen und Charakter." *Archivum Fratrum Praedicatorum* 55 (1985): 49–65.
———. "Albertus Magnus über die Ewigkeit aus philosophischer Sicht." *Archivum Fratrum Praedicatorum* 56 (1986): 31–48.
———. "Gott und die Welt: Zum achten Buch der Physik des Albertus Magnus (nach dem kritisch erstellten Text)." In *Mensch und Natur im Mittelalter*, ed. Albert Zimmermann and Andreas Speer, 281–301. Miscellanea Mediaevalia, 21.1. Berlin: Walter de Gruyter, 1991.
———. "Der 'Liber de causis'-Kommentar Alberts und seine naturphilosophischen Kommentare." *Documenti e studi sulla tradizione filosofica medievale* 6 (1995): 39–105.
Hudry, Françoise. "Le *Liber XXIV philosophorum* et le *Liber de causis* dans les manuscrits." *Archives d'histoire doctrinale et littéraire du moyen âge* 59 (1992): 63–88.
Hyman, Arthur. "Maimonides on Creation and Emanation." In *Studies in Medieval Philosophy*, ed. John F. Wippel, 45–61. Studies in Philosophy and the History of Philosophy, 17. Washington: Catholic University of America Press, 1987.
Imbach, Ruedi. "Le (néo-)platonisme médiéval, Proclus latin et l'école dominicaine allemande." *Revue de théologie et de philosophie* 110 (1978): 427–48.
Janssens, Jules. "Le *Dānesh-Nāmeh* d'Ibn Sīnā: Un texte à revoir?" *Bulletin de philosophie médiévale* 28 (1986): 163–77.
———. "Creation and Emanation in Ibn Sīnā." *Documenti e studi sulla tradizione filosofica medievale* 8 (1997): 455–77.
Joël, M[anuel]. *Verhältniss Albert des Grossen zu Moses Maimonides: Ein Beitrag zur Geschichte der mittelalterlichen Philosophie*. Breslau: H. Skutsch, 1863. Reprint in vol. 1 of idem, *Beiträge zur Geschichte der Philosophie*, Breslau: H. Skutsch, 1876. *Beiträge zur Geschichte der Philosophie* reprinted as 2 vols.

in 1 within the series "Jewish Philosophy, Mysticism and the History of Ideas: Classics of Continental Thought," New York: Arno Press, 1980.

Jolivet, Jean. "La répartition des causes chez Aristote et Avicenne: Le sens d'un déplacement." In *Lectionum Varietates: Hommage à Paul Vignaux (1904–1987)*, ed. J. Jolivet, Z. Kaluza, and A. de Libera, 49–65. Etudes de Philosophie Médiévale, 65. Paris: Librairie Philosophique J. Vrin, 1991.

Kaiser, Rudolf. "Zur Frage der eigenen Anschauung Alberts d. Gr. in seinen philosophischen Kommentaren: Eine grundsätzliche Betrachtung." *Freiburger Zeitschrift für Philosophie und Theologie* 9 (1962): 53–62.

———. "Versuch einer Datierung der Schrift Alberts des Grossen *De causis et processu universitatis.*" *Archiv für Geschichte der Philosophie* 45 (1963): 125–36.

This and the following entry are based on the author's dissertation, "Das Verhältniss Alberts des Großen en zu den Lehren des Neuplatonikers Proklos" (Bonn, 1954).

———. "Die Benutzung proklischer Schriften durch Albert den Großen." *Archiv für Geschichte der Philosophie* 45 (1963): 1–22.

Kogan, Barry Sherman. "Averroës and the Theory of Emanation." *Mediaeval Studies* 43 (1981): 384–404.

Kovach, Francis J. "The Enduring Question of Action at a Distance in Saint Albert the Great." In *Albert the Great: Commemorative Essays*, ed. Francis J. Kovach and Robert W. Shahan, 161–235. Norman: University of Oklahoma Press, 1980.

Kraus, Paul. "Plotin chez les Arabes: Remarques sur un nouveau fragment de la paraphrase arabe des *Ennéades.*" *Bulletin de l'Institut d'Egypte* 23 (1940–41): 263–95.

Kraye, Jill. "The Pseudo-Aristotelian *Theology* in Sixteenth- and Seventeenth-Century Europe." In *Pseudo-Aristotle in the Middle Ages: The "Theology" and Other Texts*, ed. Jill Kraye, W. F. Ryan, and C. B. Schmitt, 265–86. Warburg Institute Surveys and Texts, 11. London: Warburg Institute, University of London, 1986.

Lafleur, Claude, avec la collaboration de Joanne Carrier. *Le "Guide de l'étudiant" d'un maître anonyme de la Faculté des arts de Paris au XIIIe siècle: Edition critique provisoire du ms. Barcelona, Arxiu de la Corona d'Aragó, Ripoll 109, ff. 134ra–158va*. Publications du laboratoire de philosophie ancienne et médiévale de la Faculté de philosophie de l'Université Laval, 1. Quebec: Faculté de philosophie, Université Laval, 1992.

A definitive version of this work is to appear in the "Continuatio Mediaevalis" of "Corpus Christianorum."

Lafleur, Claude. "Les 'guides de l'étudiant' de la Faculté des arts de l'Université de Paris au XIIIe siècle." In *Philosophy and Learning: Universities in the Middle*

Ages, ed. Maarten J. F. M. Hoenen, J. H. Josef Schneider, and Georg Wieland, 137–99. Education and Society in the Middle Ages and Renaissance, 6. Leiden: E. J. Brill, 1995.

Leaman, Oliver. *Averroes and His Philosophy*. Oxford: Clarendon Press, 1988.

Lemay, Richard. S.v. "Gerard of Cremona." *Dictionary of Scientific Biography*.

Libera, Alain de. "Logique et existence selon saint Albert le Grand." *Archives de Philosophie: Recherches et Documentation* 43 (1980): 529–58.

———. "Théorie des universaux et réalisme logique chez Albert le Grand." *Revue des sciences philosophiques et théologiques* 65 (1981): 55–74.

———. "Ulrich de Strasbourg, lecteur d'Albert le Grand." *Freiburger Zeitschrift für Philosophie und Theologie* 32 (1985): 105–36.

———. "Philosophie et théologie chez Albert le Grand et dans l'école dominicaine allemande." In *Die Kölner Universität im Mittelalter: Geistige Wurzeln und soziale Wirklichkeit*, ed. Albert Zimmermann, 49–67. Miscellanea Mediaevalia, 20. Berlin: Walter de Gruyter, 1989.

———. *Albert le Grand et la philosophie*. A la recherche de la vérité. Paris: Librairie Philosophique J. Vrin, 1990.

———. "Albert le Grand et Thomas d'Aquin interprètes du *Liber de causis*." *Revue des sciences philosophiques et théologiques* 74 (1990): 347–78.

———. "*Ex uno non fit nisi unum*: La *Lettre sur le Principe de l'univers* et les condamnations parisiennes de 1277." In *Historia philosophiae Medii Aevi: Studien zur Geschichte der Philosophie des Mittelalters*, ed. B. Mojsisch and O. Pluta, 1:543–60. Amsterdam: B. R. Grüner, 1991.

———. "Albert le Grand et le platonisme: De la doctrine des idées à la théorie des trois états de l'universel." In *On Proclus and His Influence in Medieval Philosophy*, ed. E. P. Bos and P. A. Meijer, 89–119. Philosophia Antiqua, 53. Leiden: E. J. Brill, 1992.

———. "Albert le Grand ou l'antiplatonisme sans Platon." In *Contre Platon*, vol. 1, *Le platonisme dévoilé*, ed. Monique Dixsaut, 247–71. Paris: Librairie Philosophique J. Vrin, 1993.

Loë, Ludwig Dietrich (*in religion* Paulus von). "De vita et scriptis B. Alberti Magni." *Analecta Bollandiana* 19 (1900): 257–84; 20 (1901): 273–316; 21 (1902): 361–71.

Lohr, Charles H. "The Pseudo-Aristotelian *Liber de causis* and Latin Theories of Science in the Twelfth and Thirteenth Centuries." In *Pseudo-Aristotle in the Middle Ages: The "Theology" and other Texts*, ed. Jill Kraye, W. F. Ryan, and C. B. Schmitt, 53–62. Warburg Institute Surveys and Texts, 11. London: Warburg Institute, University of London, 1986.

Lossky, V. "La notion des 'analogies' chez Denys le Pseudo Aréopagite." *Archives d'histoire doctrinale et littéraire du moyen âge* 5 (1930): 279–309.

Maccagnolo, Enzo. "David of Dinant and the Beginnings of Aristotelianism in Paris." In *A History of Twelfth-Century Western Philosophy*, ed. Peter Dronke, 429–42. Cambridge: Cambridge University Press, 1988.

Madec, Goulven. "Yliatim." *Archivum Latinitatis Medii Aevi* 43 (1981–82): 119–21.

Mahoney, Edward P. "Metaphysical Foundations of the Hierarchy of Being According to Some Late-Medieval and Renaissance Philosophers." In *Philosophies of Existence, Ancient and Medieval*, ed. Parviz Morewedge, 165–257. New York: Fordham University Press, 1982.

Manser, Gallus M. *Das Wesen des Thomismus*. 3d ed. Thomistische Studien, 5. Fribourg: Paulusverlag, 1949.

Maquart, F.-X. "Aristote n'a-t-il affirmé qu'une distinction logique entre l'essence et l'existence?" *Revue Thomiste* 31 (1926): 62–72.

———. "Deux autres arguments de M. Rougier." *Revue Thomiste* 31 (1926): 267–76.

———. "Un dernier argument de M. Rougier." *Revue Thomiste* 31 (1926): 358–66.

Maritain, Jacques. *Bergsonian Philosophy and Thomism*. Trans. Mabelle L. Andison in collaboration with J. Gordon Andison. New York: Philosophical Library, 1955.

Masnovo, Amato. *Da Guglielmo d'Auvergne a S. Tommaso d'Aquino*. Vol. 3, *L'Uomo*. Pubblicazioni dell'Università Cattolica del Sacro Cuore, n.s., 10. Milan: Società editrice "Vita e Pensiero," 1945.

McInerny, Ralph. *Boethius and Aquinas*. Washington, D.C.: Catholic University of America Press, 1990.

Meersseman, G. *Introductio in Opera Omnia B. Alberti Magni O.P.* Bruges: Beyaert, 1931.

———. *Geschichte des Albertismus*. Heft 1, *Die Pariser Anfänge des Kölner Albertismus*. Institutum Historicum F.F. Praedicatorum Romae ad S. Sabinae: Dissertationes Historicae, 3. Paris: R. Haloua, 1933.

Munk, S. *Mélanges de philosophie juive et arabe*. Paris: A. Franck, 1859. Reprint, Paris: Librairie Universitaire, 1927.

Nardi, Bruno. *Studi di filosofia medievale*. Storia e Letteratura, 78. Rome: Edizioni di Storia e Letteratura, 1960.

Noone, Timothy B. "Albert the Great on the Subject of Metaphysics and Demonstrating the Existence of God." *Medieval Philosophy & Theology* 2 (1992): 31–52.

Opelt, Ilona. "Zur Übersetzungstechnik des Gerhard von Cremona." *Glotta: Zeitschrift für griechische und lateinische Sprache* 38 (1960): 135–70.

Pagnoni-Sturlese, Maria Rita. "A propos du néoplatonisme d'Albert le Grand: Aventures et mésaventures de quelques textes d'Albert dans le Commentaire sur Proclus de Berthold de Moosburg." *Archives de Philosophie: Recherches et Documentation* 43 (1980): 635–54.

Park, Katharine. "Albert's Influence on Late Medieval Psychology." In *Albertus Magnus and the Sciences: Commemorative Essays, 1980*, ed. James A. Weisheipl, 501–35. Studies and Texts, 49. Toronto: Pontifical Institute of Mediaeval Studies, 1980.

Pattin, Adriaan. "De hiërarchie van het zijnde in het *Liber de causis*." *Tijdschrift voor Philosophie* 23 (1961): 130–57.

———. "Over de schrijver en de vertaler van het *Liber de causis*: Studie over de vijf eerste proposities." *Tijdschrift voor Philosophie* 23 (1961): 323–33, 503–26.

———. "De *Proclus Arabus* en het *Liber de causis*." *Tijdschrift voor Filosofie* 38 (1976): 468–73.

———. Review of *De causis et processu universitatis a prima causa*, ed. W. Fauser. *Tijdschrift voor Philosophie* 56 (1994): 766–69.

———. "Autour du *Liber de causis*: Quelques réflexions sur la récente littérature." *Freiburger Zeitschrift für Philosophie und Theologie* 41 (1994): 354–88.

Pearson, Paul. "Creation Through Instruments in Thomas' Sentence Commentary." In *Philosophy and the God of Abraham: Essays in Memory of James A. Weisheipl, OP*, ed. R. James Long, 147–60. Papers in Mediaeval Studies, 12. Toronto: Pontifical Institute of Mediaeval Studies, 1991.

Peghaire, Julien. "L'axiome 'Bonum est diffusivum sui' dans le néo-platonisme et le thomisme." *Revue de l'Université d'Ottawa* 1 (1932): 5*–30*.

Pegis, A. C. "Necessity and Liberty: An Historical Note on St. Thomas Aquinas." *The New Scholasticism* 15 (1941): 18–45.

Pelster, F. *Kritische Studien zum Leben und zu den Schriften Alberts des Grossen*. Freiburg-im-Breisgau: Herder, 1920.

———. "Zur Datierung der Aristotelesparaphrase des hl. Albert des Grossen." *Zeitschrift für katholische Theologie* 56 (1932): 423–36.

———. "Beiträge zur Aristotelesbenutzung Alberts des Grossen." *Philosophisches Jahrbuch* 46 (1933): 450–63; 47 (1934): 55–64, 458–63.

Philalethes [King Johann of Saxony]. "Ueber Kosmologie und Kosmogenie nach den Ansichten der Scholastiker in Dante's Zeit, zu Gesang I des Paradieses." Note in *Dante Alighieri's Goettliche Comoedie. Dritter Theil, Das Paradies.* Metrisch übertragen und mit kritischen und historischen Erläuterungen versehen von Philalethes. Dresden and Leipzig: Arnoldische Buchhandlung, 1849. 2d ed., 1865–66. Reprint of 2d ed., Leipzig: B. G. Teubner, 1904.

Price, Betsy Barker. "The Physical Astronomy and Astrology of Albertus Magnus." In *Albertus Magnus and the Sciences: Commemorative Essays, 1980*, ed. James A. Weisheipl, 155–85. Studies and Texts, 49. Toronto: Pontifical Institute of Mediaeval Studies, 1980.

Rohner, Anselm. *Das Schöpfungsproblem bei Moses Maimonides, Albertus Magnus und Thomas v. Aquin: Ein Beitrag zur Geschichte des Schöpfungsproblems im Mittelalter.* Beiträge zur Geschichte der Philosophie des Mittelalters, 11.5. Münster: Aschendorff, 1913.

Roland-Gosselin, M.-D. *Le "De Ente et Essentia" de S. Thomas d'Aquin.* Bibliothèque Thomiste, 8. Kain: Le Saulchoir, 1926.

Rosenthal, Franz. "Aš-Šayḫ al-Yūnānī and the Arabic Plotinus Source." *Orientalia,* n.s., 21 (1952): 461–92; 22 (1953): 370–400; 24 (1955): 42–66.

Rothschild, Jean-Pierre. "Un traducteur hébreu qui se cherche: R. Juda b. Moïse Romano et le *De causis et processu universitatis* II, 3, 2 d'Albert le Grand." *Archives d'histoire doctrinale et littéraire du moyen âge* 59 (1992): 159–73.

———. "Les traductions du *Livre des causes* et leurs copies." *Revue d'histoire des textes* 24 (1994): 393–484.

Rowson, Everett K. "An Unpublished Work by al-ʿĀmirī and the Date of the Arabic *De causis.*" *Journal of the American Oriental Society* 104 (1984): 193–99.

Saffrey, Henri-Dominique. "L'état actuel des recherches sur le *Liber de causis* comme source de la métaphysique au moyen âge." In *Die Metaphysik im Mittelalter: Ihr Ursprung und ihre Bedeutung,* ed. Paul Wilpert, 267–81. Miscellanea Mediaevalia, 2. Berlin: Walter de Gruyter, 1963.

Saranyana, José Ignacio. "Sobre la contribución de Alberto Magno a la doctrina del 'actus essendi.'" In *Albert der Grosse: Seine Zeit, sein Werk, seine Wirkung,* ed. Albert Zimmermann, 41–49. Miscellanea Mediaevalia, 14. Berlin: Walter de Gruyter, 1981.

Serra, Giuseppe. "Alcune osservazioni sulle traduzioni dall'arabo in ebraico e in latino del *De generatione et corruptione* di Aristotele e dello pseudo-aristotelico *Liber de causis.*" In *Scritti in onore de Carlo Diano,* 423–27. Bologna: Pàtron, 1975.

Sturlese, Loris. "Saints et magiciens: Albert le Grand en face d'Hermès Trismégiste." *Archives de Philosophie: Recherches et Documentation* 43 (1980): 615–34.

———. "Proclo ed Ermete in Germania da Alberto Magno a Bertoldo di Moosburg: Per una prospettiva di ricerca sulla cultura filosofica tedesca nel secolo delle sue origini (1250–1350)." In *Von Meister Dietrich zu Meister Eckhart,* ed. Kurt Flasch, 22–33. Corpus Philosophorum Teutonicorum Medii Aevi, Beiheft 2. Hamburg: Felix Meiner Verlag, 1984.

———. "Il dibattito sul Proclo latino nel medioevo fra l'università di Parigi e lo Studium di Colonia." In *Proclus et son influence: Actes du Colloque de Neuchâtel, juin 1985,* ed. G. Boss and G. Seel, 261–85. Zurich: Editions du Grand Midi, 1987.

―――. "Il razionalismo filosofico e scientifico di Alberto il Grande." *Documenti e studi sulla tradizione filosofica medievale* 1 (1990): 373–426.

―――. *Die deutsche Philosophie im Mittelalter: Von Bonifatius bis zu Albert dem Großen (748–1280)*. Munich: C. H. Beck, 1993.

Snyder, Steven C. "Albert the Great: Creation and the Eternity of the World." In *Philosophy and the God of Abraham: Essays in Memory of James A. Weisheipl, OP*, ed. R. James Long, 191–202. Papers in Mediaeval Studies, 12. Toronto: Pontifical Institute of Mediaeval Studies, 1991.

Sweeney, Leo. "The Doctrine of Creation in *Liber de Causis*." In *An Etienne Gilson Tribute Presented by His North American Students with a Response by Etienne Gilson*, ed. Charles J. O'Neil, 274–89. Milwaukee: Marquette University Press, 1959.

―――. "A Controversial Text on 'Esse primum creatum' in Albert the Great's *Liber de causis et processu universitatis*." *Proceedings of the PMR Conference* 5 (1980): 137–49.

―――. "*Esse Primum Creatum* in Albert the Great's *Liber de Causis et Processu Universitatis*." *The Thomist* 44 (1980): 599–646.

―――. "The Meaning of *Esse* in Albert the Great's Texts on Creation in the *Summa de Creaturis* and *Scripta Super Sententias*." In *Albert the Great: Commemorative Essays*, ed. Francis J. Kovach and Robert W. Shahan, 65–95. Norman: University of Oklahoma Press, 1980.

―――. "Are Plotinus and Albertus Magnus Neoplatonists?" In *Graceful Reason: Essays in Ancient and Medieval Philosophy in Honour of Joseph Owens, CSSR*, ed. Lloyd P. Gerson, 177–202. Papers in Mediaeval Studies, 4. Toronto: Pontifical Institute of Mediaeval Studies, 1983.

Taylor, Richard Charles. "A Note on Chapter I of the *Liber de causis*." *Manuscripta* 22 (1978): 169–72.

―――. "Saint Thomas and the *Liber de causis* on the Hylomorphic Composition of Separate Substances." *Mediaeval Studies* 41 (1979): 509–13.

―――. "Neoplatonic Texts in Turkey: Two Manuscripts Containing Ibn Ṭufayl's *Ḥayy Ibn Yaqẓān*, Ibn al-Sīd's *Kitāb al-Ḥadāʾiq*, Ibn Bājja's *Ittiṣāl al-ʿAql bi-l-Insān*, the *Liber de causis*, and an Anonymous Neoplatonic Treatise on Motion." *Mélanges de l'Institut Dominicain d'Etudes Orientales du Caire* 15 (1982): 251–64.

―――. "The *Liber de causis*: A Preliminary List of Extant Manuscripts." *Bulletin de philosophie médiévale* 25 (1983): 63–84.

―――. "'Abd al-Latif al-Baghdadi's Epitome of the *Kalam fi mahd al-khayr (Liber de causis)*." In *Islamic Theology and Philosophy: Studies in Honor of George F. Hourani*, ed. Michael E. Marmura, 236–48, 318–23. Albany: State University of New York Press, 1984.

———. "The Kalām fī maḥḍ al-khair (*Liber de causis*) in the Islamic Philosophical Milieu." In *Pseudo-Aristotle in the Middle Ages: The "Theology" and Other Texts*, ed. Jill Kraye, W. F. Ryan, and C. B. Schmitt, 37–52. Warburg Institute Surveys and Texts, 11. London: Warburg Institute, University of London, 1986.

———. "Remarks on the Latin Text and the Translator of the *Kalām fī maḥḍ al-khair/Liber de causis*." *Bulletin de philosophie médiévale* 31 (1989): 75–102.

———. "A Critical Analysis of the Structure of the *Kalām fī mahd al-khair (Liber de causis)*." In *Neoplatonism and Islamic Thought*, ed. Parviz Morewedge, 11–40. Studies in Neoplatonism: Ancient and Modern, 5. Albany: State University of New York Press, 1992.

Teske, Roland J. "William of Auvergne's Use of Avicenna's Principle: '*Ex uno, secundum quod unum, non nisi unum.*'" *The Modern Schoolman* 71 (1993–94): 1–15.

Théry, G. *Autour du décret de 1210: I. David de Dinant: Etude sur son panthéisme matérialiste*. Bibliothèque Thomiste, 6. Kain: Le Saulchoir, 1925.

———. "Edition critique des pièces relatives au procès d'Eckhart contenues dans le manuscrit 33 b de la bibliothèque de Soest." *Archives d'histoire doctrinale et littéraire du moyen âge* 1 (1926–27): 129–268.

Thomassen, Beroald. *Metaphysik als Lebensform: Untersuchungen zur Grundlegung der Metaphysik im Metaphysikkommentar Alberts des Grossen*. Beiträge zur Geschichte der Philosophie und Theologie des Mittelalters: Texte und Untersuchungen, neue Folge, 27. Münster: Aschendorff, 1985.

Trouillard, Jean. "Procession néoplatonicienne et création judéo-chrétienne." In *Néoplatonisme: Mélanges offerts à Jean Trouillard*, 1–30. Les Cahiers de Fontenay, 19–22. Fontenay aux Roses: E.N.S., 1981.

Vajda, Georges. "Les Notes d'Avicenne sur la *Théologie d'Aristote*." *Revue Thomiste* 51 (1951): 346–406.

van den Bergh, S. S.v."Djins." *Encyclopaedia of Islam*, new ed.

Van Steenberghen, Fernand. "La filosofia di Alberto Magno." *Sapienza* (Naples) 18 (1965): 381–93.

———. "Albert le Grand avait-il une philosophie personelle?" *Académie royale de Belgique: Bulletin de la Classe des Lettres*, 5e série 52 (1966): 15–30.

———. *La philosophie au XIIIe siècle*. Philosophes Médiévaux, 9. Louvain: Publications Universitaires, and Paris: Béatrice-Nauwelaerts, 1966.

Pages 292–306 are nearly identical with the preceding item.

———. "Albert le Grand et l'aristotélisme." *Revue internationale de philosophie* 34 (1980): 566–74.

Vansteenkiste, C. "Intorno al testo latino del *Liber de causis*." *Angelicum* 44 (1967): 60–83.

———. "Il nono volume del nuovo Alberto Magno." *Angelicum* 50 (1973): 249–59.
Vasoli, Cesare. "L'immagine di Alberto Magno in Bruno Nardi." *Freiburger Zeitschrift für Philosophie und Theologie* 32 (1985): 45–64.
Verbeke, Gérard. "Le hasard et la fortune: Réflexions d'Albert le Grand sur la doctrine d'Aristote." *Rivista di filosofia neo-scolastica* 70 (1978): 29–48.
Wéber, Edouard. "La relation de la philosophie et de la théologie selon Albert le Grand." *Archives de Philosophie: Recherches et Documentation* 43 (1980): 559–88.
———. "Langage et méthode négatifs chez Albert le Grand." *Revue des Sciences Philosophiques et Théologiques* 65 (1981): 75–99.
Weisheipl, James A. "Albertus Magnus and the Oxford Platonists." *Proceedings of the American Catholic Philosophical Association* 32 (1958): 124–39.
———. "The *Problemata determinata XLIII* ascribed to Albertus Magnus (1271)," *Mediaeval Studies* 22 (1960): 303–54.
———. "The Celestial Movers in Medieval Physics." *The Thomist* 24 (1961): 286–326.
———. "Albert's Disclaimers in the Aristotelian Paraphrases." *Proceedings of the PMR Conference* 5 (1980): 1–27.
———. "The Life and Works of St. Albert the Great" and "Albert's Works on Natural Sciences (*libri naturales*) in Probable Chronological Order." In *Albertus Magnus and the Sciences: Commemorative Essays, 1980,* ed. James A. Weisheipl, 13–51 and 565–77. Studies and Texts, 49. Toronto: Pontifical Institute of Mediaeval Studies, 1980.
———. "Albertus Magnus and Universal Hylomorphism: Avicebron: A Note on Thirteenth-Century Augustinianism." In *Albert the Great: Commemorative Essays,* ed. Francis J. Kovach and Robert W. Shahan, 239–60. Norman: University of Oklahoma Press, 1980.
———. "The Axiom 'Opus Naturae Est Opus Intelligentiae' and Its Origins." In *Albertus Magnus — Doctor Universalis: 1280/1980,* ed. G. Meyer and A. Zimmermann, 441–63. Walberberger Studien: Philosophische Reihe, 6. Mainz: Matthias-Grünewald-Verlag, 1980.
Wieland, Georg. *Untersuchungen zum Seinsbegriff im Metaphysikkommentar Alberts des Grossen.* Beiträge zur Geschichte der Philosophie und Theologie des Mittelalters, neue Folge, 7. Münster: Aschendorff, 1972.
———. Albert der Große und die Entwicklung der mittelalterlichen Philosophie." *Zeitschrift für philosophische Forschung* 34 (1980): 590–607.
———. "The Reception and Interpretation of Aristotle's *Ethics.*" In *The Cambridge History of Later Medieval Philosophy: From the Rediscovery of Aristotle to the Disintegration of Scholasticism, 1100–1600,* ed. Norman Kretzmann,

Anthony Kenny, Jan Pinborg, and Eleonore Stump, 657–72. Cambridge: Cambridge University Press, 1982.

Wielockx, Robert. "Gottfried von Fontaines als Zeuge der Echtheit der Theologischen Summe des Albertus Magnus." In *Studien zur mittelalterlichen Geistesgeschichte und ihrer Quellen*, ed. Albert Zimmermann, 209–25. Miscellanea Mediaevalia, 15. Berlin: Walter de Gruyter, 1982.

———. "Zur *Summa Theologiae* des Albertus Magnus." *Ephemerides Theologicae Lovanienses* 66 (1990): 78–110.

Wippel, John F. "Thomas Aquinas on the Distinction and Derivation of the Many from the One: A Dialectic between Being and Nonbeing." *Review of Metaphysics* 38 (1985): 563–90.

———. "The Latin Avicenna as a Source for Thomas Aquinas's Metaphysics." *Freiburger Zeitschrift für Philosophie und Theologie* 37 (1990): 51–90.

Włodek, Sophie. "Albert le Grand et les albertistes du XVe siècle: Le problème des universaux." In *Albert der Grosse: Seine Zeit, sein Werk, seine Wirkung*, ed. Albert Zimmermann, 193–207. Miscellanea Mediaevalia, 14. Berlin: Walter de Gruyter, 1981.

Wolfson, Harry A. "The Meaning of *Ex Nihilo* in the Church Fathers, Arab and Hebrew Philosophy, and St. Thomas." In *Mediaeval Studies in Honor of Jeremiah Denis Matthias Ford*, ed. Urban T. Holmes, Jr., and Alexander J. Denomy, 353–70. Cambridge: Harvard University Press, 1948.

———. "The Meaning of *Ex Nihilo* in Isaac Israeli," *Jewish Quarterly Review*, n.s., 50 (1959–60): 1–12.

———. "The Identification of *Ex Nihilo* with Emanation in Gregory of Nyssa." *Harvard Theological Review* 63 (1970): 53–60.

Zambelli, Paola. "Le stelle 'sorde e mute' ed i loro 'motori' alle origini della scienza moderna? Un case-study storiografico." In *Historia philosophiae Medii Aevi: Studien zur Geschichte der Philosophie des Mittelalters*, ed. B. Mojsisch and O. Pluta, 2:1099–1117. Amsterdam: B. R. Grüner, 1991.

Zimmermann, F. W. "The Origins of the So-Called *Theology of Aristotle*." In *Pseudo-Aristotle in the Middle Ages: The "Theology" and Other Texts*, ed. Jill Kraye, W. F. Ryan, and C. B. Schmitt, 110–240. Warburg Institute Surveys and Texts, 11. London: Warburg Institute, University of London, 1986.

Index of Subjects

activity: God's as not distinct from his substance, 10, 21, 24, 27, 94n51; as not more perfect than substance, 9, 12; *ultra genus*, 20–21
alatyr, 56, 90n29
analogy, 20–21, 31–34, 43–44, 51, 75, 79–80, 104n29, 116nn38–41, 117n46, 118n47, 127nn28, 30
angels, 65, 139n35
anniyya, 24, 28, 108n9
artisan, example of, 15–16, 57–58, 75, 135n18

being: as first created thing, 7, 38–41, 43–45, 51, 62, 74–77, 79; as indeterminate, 7–8, 30, 38, 40, 89n27, 93n45; relation to life and intellect, 9, 74, 89n27; 93n45. See also *anniyya; ens; esse;* essence; existence; *huwiyya; id quod est*

cause: and effect, contact between, 27–29, 30, 112n20, 113n26; and effect, mutual indwelling, 9, 30; and effect, proportion between, 6–7, 33, 56, 64; efficient, 18, 60–64, 67, 119n3, 137n26, 139n34, 140n3; exemplar, 33; final, 60; formal, 55–56, 140n3; instrumental, 15, 61–62; by intellect, 68, 70; by nature, 68, 73, 142n17; *per se*, 68, 70–71; primary, 6, 11–12, 19, 27–30, 55; without relation to effect, 10, 24, 28–30, 43; secondary, 6, 11, 13, 18–19, 27–30, 53–55, 58–60, 79, 100n17, 114n28, 144n23; undiminished by flowing, 16; univocal and equivocal, 15, 33–34, 102n21, 118n47
communicability, 19, 21–24, 28–31, 66, 107n7, 112n21, 113n25, 115nn33–34
contemplation, 11, 53–54, 57–58, 60, 95n54, 102n22, 131n6, 135n19
continuator, 28–30, 32, 94n49, 113n26, 114n28
contraction, 59, 141n13
creation: distinguished from concreation, 73, 145nn25–26; by creatures, 2–3, 13, 39, 53–56, 79–80, 130n1; as emanation, 18–19, 79; in Eriugena, 1; distinguished from generation, 95n55, 131n3; distinguished from information, 10, 13, 43, 50, 56, 67, 74–75, 145n26; in the Judeo-Christian tradition, 2; in the *Liber de causis*, 7–8, 10, 13; and philosophy, 130n1; in Plotinus, 2

disclaimers, 4, 13, 64
distance, 13, 21, 37, 54, 57, 72, 79, 101n18, 102n22, 144n23

eduction, 15–16, 98n8, 135n18
emanation: as coming to an end, 59, 115n33; and eduction, 15–16, 98n8, 135n18; and efficient, formal, and final causation, 17; and equivocal causation, 15, 32; not from material things, 19–20, 103n23; and metaphor, 19–21, 97n1; and necessity, 1–2, 13, 71–72, 100n17; and order, 2, 18–19; and pantheism, 1–2, 23–24; recipient of, 17–18, 31–32, 75, 100n16, 140n3; in Scripture, 1; and undiminished font, 16, 79; and unity of efflux, 10, 12–13, 35–37, 139n2; and univocal causation, 15–16, 30, 32; its vehicle, 30; words and images for, 1, 2, 16, 19, 97n1
ens, 24–25, 28–29, 44, 47, 74–75, 108n10, 126n23, 129n36
Epicureans, 106n2
Epistula de principio universi esse, 3, 36–37, 63–64, 84nn9, 11, 121n7
esse, 24–30, 40, 43–47, 49–52, 56, 67, 69, 74–75, 108nn9–10, 109n12, 110n15, 112nn21, 23, 113n25, 114n30, 115n34, 125nn22–23, 129nn34, 36, 130n39, 138n29; *esse naturale* and *esse naturae*, 46
essence, 47, 70, 108n11, 111n16, 112n21; as from Intellect, 2; and order, 18; as possibility for existence, 17–18, 57, 67, 75. *See also anniyya*; being; *ens*; *esse*; existence; *huwiyya*; *id quod est*
existence, 46–47, 57, 74–75, 79, 108n11, 109n12, 111n16; and the One, 2, 109n11. *See also anniyya*; being; *ens*; *esse*; essence; *huwiyya*; *id quod est*

forms, 134n16, 135n18; before, in, and after things, 41–42, 44–45, 51, 69, 77, 80, 123nn18–19, 125n20; celestial, 135n20; in Eustratius, 41; in Ibn Sīnā, 41, 46–47; in the *Liber de causis*, 7–11, 40; as light, 21; in the mind of the artisan, 15–16, 41; in Plotinus, 38, 40, 51; threefold consideration of forms before things, 41–42, 45–47, 50–52, 75
fundamentum, 110n16

God: as form, 29–30; and his governance, 10–11, 24, 27–30, 79; and infinity, 10, 27, 30; as mover of outermost sphere, 60–64, 137n26, 138nn30, 32, 139n34; and his simplicity, 24, 27, 30, 35, 43, 68, 71. *See also* activity; cause; communicability; incommunicability; ineffability; intellect; knowledge; necessity; omnipresence; One; pantheism; relation; Trinity; will; wisdom
goodness: as God's being, 10, 27; as self-diffusive, 10, 22, 72

henads, 45, 96n58
heresy, 13, 37, 51–52, 64
hierarchy: and analogy, 31–32; and mediation, 54–56; and relation of adjacent orders, 10
huwiyya, 24, 28, 108n9, 126n23
hyliatin, 26–27, 69, 91n35, 109n13, 110n16

identity, principle of, 17
id quod est, 24–30, 67, 108n10, 109n12, 110n16, 112n23, 113n25, 114n30, 115n34
incommunicability, 22–23, 27–28, 30–31, 45, 66, 107n7, 113n25
ineffability, 8, 10, 119n3, 127n27
infinity: and being, 40; and Life, 93n45; as pure or participated, 9–10
information, as distinguished from creation, 10, 13, 43, 50, 56, 67, 74–75
intellect: in Albert's usage, 101n20; in the *Liber de causis*, 6–10, 40, 74, 77,

INDEX OF SUBJECTS   171

93n45; in Plotinus, 2, 38, 40, 51, 77; in Proclus, 89n27; universally acting, 19, 41, 57–58, 68, 111n19
intelligence: in Albert's usage, 101n20, 122n16; as concept, 39–41, 51, 75, 77, 122n14, 136n22; as intellective substance, 48–49, 51, 53–62, 64–65, 75–77, 131n6, 135n20, 138n29

knowledge: divine and human, 69, 141nn8–10; and Intellect, 9, 41, 92n37; and soul, 91n33

Liber de causis: and Albert's contemporaries, 2–3, 13, 39, 48; as completion of Aristotle's *Metaphysics*, 4, 47, 52, 74–75, 87n18, 118n46; summary of, 6–12
light, 16, 19, 20–21, 31, 35, 41–42, 58–60, 69, 71, 100n17, 103nn23, 26, 105n34, 116n36, 124n18, 135n20, 136n23

matter, 15–16, 18–19, 23, 26, 69, 91n35, 103n23, 109n14, 110n16, 135n18
mediation, 7, 9–13, 137n24
mediator, 114n28
metaphor, 19–21, 97n1, 103nn24, 26, 105nn32–33, 112n20
metaphysics, subject of, 47, 74–75

necessity: and emanation, 1–2, 71–72, 100n17; in God, 54; in intelligences, 53–54, 58; and natures, 68, 142n17

omnipresence, 11, 27, 30
One, the: in the *Liber de causis*, 7, 10, 12; in Plotinus, 2, 36, 38, 51
order, 18, 56, 68–69, 93n46. *See also* hierarchy

pantheism, 30, 35, 107n7, 113n26, 114n29, 118n47; and emanation, 1, 23–24; and Plotinus, 2

paraphrases, Albert's Aristotelian: characteristics of, 5, 64, 138n32; disclaimers in, 4, 13–14; scope of, 3–4
participation: and "acquisition," 6, 96n58; and the imparticipable, 44–46, 51, 96n58
Peripatetics, 16, 61–65, 68, 79–80, 99n9, 105n33, 106n2, 123n18, 146n30
Platonists, 61–65, 73, 79–80, 105n33, 123n18, 146n30
possibility: and order, 18, 102n21; of a thing as from the thing, 17–18, 53–54, 58, 67, 140n3
potency: as concreated, 73; as increasing along the causal chain, 57; of subject, 15–16, 18
power: as diminished along the causal chain, 7, 13, 72
principle, 15–17, 44
privation, 72, 136n21
procession, 16, 57, 99n9, 102n22, 127n28; processions, 31, 44–47
Pythagoreans, 131n4

reception according to the mode of the recipient, 9–13, 18, 31–32, 54–56, 60, 67, 72–73, 79, 102n21, 115n34, 139n2
recipient of emanation, 17–18, 31, 50, 70, 75, 100n16
relation, 94n49, 95n54, 127n25, 141n8; of cause to effect not found in God, 10, 24, 28–29, 43, 126n24; of likeness of God unilateral, 33, 117n43
resolution, 43, 49–50, 125n22, 129n38
reversion: 2, 8–9, 12

self-constitution, 9, 11–13, 17, 38, 67, 95n55, 96nn57, 59
self-multiplication, 19, 34
self-sufficiency, 9–11, 66, 94n52
shadow, 19, 21, 35, 69–70, 73–74, 79, 102nn21–22, 141nn11, 13

signification: distinction between perfection signified and mode of signifying, 20–21

soul: as between sensibles and intelligibles, 9; as between time and eternity, 6, 12; as concept, 41; and discursive thought, 91n33; and emanation, 83n4; grades of, 7–8, 10; human, 48, 134n14; illumination of, 57; and need for body, 19, 92n41; "noble," 7–8, 56, 134n14, 135n20; origin of, 54–56

spheres, 54–56, 58, 60–65, 72, 131nn5–6, 135n20, 137n25, 138nn28–29, 31–32, 139n34

Stoics, 80, 106n2, 123n18

stramentum, 7, 90n30

supposit, 26–27, 29, 69, 110n16, 113n25

theologians, 13–14, 37, 62, 65, 134n15

Trinity, 113n25, 115n34, 143n17

universality, causal and predicative, 33–34, 42–43, 118n48. *See also* forms

will, 68, 70–72, 139n34, 140nn4–5, 142n17

wisdom, 68–70, 72–73, 144n23

Index of Persons

Abū Ma'šar, 139n34
"Alexander," 24
Ambrose, 124n18
Anaxagoras, 136n20, 138n30
Antiphon, 135n18
Aquinas, Thomas, 3, 76, 79, 82n11, 85n15, 88n21, 93n43, 96n61, 99n9, 105n33, 108n11, 121n11, 125n20, 128n32, 130n1, 137n26, 145n25, 146n30
Aristotle, 3–5, 13–15, 17, 21–22, 26, 32, 36, 41–42, 47, 51, 54–56, 61–64, 70, 73–76, 79–80, 87n18, 98n7, 101nn19–20, 103n23, 105n33, 109nn11, 14, 110n16, 112n20, 116n38, 118n48, 119n3, 120n6, 123nn18–19, 126n24, 130n1, 131n5, 135nn18, 20, 137n24, 138n32, 139n34, 144n23
Asclepius, 23
Augustine, 13–14, 20, 101n18, 103n26, 105n33, 121n8, 126n24, 135n19, 145n25
Avendaud, 84n10, 85n14, 86n17
Averroes. *See* Ibn Rušd
Avicebron. *See* Ibn Gabirol
Avicenna. *See* Ibn Sīnā

Bacon, Roger, 97n1, 121n11
Badawī, 'Abd al-Raḥmān, vii
Bardenhewer, Otto, vii, 85n14, 90n29, 94n47

Basil the Great, 1
al-Battānī, 139n34
al-Biṭrūǧī, 54–55, 132nn7–8
Boethius, 1, 25–26, 101n18
Booth, Edward, 125n20

Craemer-Ruegenberg, Ingrid, 87n20

David of Dinant, 24
David the Jew, 3, 37, 63, 79–80, 85n14, 86n17
Degen, Ernst, 88n21
Dionysius, pseudo, 1–3, 13, 20, 22, 31, 33, 37, 42, 44–47, 51, 71, 76, 80, 96nn58, 1, 99n9, 101n18, 105nn32–33, 1, 116n41, 117nn43, 46, 119n49, 126n24, 128n32, 129nn36, 38, 137n24, 139n1, 143n18, 145n28, 146nn30–31
Duhem, Pierre, 13–14

Eckhart, 99n12
Eriugena, 1, 107n7, 111n18
Eustratius, 41, 44, 47, 51, 123nn18–19, 125n20

al-Fārābī, 3, 5, 22, 53, 61–62, 79–80, 85n12, 98n6, 106n2, 120n6, 121n7, 131nn3, 6, 132n8, 137n26
Fauser, Winfried, 88n21, 92n42, 94n52

173

INDEX OF PERSONS

Ğābir b. Aflaḥ, 139n34
al-Ġazālī, 3, 5, 15, 22, 37, 48, 53, 65, 79, 81n1, 84n12, 87n17, 106n2, 120n6, 130n2
Gerard of Cremona, 3, 25, 62, 84n8, 91n35, 92nn39–40, 93n43, 94nn49, 52, 95nn54, 56, 108n9, 126n23
Gerson, Lloyd, 2
Gilbert of Poitiers, 25, 105n32
Grabmann, Martin, 13
Gundisalvi, 84n8

Henry of Ghent, pseudo, 97n1, 122n11, 130n39
Hermes Trismegistus, 23, 106nn2–3

Ibn Gabirol, 13, 36, 68, 70, 97nn1, 3, 99n9, 101n19, 102n21, 140nn4–5
Ibn Rušd, 48, 71, 120n6, 131n3, 137n26, 141n9
Ibn Sīnā, 3, 5, 15, 17, 22, 25, 36–37, 41, 44, 46–48, 51, 53–57, 60–63, 65, 71, 79–80, 85n12, 87n17, 96n1, 100n16, 106n2, 107n7, 109n12, 120n6, 121n7, 123nn18–19, 128n34, 129n35, 131nn3, 6, 132n8, 135nn18, 20, 137n26, 138nn30, 32, 141n9, 146n30
Isaac Israeli, 65, 95n55, 102n21

James of Venice, 39
Janssens, Jules, 83n3
Jean de Maisonneuve, 98n4
John of Dacia, 85n15, 86n16, 96n60
John of Damascus, 121n8, 143n17
John of Jandun, 83n4
John Sarrazin, 108n7

Kaiser, Rudolf, 88n21
Kraemer, Joel, 92n38

Libera, Alain de, 89n24, 98n4, 99n8, 101n18
Lucan, 23–24

Maimonides, 36, 48, 65, 68–70, 97n1, 98n5, 101n18, 105n33
Maquart, F.-X., 109n11
Māšāʾallāh, 90n29, 137n25
Meersseman, G., 87n18

Pattin, Adriaan, vii, 82n10, 92n42, 94n52
Peter Comestor, 124n18
Peter Lombard, 107n7, 111n17, 124n18
Plato, 4, 22, 41–42, 44, 53, 61, 64, 73, 106n2, 117n43, 120n5, 123nn18–19, 131n3, 135n18
Plotinus, 1–2, 7, 36, 38, 40, 51, 77, 80, 85nn12, 15, 90n32, 91nn33, 35, 92n36, 93n45, 95n54, 96nn58–59, 101n18, 102n21, 109nn11, 14
Plutarch of Chaeronea, 24
Porphyry, 71, 106n2, 146n1
Priscian, 104n28
Proclus, 3, 6–7, 45–46, 76, 79, 88n21, 89n27, 90n32, 92n35, 93n45, 95n54, 96n58, 101n20, 112n23, 117n43, 126n24
Ptolemy, 54, 131n5, 137n25, 139n34
Pythagoras, 106n2

Siger of Brabant, 100n14, 120nn4, 6, 121n9, 140n3
Socrates, 106n2

Ṯābit b. Qurra, 131n5
Taylor, Richard C., vii, 91n33, 92n41, 94n47, 95n54
Tempier, Etienne, 37
Thales, 106n2
Themistius, 106n2
Theophrastus, 71

Ulrich of Strassburg, 64, 98nn4, 7, 99nn9–10, 102n22, 129n39, 138n27, 141n13, 144n23, 145n25

Vansteenkiste, C., 90n29

Wieland, Georg, 121n9
William of Auvergne, 97n1,
  100nn16–17, 115n34,
  121n10, 132n8, 140n4,
  142n15
William of Moerbeke, 3, 88n21

Zeno, 106n2

Index of Texts

Albert

De caelo et mundo 2.2.6   138n32

De causis et proc. univ.
1.1.6	36, 67–68
1.1.8	17, 25–26
1.1.10	13, 17, 25, 37, 76
1.1.11	17–18
1.2.1	26, 111n19
1.2.5	30
1.2.6	30, 69, 141n9
1.2.8	68
1.3.1–2	71–72
1.3.4	68
1.3.5	53, 55
1.4.1	15–16, 97n3, 98nn4–7, 99nn9–10
1.4.2	17–19, 31, 34, 101n18, 102n22, 115n34
1.4.3	23, 31
1.4.4	18–19, 21, 34, 73
1.4.5	17, 23–24, 35, 57
1.4.6	32, 57
1.4.8	57–58, 65
2.1.1	3–4, 21, 64
2.1.2	17, 30
2.1.5	34, 41
2.1.6	64, 69, 73–74
2.1.13	53, 55–57
2.1.14	72
2.1.17	43, 50, 74
2.1.18	43–44, 47
2.1.19	39, 125n22
2.1.20	41–42, 74
2.1.21	42, 76
2.1.24	48
2.2.7	48–49
2.2.17	54–55, 74
2.2.18	26–27
2.2.37	72
2.2.44	31–32, 69
2.3.3	33
2.3.10–14	73–74
2.4.1	27–28, 30
2.4.2	66, 69, 72, 139n2
2.4.3	29
2.4.4	25
2.4.7	66
2.4.11	30
2.4.12	66, 69–70, 73
2.4.14	71
2.5.2	69–70
2.5.18	60
2.5.24	4, 65, 87n18

Metaph.
1.1.1	47
1.1.2	45, 47, 128n32
4.3.9	16
7.5.10	16
8.1.1	17

Metaph. (cont.)

11.2.12	62–63
11.2.17	61, 63
11.2.19	59
11.2.20	58–59, 61
11.2.21	62
11.3.7	61–63

Phys. 8.1.15   64

Probl. determ.

1	64
7	60

Sent.

1.4.3 solutio, ad 6	113n25
1.8.30 sed contra, reply	33, 118n47
1.19.14 solutio	113n25
1.19.15 ad quaest.	113n25
2.2.1	64–65
2.3.4 solutio	110n16
2.14.6	64

Summa

1.3.13.1	20
1.14.56 solutio, ad 1, ad quaest. 2	20–21
1.14.58.1.1 ad 1	20
2.1.4.3 obj. 7	24

Super Dion. De div. nom.

1.57	33
2.37	113n25, 115n30
2.83	42
4.51	127n28
5.9	127n30
5.16	42
5.22	115n30
7.20	139n34
11.24–26	45–46
13.22	33

Super Dion. De myst. theol. 3   20

Anonymous

Liber de causis

1	6, 55–56, 74–75, 79
2	6
3	6–7, 13, 55
4	6–8, 11, 39–40, 50, 77, 122n17
5	8, 16, 48
6	8, 49
7	8
8	8, 11, 26–27, 37, 109n11
9	8–9
10	9
11	9
12	9
13	9
14	9, 11
15	9–10, 16
16	10
17	10, 50, 55, 74, 76, 126n23, 145n28
18	10, 115n33, 137n24
19	10, 24–25, 27–30, 37, 66, 71–72, 76, 108n10, 112n23, 114n28, 126n24, 139n2
20	11, 66
21	11
22	11, 71
23	11, 30, 72–73, 79
24	11
25	11
26	11
27	11–12
28	11–12
29	12
30	12
31	12

MS Ripoll 109, 134ra–158va   4, 86n16

Aquinas, Thomas

In Librum de causis expositio 4   128n32

Metaph. 12.9   76

Aristotle

Cael.

2.6 ($288^{b}3$–5)	62, 138n32
2.12 ($292^{a}22$–$^{b}24$)	55

De An. 2.4 (415^{b}13)   74

De gen. et corr.
  1.6 (322^{b}23–323^{a}33)   112n20
  2.10 (336^{a}27)   13, 36

Metaph.
  5.18 (1022^{a}25–35)   17
  7.3 (1029^{a}20–25)   110n16
  7.7 (1032^{b}11–14)   16, 98n7
  7.17 (1041^{a}9–20)   17
  12.7 (1072^{b}28–29)   61, 138n27
  12.8 (1073^{a}27–28, 1074^{a}31–37)   36

Phys.
  8.1 (251^{a}22–28)   61
  8.6 (260^{a}18–19)   36

Dionysius, pseudo

Div. nom.
  4.1   71
  5.5   77
  5.6   42, 76
  5.8   46
  11.6   45–46

Ibn Sīnā

Sufficientia 1.7   46, 128n34

Maimonides

Guide of the Perplexed 2.22   36

Wisdom of Solomon 7.25   1, 115n34

www.ingramcontent.com/pod-product-compliance
Lightning Source LLC
Chambersburg PA
CBHW021356300426
44114CB00012B/1251